Praise for *The Expe*

I am not sure I have ever read a sharper book on instruction than *The Expert Teacher,* written by a master classroom educator with remarkable depth of knowledge in educational research.

The book offers a powerful fusion of hands-on experience and underpinning research, and I love the fierce attention to detail in Darren's analysis of exactly what makes a lesson succeed in terms of student understanding. Darren achieves this not just by suggesting practices such as analogies, examples, diagrams and confronting misconceptions, but also by teasing apart exactly what makes those practices effective or not.

I have spent over 40 years in education considering what makes a beautiful lesson, and I still found myself surprised and enlightened by what I encountered on almost every page. It's hard to imagine any teacher reading this book without becoming profoundly more intentional in building and leading effective lessons.

Ron Berger, Chief Academic Officer, EL Education

Darren Mead brings his lifelong professional obsession with pedagogical perfection to life in an accessible and intelligent book which, much like the man himself, is unassuming and not beholden to fashionable ideas.

Alistair Smith, trainer, author and
designated learning consultant to the Football Association

Reading this book is like sitting in the theatre of the mind of one of the most nuanced, thoughtful and eclectic educators in the world. Darren manages to take everything you took for granted about planning lessons and help you realise that not only is it the most important part of the job, but it can always be done better.

Unlike some other texts which espouse solely academic theory, *The Expert Teacher* is a true handbook that should be read, revisited, sticky-noted and kept on every teacher's person at all times. And while serious in intent, the book is peppered with anecdotes, metaphors and even the occasional simile which will have you laughing out loud.

A truly wonderful companion for all those who believe that every child deserves a teacher who designs wonderful, purposeful and responsive learning experiences.

Chris Harte, Director, Unstuck Learning Design

The Expert Teacher is a wide-ranging and erudite volume on what it means not just to know the content of our subject, but to understand how to teach our subject. It successfully combines links to academic research with a distillation of both Darren's and others' years of practice and collaboration, and ultimately provides a framework for improvement for all teachers.

Through the lens of pedagogical content knowledge, we are taken through our students' learning journey and their misconceptions to the destination where the important knowledge and skills have been embedded and become part of their constitution. The distinction of the expert teacher from the novice teacher is humanely explored too, making it clear that – just as our students have a hard path to follow – all teachers must accept the hard graft required to gain expertise in our chosen profession.

This book will prove to be thought-provoking and challenging, and is worth careful contemplation and regular revisiting.

David Paterson, science teacher, Aldenham School,
author, blogger and teacher trainer

Darren Mead has always used a vast evidence base to craft learning experiences for his students. In *The Expert Teacher* he distils and explains what the educational community has learned to date, and effectively translates it into simple-to-implement actions.

Sometimes irreverent, always sage, he exposes and explores the true complexity of quality teaching, while also showing how to tweak existing practice (without increasing workload!). He provides a plethora of tools to aid this process, and helps us to decide when and how to use them at different stages of the learning process.

Darren reveals why expert teaching is an intellectually, emotionally and logistically demanding endeavour, and why becoming an expert in this profession requires extraordinary social sensitivity, real-time assessment-led responsiveness and subject pedagogical expertise. It invigorates the intellectual task of creating balance between planning for the learner and the learning, and offers a one-stop repository for stimulating professional dialogue around the challenges of expert teaching and learning. Misguided, non-evidence-based, received wisdom gets short shrift and is eruditely debunked.

The Expert Teacher raises the bar of expectation for teachers, and brings clarity of insight to the canon of educational research, as well as to the fields of sociology and psychology. It is perfect for those who wish to continue to hone their craft and move themselves and others to the highest levels of professionalism.

Fergus Hegarty, Director of Science, Laidlaw Schools Trust, and Chair, Association of Science Education – North East region

Darren Mead's tour de force, *The Expert Teacher,* illuminates the complex business of teaching and learning with absolute clarity – and is a must-read for teachers aiming to develop a real professionalism in the classroom.

Painstakingly researched, the book equips the reader with a whole armoury of structuring tools and frameworks, all made accessible by Darren's well-chosen and illuminating applications and anecdotes. The book's content and message is also well-balanced, with its nourishing imperative to think deeply and rigorously about the journey of knowledge acquisition wisely countered by its permissive advocacy of tinkering with 'the exquisite lesson plan' mid flow if and when it simply isn't working. A further energy within this wonderful book is a vein of scurrilous and irreverent humour, which provides welcome – and nearly always well-judged – colour.

The moment has definitely arrived for this book to make a significant contribution to the evolution of the teaching profession.

Mark Moorhouse, Head Teacher, Matthew Moss High School

To observe an expert teacher can be a confounding experience for some: 'The students just got it', 'He really has their behaviour under control', 'I could never teach like her!' In *The Expert Teacher,* Darren Mead reminds us that these outcomes and expert teacher behaviours – and the planning of superb lessons – can be learned, but require careful consideration of the content to be studied: how it is best sequenced, taught and learned, and its relative conceptual importance. This is the tacit knowledge of the expert, a maestro. To possess this knowledge is remarkable enough; to be able to communicate it is a gift – though not to the possessor, but to those who they teach.

Rimsky-Korsakov gave us this gift in his teachings and writings on the orchestra. In *The Expert Teacher*, Darren Mead gives teachers that same gift.

Martin Said, School Designer, XP Trust

A real strength of *The Expert Teacher* is its accessibility. Developing educators can often find the language of educational writing a barrier to the ideas being expressed and be turned off; here, however, we have a book written by someone who has no desire to show us how clever they are or to stray into academia at the expense of classroom practice. Darren Mead is able to encapsulate a number of ideas that cross dichotomies and manages to bring them together in a straightforward, insightful and, ultimately, readable way.

I've not experienced what Darren refers to as his 'terrible' guitar playing, but if this book is even a slight indication of the way that he approaches his work in the classroom then I have no doubts that he is very much an expert teacher.

Colin Goffin, Vice Principal and Alternate Provision Lead, Inspiration Trust

The Expert Teacher is a unique book which offers both a synthesis of educational research and a practical insight into what works in the classroom.

Essential reading for those teachers, subject leaders and senior leaders in education who want to go beyond the quick fix and tips and tricks and take their first steps to truly understanding what mastery looks like in practice.

Mark Lovatt, teacher, author and former principal

The Expert Teacher

Using Pedagogical Content Knowledge to Plan Superb Lessons

Darren Mead
edited by Phil Beadle

independent
thinking press

First published by
Independent Thinking Press
Crown Buildings, Bancyfelin, Carmarthen, Wales, SA33 5ND, UK
www.independentthinkingpress.com
and
Independent Thinking Press
PO Box 2223, Williston, VT 05495, USA
www.crownhousepublishing.com

Independent Thinking Press is an imprint of Crown House Publishing Ltd

British Library of Cataloguing-in-Publication Data
A catalogue entry for this book is available from the British Library.

Print ISBN 978-178135311-0
Mobi ISBN 978-178135333-2
ePub ISBN 978-178135334-9
ePDF ISBN 978-178135335-6

LCCN 2019936415

Printed and bound in the UK by
TJ International, Padstow, Cornwall

For Tomas and Mandy

Contents

Contents

Foreword

It's early 2012, and I am trawling the internet for ideas about metacognition. I am in the middle of writing a book (for money – but not for much of it) that is going to be called *The Mighty Book of Plenary* and which eventually ends up being called *The Book of Plenary: Here Endeth the Lesson*. I already know quite a bit about the theoretical basis of metacognition and have read enough boring, excessively dense academic papers on it to know that anyone who says to you that it's 'thinking about thinking' isn't thinking – that would be meta-thought, you sillies.

What I want are ideas from someone who has been trying stuff out in the classroom, who has read the theoretical stuff and tried to make it concrete, realistic, doable. I keep coming back to the same blog. It is called *Pedagogical Purposes* and the bloke writing it seems a bit different. Genuinely, the point of the blog is not to promote his brand, his career, his ideas. Genuinely, he is using it to share his professional learning. He is also – genuinely – a little odd. His name is Darren Mead and he claims to be a former circus strongman. From his picture, you can't be sure if he is lying.

I get a bit stuck with this blog because the level of learning in it is quite a way above mine. He has clearly read a lot of books and academic papers. But not only this, he has digested them and shares whether and how he feels they work in the classroom. He doesn't seem to have any overriding ideology, he belongs to no club; he just wants to help.

It's 2013. I approach Darren, who, it turns out, is a science teacher in the far, cold part of the North where people speak a different language, to see if he wants to write a book. 'Why aye' he replies.

It's 2014 and I am speaking at a conference for the Essex Secondary Head Teachers' Association. I am on after Alistair Smith and am nervous as, in terms of speaking, Alistair is a legend to my mildly experienced ingénue. He starts off his speech by talking about the best teacher he has ever seen: someone he has seen recently who has blown him away! He says something along the lines of, 'He is the Jimi Hendrix of teaching. He can play it left-handed. He can play it right-handed. He can play it behind his back.' The teacher he is talking about is Darren Mead.

I don't tell Alistair that, by this time, Darren and I have been working for a year on this book. You will note that that was, at the very least, by the time you read this, five years ago. This book has taken six years from the initial approach to publication.

There are many reasons for this. Not the least is that Darren is a man of great enthusiasms, and his original text was the size of three books (there are another two books waiting to go if this one does as well as it should – his ideas on assessment (in particular) are profound). He is also very clever indeed and knows more than could possibly be fit into one book. The process of delivering this tome you are now holding has been a long one: Darren and I have skills in almost oppositional areas. He is about depth of detail where I like things artfully expressed. Hopefully, what you are holding is a worthy eventual compromise.

What it most certainly isn't, however, is a text for beginners. Darren is the one British teacher whose book, should it have existed, I would have rushed to the shops to buy as he knows more (I think) than anyone else in the profession about the theoretical basis of teaching. But, most importantly, that research hasn't just confined itself to the library. Everything Darren has to share has been trialled time and time again in the classroom. As a result, what you have in your hands is a book that I hope will be perceived to be exactly what it is – a serious piece of work by a serious person – and what it could be – a highly influential text. You'll not, I wager, find it easy reading, and you'll not, I imagine, have it by the bog for a light read (though there are funnies). But if you dive in, you'll learn lots of things you didn't know. If you dive in, you'll know some (a fraction) of what the man who might reasonably claim (though he wouldn't as he's actually quite shy) to be one of the most universally respected teachers that the world of education knows. If you dive in, you'll be on the way to the kind of expertise that Darren has. And that, dear teacher, is no small thing.

Phil Beadle

Acknowledgements

I have been fortunate to have worked with some inspirational people over my years in the classroom, too many to mention here. However, I will be forever thankful for the start I got as a student teacher from my professional mentors: John Burford, Mark Lovatt, Sarah Napthen and Rob Scott – experts in every sense of the word. I must also give an honourable mention to the original fire-starter, Alistair Smith. I was lucky enough to work alongside some amazing teachers at Cramlington Learning Village for 20 years, and I am grateful for the conversations, support and collaboration from which I learned so much. Thank you to Wendy Heslop and her staff.

Sadly, two of the great educators I have been blessed to work with are no longer with us. Dee Palmer Jones and Derek Wise CBE continue to be reference points in everything I do in my classroom. 'What would Dee do?' and 'What would Derek say?' are constant prompts in my and many others' thinking, and is a testament to their expertise and downright wisdom.

I am also thankful for the unique collaboration and support from the board members of the Two Jumps Learning Trust: Simon Brown, Chris Harte, Fergus Hegarty, Ian Neslon, Graeme Porter and Martin Said. I am grateful too to my colleagues from the old Teacher Effectiveness Enhancement Programme training days – Ken Brechin, Julie Mosley, Cath Rothwell and Trish Wright – and to our colleagues and friends from the Project for Enhancing Effective Learning, Ian Mitchell and the inspirational Jill Flack.

Thank you also to Phil Beadle for taking a random interest in what I do and for extending the offer of writing a book about it. Derek Wise once said to me, 'Darren, I know we can't teach you anything, but please let us support you in working out what you think is important,' which startled me somewhat as I thought I had concealed my stubborn single-mindedness rather well. Phil has done exactly this.

Finally, and most importantly, I want to thank my family for their love, support, encouragement and food. I love you Mandy, Tomas, Linda, Keith, Andrea, Mark and Rafa.

Introduction

An ode to lesson planning

Drive-through restaurants, click of a mouse shopping, no nails adhesive, get rich quick, open top bus tour, the 60 second news.

Silver service, personal shopper, bespoke carpentry, investments, exploring, a newspaper.

The second list appears marginally indulgent, but had we the time and money we would choose it over the former in an instant. Furthermore, most of us would actively avoid the first list (with the exception of no nails adhesive – a wondrous material), and herein lies the message: lesson planning is not a quick event; it is something to be indulged in, considered and practised, adagio. Amid the frantic pace and creeping pressure of being a teacher, this is our moment to slow down, reflect, research, collaborate and think. This is our choice.

Here is my belief: lesson planning should be not be simplified – it should be made complex and rich. Complex planning necessitates that we, the professionals, understand how learning happens, how our students 'work', how our subjects (specifically) are learned and how they can be taught better. Then, and only then, will we be able to plan lessons that are complete.

It is in our planning that we become professional; for me, it is impossible to extricate professional learning from the planning we do. Our professional kudos is wrapped up in our ability to work out how to teach groups of individuals intricate and, at times, abstract ideas so that they understand, remember, apply and enjoy them. Our professionalism is all this and more. We manage emotions, conflicts, motivation, community and identity. This is the beautiful complexity we were first drawn to. To do all of this – and we cannot unravel it – is hard yakka: it takes time, knowledge and time. Yes, time: lots of it; it takes a whole career's worth of time to get this art half right.

Ask yourself this, 'When do I really get to reflect about how I do my job?' If I am honest, it is when I am planning lessons. Although I don't really want to plan lessons – those arbitrary divisions of time; what I want to plan is how each bit of content is learned. It is actually impossible to plan an individual lesson as they don't exist in the learning world. When planning, I ponder: what went well? Whom did it go well for? What bombed? Did I have the right information to make good decisions today? Was all the information available to the students so they could make sense of it? How many times did they get each bit of vital information? All the questions I cannot possibly answer during a lesson, while I'm staving off the dominant question that we ask all lesson, every lesson: 'Is it OK to move on?' Classrooms are busy and complex, so succumbing to the overriding temptation of getting through the plan no matter what else happens is an understandable preoccupation. But is it the right one? Good planning and an understanding of how learning takes place help to prevent the thought of starting the next activity from becoming too dominant.

Never worry that you spend too long on a lesson plan, even in the sometimes overwhelmingly busy working day of a classroom teacher. It is an investment in you and your students – and as the famous shampoo vendor L'Oréal says, 'You're worth it.' In the long run, your planning and resources will be recycled and time will be saved, and you will be better at teaching that particular concept. Time constraints do have benefits; after all, necessity is the mother of invention. A lack of time encourages us to plan collaboratively and learn from someone else's experience (or allow them to learn from ours), and it is our students who benefit. Spending an age on a plan can lead teachers towards the fatal predilection of overly zealous and blind adherence to that plan. However, it is worth knowing that this is more likely if the plan is merely a series of activities. If the plan is built around what needs to be done to learn a concept, and furthermore, what the emerging understanding(s) might look like, then we can do the apparently contradictory thing of sticking to the plan and being entirely flexible and responsive at the same time.

All of the planning decisions we make are based on our pedagogical content knowledge. Pedagogical content knowledge is what we know about how learning happens, what we know about how our subjects are learned and what we know about the learners in front of us. This is practical knowledge. It is how we transform our subject knowledge into multiple ways of representing it in teachable ways. It is how we take the implicit expert thinking of a subject specialist and make it explicit through modelling. It is how we find out our students' prior conceptions and tailor their experiences in order for them to learn – and potentially reorganise their understanding when their preconceptions turn out to be misconceptions. Knowing how to do this is pedagogical content knowledge. Clearly, the role of pedagogical content knowledge in planning is central. To access it we have to stop, think and reflect on what students tend to already know, what they generally find difficult, what has helped in the past, what are the parts that make up the whole knowledge and what sequence the concepts should be taught in. This may require some research and discussions with other subject specialists. It takes time.

Questioning

From our pedagogical content knowledge we also get the knowledge to ask useful questions. There is a certain truth in the idea that many of our best questions are thought up on the spot as part of a dialogue. However, in order to more regularly ask purposeful questions, the planning is best done before the lesson. This allows us to consider:

- Why we are asking the question: is it to gather information on student learning? Is it to encourage students to think about an idea? Is it to consolidate learning? Is it to engage students with a new idea? Is it to reveal prior knowledge?

- Who is/are the question(s) for: the whole class or just a selected group of students?

- What response are we expecting to hear if they understand the concepts, if they know the concept, or if they are retaining a misconception or making a common mistake?

In the worst-case scenario, a teacher asks rhetorical questions to individuals as an attention keeping device, playing the baked potato skinned host of a bizarre quiz show, 'Guess What's In My Head?' The prize being that the teacher will continue with their explanation once a single correct answer has been given. In short, the questioning lacks pedagogical purpose. These questions are probably recall questions, perhaps on what has just been said or even about concepts the students should (already) know. If the only mechanisms a teacher has to ensure that key ideas are being recalled to aid long-term retention are some off-the-cuff questions flung at little Darren, who is staring out of the window, then all we can do is rue 30 lost opportunities.

If the aiding of retention is the purpose of the questioning, then the identification of the facts to be recalled should really be identified before the discussion, not when our attention is focused on who is paying attention. This allows us to couple the right question with the right mechanism. So, a question that recalls a key fact that will be useful in learning the new knowledge (e.g. that chlorophyll makes plants green), and the appropriate mechanism to ensure that all students have the opportunity to recall the information (e.g. think-pair-share, a random name generated with a 30 second think time or a choice of A, B, C answers) can then be matched to the content according to the teacher's professional knowledge as to which will serve this purpose best.

Effective teacher behaviours

Try an internet search of 'Who am I in ...?' and marvel at the myriad of unheard of TV shows where you can take a quiz to work out which character you would be in this show. (Apparently, I'm 53% Mickey Mouse, with which I'm fine.) As teachers, we are all character actors and on any one day will have to be most things to most people. Unfortunately, we tend to perceive how a fellow teacher acts as being a manifestation of their innate personality and ascribe their success to this. I have lost count of the number of conversations I've had about behaviour management after I have sent a willing newly qualified teacher to go and watch how a more experienced member of staff manages behaviour, only to be told that 'there weren't any problems', suggesting that the many nuances of the teacher's strategies were entirely missed.

Thankfully, there is a huge body of research on effective teacher behaviours, most notably from McBer (2000) and Muijs and Reynolds (2011), which suggests that an effective maths teacher might act in differing ways to an effective English teacher, with there being an area of overlap between all effective teachers. The key message here is that the behaviours of the most effective teachers are not based on their personalities but can be learned. The effective teacher behaviour research exemplifies the difficulties that teachers can have in applying research to practice, because this goes beyond knowledge and into the realm of our beliefs. This makes teaching a unique field of expertise. When student medics enter an operating theatre the environment and procedures are alien to them; they are an outsider learning to become an insider. As a student teacher, the classrooms, corridors, halls and desks are very familiar to us – we are already insiders and we bring with us an array of beliefs. This is not, of course, an argument for teachers having to enter voluntary psychoanalysis in order to uproot and reconstruct our belief systems in order to plan a lesson; however, sometimes we fail to see how we can do things better because of our certainties and our beliefs about learning and schooling. Our beliefs can act as filters to new information and experiences.

There are undeniable commonalities in the behaviours of the most effective teachers. A very brief summary of effective teacher behaviours might look like this. Effective teachers are confident in their ability and are highly committed to the success of all students. Their interactions are consistently fair and respectful, inducing a sense of trust in their classroom. They have the ability to think analytically and conceptually, allowing them to be flexible in their approaches. They act proactively and are constantly seeking out information to make good decisions. They set high standards, model them and hold others accountable. They have an overwhelming passion for learning and for what education can do. They work in teams, understand the motivations of others and seek to influence them in positive ways. They communicate clearly and are inclusive. They employ a variety of teaching methodologies that engage and stimulate thinking. They take an active interest in their own pedagogical content knowledge and use this knowledge to teach as well as they can. They create classroom communities that provide an orderly and civilised climate where students feel safe and suitably challenged. They teach, they learn and they seek to model the behaviours that exemplify these noble pursuits (McBer 2000: 2).

As expert teachers we need to have deep and rich knowledge of many pedagogies as well as of the subjects and students we teach. This is our DNA. Planning lessons is how we learn this, so I am going to take my time over this, not as an indulgence but as a right.

How to use this book

Within this book I hope you find a detailed (but not absolute) set of notes on what we know about pedagogical content knowledge, teaching and learning. Where there seems to be an answer, it has been offered; where it is vague, what we think we know has been offered. This has been done in the spirit that it is better to know what you do not know than to not know that you do not know. The intention of this book is to help teachers to reflect on what and how they plan, how they teach and how to improvise around these plans.

When I was asked by Phil Beadle to write this book, my first reaction was to ask who had turned him down first. Phil was too polite to answer but my reaction has borne me out. I knew, somehow, that writing a book that was originally called 'How to Plan Lessons' was a nigh on impossible mission. What seems like a simple process involves much knowledge about the stuff to be learned; how it is learned; the context of the school, class and students; and the relationships, thinking and motivation behind being a learner. Not to mention how assessment, examinations and schools work, and how the system does not. My initial feeling is my final feeling – that there is much to say on the subject. So, on 6 August 2014 at 8:29am, I sat down and randomly wrote questions that I thought might constitute a checklist.[1] It quickly became overwhelming and out of sequence, as many ideas ran concurrent with others. I present the list here to illustrate what goes on in teachers' heads. I am sure the list is incomplete.

- What exactly needs to be learned?

- How exactly can this be and remain useful?

- How will this connect to the bigger question or problem?

- Where is this knowledge headed towards – what are the next things to be learned in subsequent sessions?

- Do all the intentions have equal value? Are some concepts more important than others?

---

[1] Isn't Google Docs an amazing and unnerving thing!

Introduction

- What might the students already know that will be useful during learning this?

- How can this be made useful and relevant to them?

- What misconceptions might they have?

- How might these be challenged and corrected?

- What might they find difficult?

- How might this be made easier?

- Has this been oversimplified? How might they develop a more complex understanding? How do we work towards complexity?

- How best is this taught?

- How best is this learned?

- What activities will help them to learn this?

- How do I need to be to manage this learning?

- How will the students be motivated?

- What questions will be asked to develop their understanding?

- What questions will be asked to check their understanding?

- How might the uniqueness of learning be expressed by different students?

- How will the teacher collect enough information to make good decisions?

- How will the teacher collect detailed information about student learning?

- What feedback could be given to develop their understanding?

- What alternative explanations could be used to develop their understanding?

- How many exposures to each learning intention are the students getting?

- Are there any subsequent exposures to this knowledge?

- How will the students know they have learned this?

- Do they have an opportunity to make sense of this information?

- Do they have an opportunity to improve the quality of their work and/or understanding?

- Do they have an opportunity to practise and rehearse?

- Do they have an opportunity to reflect and respond to feedback?

- Which tasks are best served as group tasks? Which tasks are best served as individual tasks?

- Who is being served by each task? Is it for the students to learn or to provide me with information about their learning? Can it do both?

- How will motivation be maintained?

- How long do I expect each activity to take?

- Will the students cover all of the intentions satisfactorily in the time we have?

- Are there too many intentions for this time period?

- Which activities are OK to move on from in a slightly incomplete form? Which ones must have 100% completion?

- What do successfully completed tasks look like? What will their qualities be?

- Will increasing student ownership of the tasks/learning improve motivation and retention? How can the tasks be designed to do this?

- Do any of the tasks help to develop broader literacy and numeracy?

- What does this knowledge look like when fully formed?

- What are the intermediary steps to get there?

- Do any of the tasks help to develop literacy within my subject area?

- How do these opportunities support the original subject learning intentions?

- How can a balance be found over subject content and developing literacy?

- How can feedback be provided to develop literacy and numeracy?

- Do we all have an opportunity to be human?

- What attributes and skills would support students learning these concepts?

- How can this be scaffolded to help students develop these? How can students be supported with these?

- What feedback might develop this over time? What experiences might they need to become better at these?

- Is our classroom community strong enough for mistakes to be made publicly?

- Is our classroom community strong enough for students to support one another?

- How will the class be managed?

- Who will sit with whom?

- How will the students be greeted and settled?

- What rituals and protocols might be useful to build and maintain our classroom community?

- How will I set the tone for today's lesson?

- What is the appropriate tone for this learning to take place in?

- How will the learning be made memorable?

- How will the students memorise the learning?

- How will all students be challenged? How will all students be supported?

- How will all students access the information?

- What questions will they ask to gain the right information?

- What signs might there be to tell me that it is time to move the whole class on?

- What signs might there be to tell me that some students need a different route?

- What questions will encourage discussions about the content knowledge?

- What questions will encourage discussions about the strategies being used?

- When a student answers a question, how will I know they know this and have not just deduced it?

- How will learning look different to performance?

- How will students learn from other students? How will I ensure that this is right?

- What questions will stimulate metacognitive thinking around this content?

- How does this lesson and its pedagogy fit in with my school's broader educative purpose?

- Over time, are my students experiencing sufficient variety in pedagogy and experiences?

- Who is this student work for?

- Is this student work significant beyond the classroom?

- Does this lesson necessitate that I am at least cognisant of their prevailing emotions?

- How might I manage the emotions in the classroom?

- How am I encouraging the students to be kind?

- How am I communicating high expectations in all aspects of how the students are in my lesson?

- How many times have the students already been exposed to this information? How well did they understand it last time?

We can't fit all of this thinking into every plan, every lesson, every day, but the more we learn, and the more we are conscious of the decisions we make, the more our vast knowledge will come to bear. Ultimately, it helps us to design what we hope will be a useful and productive lesson for our students. It also helps us to realise that the exquisite lesson plan we have crafted is actually pants. It then gives us confidence to be able to change it, mid flow, seamlessly, so that the time we get to spend with our students is valuable to them, valuable to us and valuable to the endeavour that education brings.

My initial start point was to reject the idea of a checklist, a simple set of steps that will organise our time with students but, in reality, do little to pave the way for deep professional thinking about what we do. So this book, and it is intended as more of a recipe book, exists to inform but also allows for your skill, knowledge, passion, unique abilities and professionalism. This spirit is best summed up by Claudia Roden (2005: 7) in her *Arabesque* cookbook:

> Trust your taste and allow yourself a certain freedom in the preparation of the dishes. This is in the spirit of these cuisines which, although faithful to tradition, have no absolute rules and are rich in variations and poor in precision. You are told to 'weigh with the eye' and to taste as you go along. And that is what cooking is about. We are dealing with products of nature and these vary. … Many vegetables available to us come from different countries and are grown in different soils. … They have a different taste and respond differently to cooking. Rice, even of the same variety, and same provenance varies from one year to the next and, depending on whether it is new or old [differs] in the amount of water it absorbs. Once upon a time the recommendation for many rice recipes was to add 'as much water as it takes'. There was much sense in that.

It's time to get cooking …

PART I

Pedagogical Content Knowledge: How is Your Subject Learned?

CHAPTER 1

Using Pedagogical Content Knowledge to Plan to Overcome Misconceptions

Pedagogical content knowledge is rather a mouthful to say. It might be thought of as the millefeuille[1] of educational thought, in that it is known yet remains unfamiliar. The cake of a thousand leaves is reminiscent of the many interleaved layers of understanding that a teacher has: of the content being learned, how the learning tends to happen, the strategies it is best to employ, the knowledge and learning needs of their students. Pedagogical content knowledge was developed by Lee Shulman (1986, 1987) and is a blend of subject knowledge, pedagogical knowledge and knowledge of the context in which learning takes place. It is all of these things and more; describing it as a 'blend' does not really do it justice. Although the individual elements are important in themselves, it is in combination that they become as potent as when the Ghostbusters crossed their proton beams.

At first glance, pedagogical content knowledge appears to be 'jargoneering', but the name is a useful one in terms of giving us a focus on how the content is to be transmitted so that it is learned. It is our pedagogical content knowledge that differentiates us, as teachers, from our equivalent non-teaching specialists (scientists, writers, mathematicians, economists); it is our pedagogical content knowledge that compels us to organise the transmission of knowledge in the way that we do. It is our own pedagogical content knowledge that we must employ in our planning, and it is

---

[1] The millefeuille has many names, the most humble being a custard or vanilla slice.

the students' pedagogical content knowledge that we must seek to spot in lessons so that we can speed up its acquisition.

My first, and only, formal experience of pedagogical content knowledge came early on in my career. (I say formal but, in reality, it was only as formal as a cramped science prep room can possibly be.) It involved a dear colleague, Mark Lovatt, passing me a folder with Ros Driver's *Eliciting Children's Ideas in Science* inside and being told, 'Read this. It's great for planning lessons!'[2] It was great; it still is great.

Sadly, I do not think I am alone in not having had any real training or discussion about how our subjects are learned. We tend to focus therefore on what we *do* as teachers – getting hung up on strategies, methods, teacher actions and any feedback we receive on our teaching. We call this teaching & learning: excited colleagues produce teaching & learning bulletins; we attend training in teaching & learning; we build teaching & learning toolkits; we speak of teaching & learning cycles; go on jollies to teaching & learning conferences; ruminate over teaching & learning development plans; we adhere to teaching & learning policies. And all the time we do this, pedagogical content knowledge is under our noses – ignored. What is pedagogical content knowledge? Let me tell you, dear colleague ... pedagogical content knowledge is the very ampersand between teaching & learning.

The ampersand

The great potential for formalising our use of pedagogical content knowledge is that we can move from using it instinctively and inconsistently to being able to plan with it systematically. Perhaps most importantly, it helps us to become more aware of what learning might look like in the classroom, sensitising us to misconceptions when they arise and turning them into teachable moments.

---

[2] Sadly, I can find no reference to this, but the book she co-edited, *Children's Ideas in Science*, is available from the Open University Press.

Pedagogical content knowledge most commonly manifests as one of four interacting forms:

1. Knowing how to represent knowledge so that it can be learned. This is context dependent, with teachers' prior understanding of their class(es) being a key part of how they go about representing this knowledge.

2. Knowing how to organise or sequence knowledge so that it can be learned. We have to understand how the knowledge is connected to other knowledge and other concepts. This must involve planning on a macro and micro scale so that the overarching idea and the interrelated details underneath become clearly connected.

3. Knowing which concepts and ideas are difficult to learn and, subsequently, how to help students learn them. This includes knowledge of likely student misconceptions.

4. Knowing which knowledge is important. This includes threshold concepts.

We can also add to this our knowledge of the (ever changing) curriculum and the assessment of the subject.

To be clear, the content of this book, and not just this chapter, is dedicated to understanding our pedagogical content knowledge. The next two chapters detail how we can understand the teaching of our subjects better, and the last three look at the more generic pedagogical content knowledge of the processes of how to teach and how we learn.

Planning to tackle misconceptions

What are misconceptions?

Carnegiea gigantea, the Saguaro cactus (a native of the south-western United States) is the stereotypical flora of our cartoon childhood; it is the version of cactus that marked the barren landscape through which Wile E. Coyote chased the Road Runner. Although they are surprisingly shallow rooted for a plant of that size, their rooting system is well adapted, with roots wrapping around rocks to provide anchorage. They are also incredibly robust plants. It is no surprise that Wile E. generally comes off second best when he runs into one. The Saguaro cactus itself has no awareness of how silly its choice of home is or even of how it has changed the climatic and edaphic[3] features of the Mojave Desert.

Similarly, student misconceptions are generally shrouded in a haze of blissful unawareness of their folly or illogic. Like the cactus, they too are anchored to rocks, this time of 'knowing', and like the cactus, these misconceptions can be extremely hardy. Additionally, misconceptions – like the effect the cactus has on Wile E. when he comes into close contact with one – also have the capacity to taint any ideas that come into contact with them. The cactus *belongs* in its habitat. Likewise, there can be many logical reasons for misconceptions to exist. The idea itself may be wrong but the reasoning behind it can be as right as rain.

The problem with misconceptions

Misconceptions can have a strong grounding in our students' everyday experiences. They can lie in their use of day-to-day language or in partially formed ideas that have persisted because they haven't yet been challenged. In some cases, students have actually seen the phenomena with their own eyes! And seeing, as we know, often results in believing. The word 'belief' tells us that our students' misconceptions can be deeply held to the point of feeling as if they are unquestionable. The importance of this is brought to bear by Nuthall (2007: 156): students 'evaluate [each] new experience, and what the experience implies, against their prior knowledge and beliefs'. Here, he is saying that students use their prior experiences and what they know to interpret and make sense of any new ideas being presented. If this 'knowledge' is actually incorrect, then the students will not make the correct interpretation of this information and learning won't happen. This model of learning suggests that, for learning to take place, there must be enough information to be assimilated into the

---

[3] Edaphic relates to the characteristics of the soil.

students' working memory before it can then be transferred into long-term memory. If insufficient information is available – and misconceptions will reduce the amount of correct information – then the new information is either thought of as a different version of a known idea and is absorbed into it or, alternatively, it is simply forgotten.

How misconceptions are different to mistaks[4]

Although this may sound a trifle hair-splitting, there is a useful distinction to be made between misconceptions and mistakes. Misconceptions are genuinely held beliefs: as a result, they can be difficult for students to spot and address. Their roots are in pre-conceived notions and stereotypes, our misinterpretation of concepts and facts, and our confusions about common and technical language. Mistakes, on the other hand, are often a result of carelessness or of the fact that the thing being learned is pretty difficult. Misconceptions appear to be important things to address, mistakes less so. But this is not necessarily the case. We must reference the content being learned to determine what is important.

An approach to tackling misconceptions

Time flies like an arrow. Fruit flies like a banana.

As a gentleman of a certain age, I can write this next section with a certain partially humiliated air of knowledge and wisdom. Although I am yet to suffer a proper mid-life crisis, and have thus far avoided buying a leather jacket with tassels, I have breached the other side of forty. For me, it was no big deal, I just accepted it and got on with life. However, I've observed others around me succumb to the psychological trauma of confronting the fact that they are slowly turning into old men and must now dispense with their conception of themselves as being young and replace it with an idea that is rather more disappointing.

---

4 *Sic.*

All in all, there are six more possible reactions (!) to facing the concept of being forty, most of which are about avoiding the issue in some way:

1. The more curmudgeonly will simply stick their fingers in their ears, whistle to themselves and ignore the fact that soon everyone will see them as old.

2. Others reject it claiming, 'But I feel nineteen!' Thereby blaming the accepted use of the Gregorian calendar to measure the passing of time, rather than the way they feel. Bloody Gregorians!

3. The second variety of age deniers are nowhere near as irritating, however, as the deflectors – those bastards who prefer to identify the aging process in others rather than focus on themselves. A deflector will come up with choice remarks such as, 'Well, I must say, Darren is looking rather old these days. It's the slap-head, you see.' Sad as this is, it's not as sad as their utter inability to see the relevance of aging to their own selves.

4. The most worrying way of avoiding the issue (and its implications) is to hold it in abeyance, promising to 'cross that bridge when I have to'. You wouldn't organise a pension on the day you retire, so do you really want the enormity of not being young any more suddenly befalling you at the exact point that you find yourself unable to hold yourself up in Morrisons without the aid of a shopping trolley? No. Thought not. People will stare at and mock your tears.

5. The more ingenious of us will attempt to reinterpret the facts in a manner that allows their belief of themselves as still being young to remain unaffected. Statements such as, 'Fifty is the new forty' and other such bollocks can be heard coming from the mouths of these fellers.

6. The classic line 'Life begins at forty' gives us another type of reinterpreter – one who makes surface changes to the way in which they view life's ugly landmarks. Avoid these idiots like you would a leprous dog.

If I sound at all bitter here, I am not. I am just old.

Learners do a version of all of these things when faced with a new idea that conflicts with something they previously believed, even when the idea presented to them is as true as the passing of time. Some spot the beauty in the new idea and accept it readily, but not many. Most will either ignore it, reject it, exclude it, hold it in abeyance or reinterpret it. Few will readily accept the new idea as their new belief because it overrides what they hold to be true (Chinn and Brewer 1993).

Beliefs are strong, therefore (at the risk of sounding like an odd kind of superhero – one who does wear tights but only when the cold winter nights bite) our pedagogy must be too. Beliefs are also notoriously difficult to shift by logic and reason alone so, more than ever, we need to structure our students' interactions with the right (and wrong) conceptions. Pedagogical content knowledge – or, more precisely, our knowledge of potential misconceptions – provides a useful start point.

Detailed information about subject-specific misconceptions are easy to search for, being readily available on the internet, and will become well-known to you the longer you teach your subject. After a couple of years of teaching, you will often find yourself thinking, 'They always make the same mistake or have the wrong idea.' It is a genuinely sensible thing to wonder why they always do that. Each teacher experiences these moments, so asking colleagues about common student misconceptions can be a treasure trove too. Once we are aware of them, we can then go on to help students become aware of their own misconceptions. We can scrutinise resources for potential errors; we can design our instruction to reduce the chances of students misinterpreting the information we've provided; and we can therefore avoid reinforcing or forming misconceptions.

Posner and Strike (1992: 149) suggest that the following conditions must be met if students are to correct their misconceptions (or have them corrected):

- *'The student must experience some dissatisfaction with their current conception' or understanding.* Students are unlikely to be aware of these dissatisfactions, and it therefore falls to us to make them purposefully aware of the ones they hold. This can be difficult because 'theories' work for them perfectly well in their everyday lives, so we have to tutor our students to become critical of their own thinking.

- *The new conception must be intelligible or understandable to learners.* This is where our skill in representing ideas specifically tailored to the learning needs of the students in front of us comes to the fore. Our assessment practices need to allow students (and teachers) to see that they are 'getting it'.

- *The new conception must appear initially plausible*; it must seem to be a better possible answer than the misconception. Keeping our instruction 'real' and rooted in what is known (i.e. their prior knowledge), making connections clear and using concrete examples all help students to alter their understanding of things.

- Finally, *the new conception should suggest the possibility of being fruitful or useful to them as learners.* We can do this by helping students to transfer their new understanding and applying it to new examples.

The remainder of this chapter will be organised around the following ideas to aid the planning for tackling student misconceptions:

- How can we make students aware of misconceptions?

- How could deliberately leading them towards a moment of ambiguity help?

- How does making our teaching 'real' and connected help?

- Why should we make misconceptions the focus of our assessment?

- How might the development of students' critical thinking help?

Making students aware of misconceptions

When teachers purposely pay attention to anticipated student misconceptions, it is more likely that accurate student learning will occur – although it is worth pointing out the academic distinction between the term 'misconception' and the complementary idea of the 'alternative conception'. Alternative conception is seen as a gentler, more politically correct term, as the incorrect idea held by the student may well be based on observation and logic. While I won't be using the term alternative conception, I do feel that a sensitive approach to what the students might think is proper and professionally appropriate.

The ultimate goal is to safely leave the students with some sense of dissatisfaction with their current thinking, and it is therefore important to normalise the idea that we all have misconceptions because this helps to avoid making them feel as if they are stupid. Phrases such as, 'Common errors in this area include ...', 'People often think that ... but they would be wrong' or 'I was expecting you to say that' all help to convey this intention.

The mind reader game

The mind reader game is a good way of engaging students in the process of exploring their misconceptions (and those of others). The quiz show *QI* does this entertainingly: when the contestants say an obvious but incorrect answer it flashes up behind them demonstrating that their response (misconception) was entirely expected, and a loud siren peals to further imbue the misconception with comedy. In the classroom, a simple 'A-ha!' and the flipping round of a piece of paper with the wrong idea written on it suffices quite brilliantly. It is important here to flash a quick smile accompanied by a comment along the lines of, 'You wouldn't believe how many people think that' or asking, 'Who else thought this?' Lots of hands usually go up – making it normal, making it safe.

This exposure and erosion of misconceptions can only take place in an environment of complete trust, not only by the students in you but also in each other. We're attempting to expose 'the things you don't know that you thought you knew', and students' emotional landscapes have to be protected so they do not feel humiliated.

With this in mind, it is also worth considering the frequency with which we use this kind of exposure, as well as how we go about structuring the classroom environment and conversation. In order to ensure that these are honest, open and safe, it helps if you:

- Remove any sense of there being any secret teacher(y) business: say what you are going to do and why you are doing it.[5]

- Make it clear how useful it is to you, as a teacher, and to other learners.

- Help them to see how their understanding has developed regularly. Make them see how learning should change how they think.

- Praise contributions. There is no need to go over the top: even with correct answers, a simple, 'Thank you, that's correct,' 'Thanks, that's a very helpful answer' or 'Thank you – how many people agree?' can be useful here. A 'less is more' approach during these moments is of use here because, ideally, you want the students to do the majority of the talking around the area in which the misconceptions lie. Teacher talk and explanation at this point of the lesson stops the students from thinking and talking with each other about their own understanding and, to an extent, stops them from properly altering their perceptions. Being silent or probing with questions allows us to observe and identify changes in student understanding as they occur.

- Make the students feel that you are omnipotent and God-like in terms of your knowledge in this area, giving them the feeling that you are waiting for them at the end of their journey. Students tend to trust people who clearly know a lot of stuff. Responding with, 'I was expecting this – it's a fairly common misconception' or 'I understand where you're coming from but that's not quite right,' builds trust. It is also important to thank the student who brought the misconception to our attention.

---

[5] As teachers, we make hundreds of decisions about how the students will learn. At worst, this can turn into students doing 'the work' because the teacher tells them to, rather than investing in it as something worthwhile. It can be overcome simply by explaining why a task is being done.

- Use 'we' and 'our'. Students feel safer as a collective. Learning is often social: we *can* learn from others; any error is valuable in challenging our collective understanding. There will also be silent students in any class but they may well be listening and thinking. As an example, during an observation I undertook of an MfL lesson, the plenary was for the students to discuss how to structure a specific version of a sentence in French. A student who had seemingly made no effort to become involved in the exchange was asked for their thoughts. He paused for a while and said, 'Well … I was going to say that I thought the verb should go after [the preposition].' At this moment my ears pricked. He continued, 'But now, after what Ellie said, I think it comes before [the preposition].'

- Select teaching material with care. If we are not careful we can tend towards picking images that represent our own stereotyped view of how something is. By way of explanation, we've already done this in this chapter: you pictured the cactus in the Road Runner cartoon. The picture in your head was a stereotype! Did that picture help you to properly understand the diversity of this particular cactus and its wide ranging habitat and adaptations? Put simply, no. It can be helpful, therefore, to provide multiple examples to students so that they can get a more rounded and detailed view of the subject than just the original 'model'.

Creating a deliberate moment of ambiguity

Although the idea of introducing deliberate ambiguity may sound counter-intuitive when tackling misconceptions, it can be a useful tool, especially when used early in a lesson. For instance, deliberately delaying asserting that a student's response is correct can help to prompt the kind of thinking required to recognise our own dissatisfaction and reconsider our current understanding.

Consider the common starter question: 'Write down five things you know about …' To do this, the student is required to recall information. It does not prompt questioning of what is really understood. It has its uses but is pretty limited in terms of tackling misconceptions.

Now consider an amended version of the same starter question: 'Write down five things you think you know about ...' This time the question has allowed the students to speculate; it has implied that it is OK to be wrong. This is the tone we want to establish when tackling student misconceptions: let's test our ideas to destruction and see if they are still standing at the end of the lesson. Even if the students write down the exact same thing they would have done with the previous question, we have set the tone for how the students will be led into tackling the troublesome in this classroom.

Finally, consider this rather extravagant starter question: 'Write down five things you think you know about ... that might help you to learn about ...' (e.g. 'Write down what you think you know about heat energy that might help you to learn about how heat energy travels from one place to another'). How about that for double ambiguity! This is a trickier proposition for students and will require more time for them to work on it, but the time spent is worthwhile because they are more likely to think about what they truly know and can then bring this into action while they begin to connect their knowledge to bigger questions or problems.

This example also implicitly reveals the subtle complexities of secret teacher business. In planning such tasks, we know that we are very much at the start of a dialogue that will be built upon throughout the lesson. We may be looking for gaps in knowledge in a formative way so that we can best support the learning of our students. Yet not one bit of this care and attention to detail is visible to the students. It is secret teacher business, and it can be opportune to demystify this at certain points. This questioning structure should make clear the direction of the lesson and where previous lessons may have been useful.

Keeping it 'real'

Concrete / familiar ———————————→ Abstract / unfamiliar

After isolating the problematic idea (the misconception), it is important to help students to integrate the correct one. We can do this by presenting the correct idea in such a way that it is consistent and connected to other knowledge, and which ensures that the new information being presented is plausible. In doing so, we allow the students to see this new explanation as better than their pre-existing one. This is best done in a concrete or 'real' way by using examples, models and analogies. Concrete examples and concrete words are better remembered than abstract ones (Fliessbach et al. 2006). These are teaching situations where we have to work from concrete to abstract (or from examples to theory) so the students can see the relevance of the new idea and, ultimately, are able to replace their erroneous thinking with the correct apprehension.

Plan activities that allow the students to apply the new correct idea in both familiar and unfamiliar situations, allowing it to supplant the old way of thinking and be seen as a better way of understanding this concept. The students should then see the new idea as plausible and fruitful.

Bridging analogies

This classic science teaching technique is where an abstract idea is taught to move the knowledge from a concrete familiar idea to an abstract unfamiliar one (Clement 1993). For example, let us consider an arse sitting on a chair. No, not an education secretary. An anatomical arse connected to a real human being. It is easy enough for us to visualise the weight of the person pushing down on the chair, but more difficult to conceive that the chair is pushing back up against the arse. (Our only real experience of this abstract concept might be from marking piles (pun intended) of books for several hours on a Sunday evening and getting to the point when we realise that, since we have been sitting on the same arse on the same chair for hours, that arse has become sore. We never blame the chair for pushing back, do we? We tend to look towards masochistic self-blame: '*I* haven't moved in hours' or '*I* have been sat funny.')

Now picture pushing down on a spring – the type you can squash – and it is easy to visualise the spring pushing back up against our weight. The coils of the spring move down then up, and we can see the effects of force. If we replace the spring with a piece of foam we can see the foam compress and reform when the weight is removed. The movement is the same but the mechanism of the movement is now more abstract. Finally, sitting on what appears to me an immoveable object of the chair's seat, we now have a concrete model of the elasticity, or the spring-like quality of the material, based on a sequential supplanting of ideas from the seen to the unseen.

Although the research base and published examples are too often science based, the principle is applicable across the curriculum if we follow these three steps in developing suitable analogies:

1. Identify an irksomely abstract idea that students struggle to get to grips with.

2. Think of a way of making it more visible or tangible to students.

3. Plan how to help students work back towards the abstract.

A nifty example comes from the editor of this manual who, when teaching the abstract and tricky idea of a parenthetical clause, uses football as a structural analogy. In his book, *Literacy*, Phil Beadle explains the analogy he uses to make the abstraction visible to his students: 'just like a footballer approaching a defender, a sentence also has a place to get to: a full stop' (Beadle 2015: 57). The writer intends the sentence to make a cohesive point before he gets to the full stop. As such, we might consider this simple A to B sentence:

The striker shoots wildly over the bar.

A → B

To add new information into this sentence, it would need to take a detour via point C. As in:

The striker shoots, distracted with thoughts of glory, wildly over the bar.

A → C → B

Finally, Phil provides a way of moving students' thinking from the analogy back to the abstract structure of the parenthetical clause. To do this he uses a real football, which serves to reinforce the analogy and engage and slow down the students to concentrate on the new and difficult idea. The students name themselves A, B or C.

Before A, B or C kick the ball they have to make up a sentence and then rehearse it while passing the ball from A to C to B, verbalising the necessary punctuation in the sentence. The physical structure provides a concrete version of the abstract sentence structure, and thereby grants the students access to it.

Focusing assessment on the misconceptions

Consider this question about your teaching: what do you value most?

a. Covering the curriculum.

b. Developing a deep and rich understanding of the subject you fell in love with all those years ago as a way of understanding the world.

c. Both.

My guess is that most of us would plump for (c) and declare ourselves idealistic pragmatists, although the demands of the job push our focus towards (a) more often than we would like. One way to serve both may be to identify when it is OK to just have the students learn some stuff, 'covering the ground' as it were, and when to identify the points in the curriculum where we might indulge ourselves, spending time on concepts we might pinpoint as problematic or which might require some time for the students to fully understand them. Understandably, we would struggle to do this with every concept we have to teach, so we must, in some way, be able to differentiate between when we are teaching for the students to know things and when we are teaching so they understand. Teaching to break down student misconceptions is one way that we teach for understanding.

One of the chief benefits of being aware of where students are most likely to go wrong is being able to throw the assessment kitchen sink in the direction of the difficulty. This doesn't make the design of the assessments any easier, but we can begin to check that the teaching has at least been intelligible and that student understanding is changing.

Implicit assessment

Not all feedback has to be given directly, and we don't always have to stop in order to reflect on what has (or hasn't) just been learned. Sometimes it is good to just remain in the moment of what is currently being learned. When I've played a duff chord on my guitar (this happens with unerring regularity), no one has to tell me that I've done so. I can recognise it myself and then make efforts to improve my, erm, fingering of that chord the next time I play it.

The term 'implicit feedback' hopefully suggests that it is embedded within the general flow of classroom discussion, so the students remain focused on the business of integrating the new idea. Learners can gain implicit feedback through the teacher's clever construction of activities, discussions and debates, as long as the ideas the students hold about a concept are readily juxtaposed with the correct answer. Students also listen to what other students are saying and, in the right conditions (in which they are aware of potential misconceptions), use what they have learned from others as feedback with which to scrutinise their own thinking (Nuthall 2007: 94).

Assertive questioning – a strategy to exemplify implicit feedback

Assertive questioning places the teacher in the role of coach for a section of a lesson: the teacher is in control of the process while the content being discussed is in the hands of the students. The teacher sets the whole class a problem that requires small teams of students to discuss and prepare a group response which will eventually be shared with the class. The students are encouraged to involve themselves and each other. A group spokesperson is appointed and their thinking must also be challenged within the group. The problem set must focus on a misconception or difficulty and must also be sufficiently complex so that it involves at least a few steps to fully explain it. While the students prepare a response, the teacher circulates, asking the teams if they need a clue and, eventually, if they need more time.

This method requires us to quell teacher instincts like finishing sentences for them. In the early stages, the method is attempting to prepare the students to set out possible alternative ideas that will be debated and clarified later in the lesson. If, at this stage, the students all come up with the same correct solution to the problem, it isn't a bad thing; it merely augments the acceptance of the new idea. However, it is more likely that we will select this kind of strategy for ideas that generally prove difficult for students to grasp. As such, we should expect misconceptions and misapprehensions to be discussed and sometimes agreed by the groups to be true.

We can lead them to this by giving them negligible preparation time along with a protracted debate section after the ideas have been shared. The phrasing of this debate matters — for example, 'So, using all the information available, what is the best answer?' is better than, 'Who is right?' During this phase of the method, the students will again receive implicit feedback. If incomplete solutions emerge from the debate, then this must be addressed in the final step when the teacher sanctions an answer. Although the final step allows us to actively teach, our start point must come from the students' current collective position. Therefore, the teacher's role is about more than telling them the correct answer; it involves highlighting contradictions and identifying correct logical thinking and gaps in the students' knowledge.

There is a nine step process to set up assertive questioning:

Step 1: Design a clear question that requires a multipart response. Ideally, this will explicitly (or implicitly) cause the students to give reasons for their answers. Divergent questions which encourage the students to apply their knowledge are useful here — for instance, 'Why are plants important in the development of the earth's atmosphere?' or 'In what ways might history have been changed had the Spanish Armada defeated the English in 1588?' One question for the entire class is enough.

Step 2: Consider the grouping of the students. Students should work in teams of three or four to formulate an answer. But you decide who works with whom.

Step 3: Set the students off in the direction of answering the question. Make it clear that all members should be ready to explain to the class their team's thinking and that you will not reveal the answer until the end of the session.

Step 4: Circulate the room, primarily to ensure that the students are on task. Check how much longer they need to complete the task. Agree deadlines.

Step 5:   Before you move on, check if any teams need more time.

Step 6:   Make it clear that you are going to be making a note of their responses but that this does not mean they are correct.

Step 7:   Nominate the students *you* want to speak, recording the responses on the board. Take several answers.

Step 8:   Evaluate the answers given so far. Do they agree and why? What is missing from the answer? How can the answer be improved? This again needs to be free from teacher guidance.

Step 9:   Now give the teacher sanctioned answer. Praise contributions and correct thinking.

Teaching critical thinking

Don't worry! This is not the dreaded return of the generic thinking skills lesson; however, it is worthwhile to look at the characteristics of critical thinkers as they seem to be well suited to broaching and overcoming misconceptions. According to Ennis (2011: 12), critical thinkers:

- Are 'open-minded' and aware of alternatives.

- Try to be 'well-informed'.

- 'Judge the credibility' of the information accurately.

- 'Identify conclusions, reasons and assumptions.'

- Assess the 'quality of an argument' well.

- Can construct and defend a 'reasonable position'.

- 'Ask appropriate clarifying questions.'

- Develop 'plausible hypotheses' and know how to test them.

- 'Define terms in a way appropriate for the context.'

- 'Draw conclusions' when needed, but only with 'caution'.

- Use all the items in this list when deciding what to believe or do.

Misconceptions (as a rule) are subject based and, in order to overcome them, the students benefit from being able to analyse, evaluate and judge the merits of different ways of explaining a concept. Ergo, critical thinking has its place within the teaching of subjects, although which elements are more useful may differ in maths, science or history.

Teacher modelling of how critical thinking manifests itself in your particular subject domain is an important way of teaching the students how to do this. They will then be better equipped to replicate it, and it helps them to see the thinking as a process. In many ways, you want the students to get into the habit of questioning everything, not to just swallow the 'teacher is always right' dogma (this is important even when the teacher is right). Obviously, this is a long-term approach and not something that just happens within the space of a lesson. But it is clear that if students can identify their own dissatisfaction with an idea, and then form better arguments based on a more evaluative way of thinking about the available evidence, then they will be better equipped to avoid misconceptions.

Put simply, critical thinking is the ability to think and communicate clearly and rationally. Dialectical approaches – the art of investigating and discussing the truth of opinions – are most suited for our purposes here in preparing students to be more discerning about what it is they know. It seems logical that, at some point in the breaking down of a misconception, the students should have a chance to evaluate their ideas against the (new) evidence. Critical thinking is difficult as a novice but not impossible, and is not in any way a fruitless exercise. Regular bouts of evaluative thinking plotted through a sequence of lessons where known misconceptions are to be tackled will prime student thinking (and begin to create the necessary classroom culture) before they enter the arena of the 'confusing'. It is the long-term blend of both skills and content that will best support learners; consequently, it is desirable (yet occasionally onerous and quite difficult) to achieve some form of alignment between the content and the skills.

The best start point in identifying what might be important for students is our pedagogical content knowledge and, in particular, what we know about how our subject is learned. We must think about the concepts in a sequence of lessons, their difficulties in being learned and then how we ourselves think through these difficulties. How we model the thinking we use to understand these concepts can then form the basis of our lesson planning. We can do this by considering how we:

- Distinguish between confusing or closely related ideas and thereby identify the problem or difficulty.

- Solve problems.

- Weigh up evidence of what is the correct way of thinking. How do we know something is right?

- Make decisions about the correctness of thinking or 'facts'.

In this way, we can illustrate how we think as experts and establish how best to structure classroom dialogue. Teacher modelling should as clearly as possible show how to test the veracity of ideas as we seek to attain the right answer. Argumentation is the 'process of reasoning systematically in support of an idea, action, or theory',[6] and, for teachers, it enjoys an overlap with explanation, which may be 'complementary and synergistic'.[7] Argumentation has been used across the curriculum in the teaching of science, mathematics and reading, and in the comprehension of history and social studies (Nussbaum 2008). The natural habitat for argument is in the discourse of the classroom between teachers and students, and between students themselves. Successful argument must be, firstly, about the idea and, secondly, collaborative, leading to 'learning gains that are more permanent' (Nussbaum 2008: 351), with student

---

[6] See https://en.oxforddictionaries.com/definition/argumentation.
[7] See http://www.nuffieldfoundation.org/practical-work-learning/how-argumentation-different-other-related-concepts.

explanation more potent than received explanation. This reminds me of the 'generation effect', as described by de Winstanley and Bjork (1997), which proved that student generated ideas are better remembered than those provided by the teacher. The idea of collaborative discourse can simply be seen as polite disagreement rather than being direct and confrontational. Politeness is more effective at generating new ideas and learning (Chui 2008), and it must be modelled by the teacher.

By definition, misconceptions are a collection of alternative ideas: they vary from one another and from the correct version. In order for students to confront their views, it is important that their views on the concept are aired. Teachers must therefore consider carefully how they construct classroom dialogue (both teacher-to-student and peer-to-peer conversations). Now, this may not come as a surprise, but there is normally only one teacher to a class of 30 students. In management speak, there is a low teacher-to-student ratio, which makes having sufficient teacher-to-student dialogue difficult; if there are 30 students in a class, there may very well be 30 distinct ideas. It is no wonder that we, as teachers, find it easy to fall into the habituated behaviour of the initiation-response-feedback (IRF) methodology. This dialogue too often turns into an all too closed discussion where the teacher expects only a single predetermined response. The IRF sequence is in clear conflict with our intentions of exposing alternative perspectives and rigorously evaluating them so that the students change their minds about what they think. If we define classroom dialogue as being the kind of stymied talk that ordinarily goes on in lessons, then we miss the potential richness that a true dialogue can bring. Thankfully, simple structures can be used to provoke students to enter into reasoning, explanation and justification. For instance, strategies like 'odd one out' can be used to raise the expectations of student responses in class discussions.

Odd one out is a simple enough technique: the students are given several ideas or examples from which to identify and justify why they think one option in three might be the odd one out (note the ambiguity of 'might' here). It is helpful if multiple correct answers are presented to the students so that more than one idea can be correct. Student responses also improve with an outline of the desired response structure, such as, 'The odd one out is ... because ...' In spite of this structure, some students will still want to just give an answer and avoid clarifying it. This can be reduced by providing them with an opportunity to discuss possible answers before responding to the group. In doing so, you can break up the IRF sequence, turning it instead into IRDF (the D standing for discussion). In the early exchanges, you may need to direct students to the response structure and insist on a 'because', but students quickly take to it.

It is worthwhile deferring the feedback part by not giving a teacher sanctioned answer straight away. This encourages the students to dwell on the concept being learned. We can do this by asking elaboration questions ('Can you tell us more?') or by eliciting responses from other students – for example, by asking, 'Has anyone got the same answer but for a different reason?' before moving on to, 'Has anyone got a different answer?' This allows for a richer set of ideas to come into the arena. This example leads us to a better working definition for classroom dialogue, where students engage in hypothetical, speculative thinking that allows them to develop ideas. It is also rich with implicit feedback. Try this method and listen for students bending the response stem into, for instance, 'I think it might be ... because' and, later, 'I agree with Bob because ...' or 'I disagree with Bob because ...'

Suddenly, it becomes clear that we cannot just plan questions. We need to plan what the ensuing discussions should achieve and, in doing so, begin to move away from the three part IRF exchanges that generally dominate classroom talk.

Mercer (2008: 1) helpfully defines three forms of discussion which have different levels of desirability within the classroom:

1. *Dispute:*
    a. Individual decision making with impoverished interactions.
    b. Competitive rather than cooperative.
    c. Little implicit feedback.

    (This version can be taken to be reminiscent of IRF.)

2. *Cumulative:*
    a. Knowledge is shared uncritically.
    b. Little implicit feedback.
    c. Ideas may be elaborated but not evaluated.

    (This is moving towards IRDF; consider the D as standing for discussion.)

3. *Exploratory:*

    a.   High levels of trust and respect.

    b.   Reasons and ideas are shared and challenged.

    c.   The group has a shared purpose.

    d.   Everyone asks questions.

    (A sophisticated version of IRDF; consider the D as standing for dialectic.)

Nuthall's (2007: 37) idea that 'social relationships determine learning' is never truer than when we are dealing with misconceptions. Exploratory talk is a way of problem solving which is based on students constructing arguments about what they believe and expressing the reasons why they believe it. It is therefore ideal for pondering misconceptions. However, we may not make the most of this as often as we should because teachers traditionally do most of the talking and, in doing so, we assume 'responsibility for the content, pacing and style of pupil contributions' (Edwards 2005: 30; quoting Barnes and Todd 1977: ix). In fact, there is a view that in these instances we underestimate students' skills in being able to initiate, elicit and extend ideas as part of their classroom dialogue. Establishing a classroom culture in which this style of exploratory talk can flourish becomes an important aspect of what teachers must do. This takes time, however, so creating some basic ground rules for (extended) classroom talk becomes an essential step for learning to take place.

We have to manage several conundrums in creating a classroom culture in which such talk flourishes:

•   How much do we stand back?

•   If we need to intervene, how and when should we do this?

•   How do we balance the right to silence with the desire for everyone to be involved?

•   How do we accommodate different types of contributors – those who come up with ideas, those who think practically about the discussion and those who reflect on the ideas?

It is nigh on impossible to get all of these elements right at any one time, but the class rules we establish can provide a decent start point. The rules might look like this:

- We listen respectfully to each other's ideas.

- We invite others to speak.

- We question the idea not the person.

- If we disagree, we must say why.

- We aim to agree in the end.

These are best established in collaboration with the class, rather than imposed on them. To develop this culture of sophisticated classroom talk, the teacher's role and their feedback during class discussions are most helpful when they do the following:

- Frame the argument (define, clarify and elicit prior understanding).

- Check student responses for meaning.

- Accept (even correct) responses early in an exchange in a tentative way – e.g. 'maybe', 'perhaps'.

- Offer new ideas as the theme develops in the dialogue, as opposed to frontloading them at the start.

- Praise the quality of the arguments and reasoning.

- Seek rebuttals and counter-arguments from students.

- Clarify and summarise the arguments and their meaning.

In all of this, it is not just the students' views that matter; the teacher's (authoritative) voice and questions are a key part of the process. We help the discussion to attain the balance needed for it to run profitably. This can be exemplified in the assertive questioning process where students and teacher have defined roles within the dialogue.

Using argument maps

Students need a range of structures to assist their critical thinking. These provide a scaffold for thinking and should be removed in the long run. This may mean that, in the short term, we design these structures for specific concepts, but we must also seek to teach the process of how to use them. After all, we know that some of the most effective activities for learning are managed by students themselves. A wonderful example comes from Will Ord (2012), who developed the delightfully flexible 'treasoning' activity which is well suited to helping students think critically *through* misconceptions. It uses a tree, its roots and the prevailing winds as an analogy to weigh up the evidence for or against an idea or concept.

Follow these five steps to set up a treasoning argument map with your class:

Step 1: The teacher draws a tree on the whiteboard and writes the argument for discussion on the board. If you are dealing with a misconception, then use the correct conception here, although this depends when in the lesson you introduce the treasoning map. It can be introduced early in the lesson, in which case you may want to start with the misconception. However, if your class has not done this kind of thinking before, or not used similar tools, then the complexity of the thinking required might get in the way of learning the concept in the first place! It is therefore recommended that it is used as a plenary tool.

Step 2: Through discussion, the teacher helps the students to explore what and how they know about this statement. It is recommended that you start with the reasons why the statement is true.

Step 3: On the roots of the tree (which, if you think about it, are anchoring and supporting the statement) write the reasons why it is *known* to be true. The strength of the evidence is represented by the depth of the roots, with deeper roots representing more important 'evidence'. It is important to engage the students in this process too.

Step 4:   The class discussion should then turn to the arguments or evidence as to why it is thought *not* to be true (if you are tackling a misconception) or simply reasons against (if you are dealing with an opinion). Once more, the strength of the evidence or reason can be represented by the strength of the wind, with strong winds being shown by thicker lines.

Step 5:   Finally, ask the students if they are now convinced that the statement is true. This can be obvious if there is no wind and lots of deep roots, although some of the previous evidence can be deep rooted and this can be useful information for future planning.

If this technique is being used to weigh up something more ambiguous (like an opinion) then there may well be equally strong arguments on each side; it is therefore a very useful pre-organiser before students tackle longer written work.

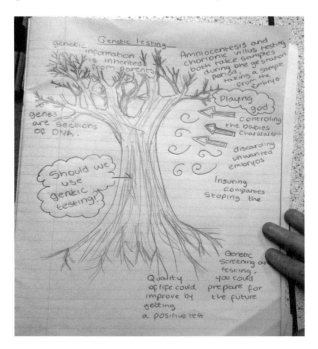

Summary

Misconceptions are deep rooted in a learner's prior experience, making them difficult to overcome. Understanding this is our first step in helping students to learn the correct conception. Since we have many strategies to correct misconceptions, our teaching needs a robust and planned approach. Our pedagogical content knowledge is central to this, and this also helps to target our assessment and feedback on problematic areas of our subjects. This involves making students aware of misconceptions, creating moments where they have to consider the evidence, and making learning concrete and clear where possible. This is more complex than it at first sounds, requiring the teacher to develop a repertoire of successful analogies and discussion structures, and to teach students how to think critically.

CHAPTER 2

Using Pedagogical Content Knowledge to Create Contexts and Connections in Learning

Experts perceive large meaningful patterns in their domain.

Glaser and Chi (1988: xvii)

The teacher's role is not only to see meaningful patterns in our domains, but to work out how we structure our teaching so that it leads towards a version of this complexity in student understanding. Once again, this is part of our pedagogical content knowledge, and we use this knowledge in two distinct ways to help our students learn: by placing new knowledge into relevant contexts and by making explicit the connections and interactions between ideas and concepts. If we plan for these during lessons and (crucially) across a series of lessons, students will begin the journey from being novices towards being experts.

Creating contexts

Placing learning in a context helps students in two main ways. Firstly, it improves student motivation by conferring importance on the tasks at hand, as the knowledge is more likely to be seen as relevant to them if it is presented in a context to which they can relate. Secondly, this context helps students to learn more efficiently by providing them with a relevant structure for the ideas being learned, which, in turn, gives them a better chance of activating the correct prior knowledge. At the heart of this chapter is Nuthall's (2007: 37) premise that 'effective activities are built around big ideas'. The 'big ideas' provide a context for learning and allow students to interpret and piece together information and ideas so that they, firstly, comprehend and, consequently, learn the new ideas.

However, it is not only content knowledge that benefits from being orientated around big ideas; the teaching of skills and attributes also requires such contextual clues. Clearly, some subjects have major skill sets that influence the teaching of the subject: physical education, drama, English and mathematics being the obvious candidates. Key skills are often entwined with content and metacognitive knowledge – for instance, knowing exactly when a specific skill should be applied.

The nature of the subject domain often asserts itself from time to time too. The idea of bias is inherent in the teaching of history because historical narratives are rarely, if ever, objective. It therefore becomes important to ask, 'Whose history is it?' throughout the curriculum in order to develop student sensitivity to bias and to prompt them to seek balance from their sources.

Contextual information is also used when we solve problems, narrowing down the field in which possible solutions might be applied. As teachers, we have much of this contextual information available to us because this is what our expertise brings. Our students, however, often struggle to see school and school tasks as anything other than a series of unrelated events, and this can result in them struggling to link past work with present work. Unfortunately, our best efforts in planning lessons will occasionally compound this difficulty. Breaking down learning intentions into learnable chunks can cause us to fail to pay regard to how to reassemble the knowledge and can result in us denying our students a view of the bigger picture.

Our practice, therefore, should contextualise the learning, making it relevant to students and allowing them the opportunity to make those manifold connections which (in many ways) define learning. Relevance is often misunderstood in teaching, and can be (mis)interpreted as making the knowledge relevant to students' lives. Personally, I am unconvinced that any effort spent making relevant correlations between the detailed aspects of the curriculum, such as parts of the longitudinal wave and the use of the semicolon, to a disaffected youth is particularly worth it. However, there may be interest in showing where the knowledge is applied in the 'real world'.

Importantly, the ideas should have relevance to the content being learned, to what the students have previously studied and to how the content works beyond the classroom. They then become useful and, as a result, stand some chance of becoming interesting; although students discern that tasks with immediate relevance are more motivating than the skill they are expected to find useful in later life. However, context is more than just a motivational technique; importantly, it is related to how we store knowledge in the schemas of our long-term memories.

Harry Brightwell moments

Schemas are theoretical mental maps which are stored in our long-term memory and organise the semantic content, specific concepts and the context in which the learning took place. The context is often provided by thoughts of 'what was I doing when I learned that?' This knowledge is another important part of our pedagogical content knowledge: how students learn. Students will remember the context in which the content was learned as much as the content itself. A conversation with my son about electrical circuits revealed this many months after he studied it in school.

> Me: So that's how you make a circuit work (*showing him how the circuit is built*). You see how all the wires make one complete loop?
>
> Tomas: Ah! That's how Harry Brightwell did it! He put the bulb on top of the battery and put wire there and there.

What he knows is entwined with what he remembers of the events of the day. This reminds me that no matter how much I want my students to be solely focused on the content of the lesson, the reality of the situation is that they also take in the richness of the classroom and its interactions. In Nuthall's (2007: 36) words, 'Students learn what they do.' This is not anywhere near as glib as it might sound and makes the construction of a potent context vital if we are to get our students to commit content to memory. The purpose of this section, therefore, is to consider how we share the clues that students need to make sense of the ideas being learned. For simplicity's sake, most of the examples described here just deal with content knowledge.

How to create a context for learning

As experienced subject experts, the connections we are generally able to make are extensive and deep. SOLO taxonomy provides a useful way of visualising how the knowledge might look, especially for the novice who will need to be told that the connections between ideas are important. SOLO taxonomy was developed by John Biggs and Kevin Collis to provide a simple, reliable and robust model of student understanding. It is comprised of three levels of understanding – surface, deep and conceptual (Biggs and Collis 1982). Its name is an acronym for Structure of the Observed Learning Outcome, and it is therefore primarily an assessment tool. It allows teachers to look at student work in terms of its *quality* rather than how many bits of this and that they have got right. The foundational stages of SOLO ('unistructural' and 'multistructural') are seen as being limited because the understanding of ideas during these phases remains disconnected; the 'relational' stage is considered to be connected but not integrated. This is desirable for learning as it is seen as 'deeper and more coherent'.[1] Although the acquisition of knowledge is not as neat as the SOLO model suggests, the taxonomy shows us that knowledge can be broken down into smaller parts and can then be reassembled; it allows us to plan with the re-assimilation of knowledge in mind.

My teacher planner, which is used to plot out medium-term plans of where the knowledge will be heading for each class, is full of one word lesson plans. ('Lesson plan' may actually be rather too strong a term but each word acts as a trigger for a substantial amount of subsequent knowledge.) At the risk of sounding dangerously middle class for a Geordie, these prompts are a bit like Radio 4's *Just a Minute*, where contestants have to speak on a subject they may not know a great deal about without repetition, deviation or hesitation. The show has run for 50 years, indicating that it must be at least occasionally amusing to those who enjoy such parlour games. I would wager that this derives from the degree of difficulty implicit in speaking fluently about something you don't know much about. Experts in a subject, however, would probably find speaking for such a limited time not at all challenging, and if I asked you to speak for a minute on a topic in your subject – enzymes, volcanoes, standard deviation, the Magna Carta, whatever – you would rightly tell me to do

---

[1] See http://pamhook.com/solo-taxonomy/ and http://www.johnbiggs.com.au/academic/solo-taxonomy/.

one as it would be impossible to fit in everything in that time. A single topic triggers a whole host of interconnected ideas and relationships; in essence, our pedagogical content knowledge is how we capture that complexity and make it understandable, teachable and, ultimately, learnable.

We do this by first establishing the broader context in which the knowledge exists. This context allows us to identify what information is relevant in our long-term memory so that we can make sense of new information by relating it to what we already know. Context can be found in many places within and between our subjects. The following table shows where it might reside, and some planning questions that might help students to unearth it are provided.

Context	Question prompts
Topic/module/ subject/domain/ school	• How does this knowledge fit with the rest of the knowledge in this module? • How does this knowledge fit with other modules or topics? • What knowledge has to be in place before this is learned? • What other knowledge might this lead to? • What makes this idea big or important for this topic?
How the knowledge is used ...	• Who uses this knowledge on a regular basis? • Where is this knowledge applied? • What does this knowledge help you to do? • What does this knowledge help you to understand? • Has this knowledge (or related knowledge) been in the news/ media recently?
Who is the learning for?	• Is there an audience for what is being learned? • Is there an authentic product linked to this knowledge?

Context	Question prompts
Students' knowledge (prior knowledge)	• What might students already know about this topic? • What experiences might they have had that could be informative? • Are there any connections to the students' everyday world? • Are there any common misconceptions associated with these ideas?
Assessment	• How is this knowledge likely to be assessed in the short term? • How is this knowledge likely to be assessed in the long term?

We have already considered much of this thinking when creating learning intentions and considering the implications of prior student knowledge, so we must now shift our focus to how we can confer relevance, usefulness and meaning to ideas being taught.

Structures to share the context of the learning

Bong … 'Here are the headlines …' Bong …

Our everyday interactions with information generally come in highly structured forms, from a news bellower belching the headlines at the top of the hour, to the chapter titles and subheadings in education books. Structure is ubiquitous, predictable and useful.

Helpful connections for students to make can be found in one of three places: connections to other bits of knowledge, connections to other parts of the module or course, and connections to the application of the knowledge. Simple strategies can be used to signpost these. For instance, the module map, which is a simplified schematic, shows the direction that learning will take over the course of a module or topic. It is, to an extent, a version of the news headlines for the duration of the topic.

The module map

Well-written module maps provide students with a big picture of what is to be learned during a topic. It can take one of two complementary forms. The first type requires us to title each lesson in the sequence in such a way that it reveals the key ideas within each lesson – very much like chapter titles in a book. Inevitably, this will make the learning appear sequential and linear, when, in reality, it probably won't be. But showing the students where ideas fit together can be helpful.

This example, taken from a Year 7 technology module, gives a clear view of the processes that students will undertake to complete a project. It gives a clear purpose to the classroom activities, modelling what engineers do and breaking down big problems into smaller but connected tasks.

The next example is based on a Year 4 Tudors module and uses big questions to highlight what the students will learn. Although this is less linear in nature, with some ideas easily switched around, there is an overall content flow to the lesson sequence.

The big picture
Lesson 1. Introduce students to the project. Link to video on YouTube: 'Rotten Teeth'.
Lesson 1. Students to identify the pin layouts for an eight pin PIC (a programmable intelligent computer such as Raspberry Pi) using the information sheet given and a set of pre-printed labels. (Reasoning)
Lesson 2. Students create flowcharts using programming editor. Students learn how to switch outputs on/off and create time delays. (Resourceful)
Lesson 2. Design the shape of the casing for the toothbrush holder using Pro/DESKTOP tutorials. (Resilience)
Lesson 3. Soldering of control circuit. You need to be able to read a circuit diagram. You should be able to identify components by their circuit symbols. (Responsible)
Lesson 4. Create an MDF case to hold the electronic circuit. Carry out research into the average family size within the group.
Lessons 5 and 6. Cut out design for facia of toothbrush holder using laser cutting machine. (Reasoning)
Finish

1. Who were the Tudors?
2. What was the War of the Roses?
3. What was Tudor life like for rich people?
4. What did Henry VIII do all day?
5. Why did Henry VIII have six wives?
6. What was Tudor life like for poor people?
7. What can Tudor inventions tell us about the lives of Tudor people?
8. What can we learn about our society from studying the Tudors?

Lesson structure and sequence and *knowledge structure and sequence* are not the same thing. To emphasise this contrast, the version of a module map below can be used instead of a linear one. This example shows many of the connections between the knowledge and is based on my own mental schemas for this topic. Its root and methodology may be different but the purpose is broadly the same: it is showing the students where the learning is going (and, in this case, coming from).

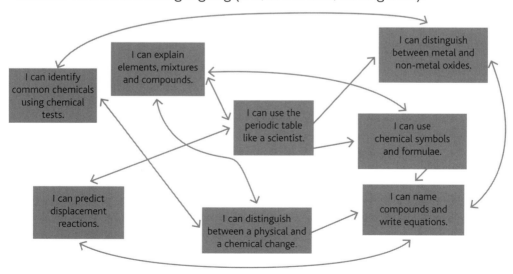

A balance must be maintained here between keeping it simple and clear enough for students and showing how the knowledge links to other bits of knowledge. This kind of map makes it easy to demonstrate where knowledge is useful in the learning of other knowledge and shows what and how other knowledge supports what we are currently learning.

As important as this is, there is perhaps a more important aspect to tools like this. Becoming good at defining learning intentions can, if we are not careful, restrict the diet of our students. Vigilance is needed here. We need to be able to demonstrate that what we are learning is greater than the sum of its parts; just like listening to an orchestra is more than a bunch of people playing a bunch of notes on an agglomeration of different bits of cat gut and wood. Cultural implications can go beyond the sum of their parts. Just ask the people of Manchester about their pride in the Hallé Orchestra, the people of Newcastle about the Royal Northern Sinfonia or the people of Kinshasa about Orchestre Symphonique Kimbanguiste, and you will see that the whole has a profundity that vastly overreaches any bald explanation of the constituent parts. So it is with the links between taught and assessed 'priorities': they are more than the sum of their parts. The gem-like quality of the periodic table, for instance, only hints at the marvel of what our universe is made from and the laws that govern it. In short, the beauty of our subjects is hidden in the interconnections, and with tools like this we are allowed to hint at and share that very beauty with our students.

A second way of conveying the detail within a bigger idea is through the written learning intentions. Simply by grouping these visually within boxes we can enable our students to see the connections within and between the bigger ideas. The 'I can' statements in the example beginning on page 52 are designed to break down (in a helpful way) what the overarching statements might conceal.[2] This method complements the breadth of the module map and reveals, to a degree, the depth of the subject. Students will probably need both at some point.

---

[2] Not everyone likes 'I can' statements, but I do, and they're not actually for the students. The 'I can' prefix reminds me constantly that what I am asking my students to learn must be actionable. Watson (2002: 208) defines learning outcomes as 'something that students can do now that they could not do previously ... a change in people as a result of a learning experience'. I tend to agree. Not everyone needs this reminder, but I do: it changes how I see assessment, how I see student knowledge, and so, for me, it is a useful part of the process.

This example is taken from a Year 8 chemistry module. Please note, that *some* of the broken down detail is rather obvious (and merely a breakdown of the bigger idea), whereas other bits (such as the 'I can use the periodic table' intention) add richness to the big idea.

I can apply the particle model to explain elements, mixtures, compounds, atoms and molecules.
I can identify common elements, mixtures and compounds.
I can define an element/compound/mixture/atom/molecule.
I can describe a model atom.
I can distinguish between atomic and molecular elements.
I can distinguish between elements, compounds and mixtures using ideas about atoms.
I can use chemical symbols and formulae.
I always use the protocols for writing symbols and formulae.
I can generalise the rule for working out a formula.
I can use the periodic table like a scientist.
I can identify where metals and non-metals are in the periodic table and describe their properties.
I can describe the organisation in the periodic table (groups and periods).
I can use valencies to work out the formula of simple compounds.
I can predict where an unknown element would be placed in the periodic table.
I can explain the differences between physical and chemical changes.
I can distinguish between a physical and a chemical change.
I can describe what happens to the atoms and molecules in physical and chemical changes.

I can name compounds and write equations.

I can use the rules to name compounds.

I can structure a simple word equation with reactants and products and + and →.

I can name all reactants and products in the following types of reaction:

- Metals and oxygen
- Metals with water
- Metals with acid
- Acids with alkalis
- Combustion
- Displacement

I can use state symbols to indicate the properties of the reactants and products in a reaction.

I can identify common chemicals using chemical tests.

I can link the results from the chemical test to identify the presence of:

- Oxygen
- Hydrogen
- Carbon dioxide
- Water

I can predict the outcomes of displacement reactions.

I can define displacement reactions.

I can describe the pattern of reactivity of group 1 alkali metals.

I can sequence the reactivity series of metals and include hydrogen and carbon.

I can apply the reactivity series to predict displacement reactions.

I can write complete word equations for displacement reactions.

> **I can distinguish between non-metal and metal oxides.**
>
> I can use the pH scale (and other indicators) to identify an acid and an alkali.
>
> I can describe the properties of an acid and an alkali.
>
> I can describe a neutralisation reaction.
>
> I know that metal oxides dissolve to make acids
>
> I know that non-metal oxides dissolve to make alkalis.

Students learn what they do

Student learning is not merely the content we teachers tend to place so much focus on. Our students also take in the whole classroom landscape and can recall surprising details about it. This is Nuthall's first premise about learning – that students learn what they do – and that they remember what they were doing when they learned something better than the thing being learned itself. You will recall my son's 'Harry Brightwell' moment, where he remembered who had come up with the idea I was explaining to him better than he remembered what he had learned in his science lesson. The following method seeks to exploit this ability and strengthen student learning.

Learning journeys

Learning journeys are a visual agenda for the classroom. For example, in the first image, the students are being prompted that two scientific models are coming up – which are key for this lesson – one based around a blender and the other a pair of scissors. When they get to the mix and match task they will instantly recognise where in the lesson they are. Likewise, in the second image, crucial content related moments are signalled, such as the set-up of the experiments, the scaffolding of reactants and products, and the particle model of a compound's molecule.

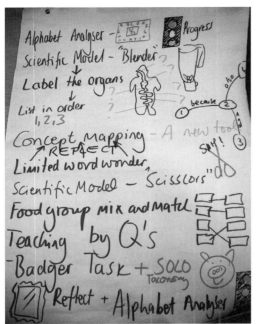
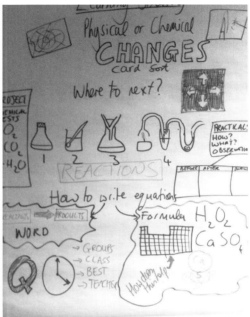

Learning journeys provide a representation of the learning and the activities, and are helpful in many ways. For students they:

- Remove secret teacher business (essential for a strong classroom culture) and help to give each class activity a positive purpose.

- Prompt student thinking and metacognition.

- Help students to spot how knowledge is being learned.

- Encourage students to see how knowledge supports the learning of other knowledge.

For teachers they:

- Clarify lesson sequences, turning the content into manageable chunks of time.

- Help us to spot the transitions.

- Aid reflection on the purpose of each activity, and how we might sell it or place it into a relevant context.

Teachers and students alike find learning journeys useful for locating their place in a lesson, with students regularly glancing at them during lessons and asking where they are. The most dramatic experience I've had that attested to their benefit was during a five day long training course I was facilitating on behalf of the Teacher Effectiveness Enhancement Programme in the charming market town of Darlington. One of the teachers on the course had an appointment during the morning of the fifth day and so arrived a little late. When she arrived, I greeted her, described what we were doing and went back to my work. Not ten minutes had passed by when she ran out crying. My instinct, like all sensitive Northern blokes, was to ask a female colleague to go and see what the problem was. As great as this idea was, my colleague explained in no uncertain terms that I was most qualified to help, so I put on my best 'are you alright?' face and waddled after the sobbing teacher. It turned out that the problem was that there was no visual agenda on display – or rather that the one we had put up had been covered by another poster! Consequently, she did not know where she was in the lesson and was bewildered to the point of losing it. Feeling truly part of a learning experience can be based on a shared sense of direction and agenda – and learning, as we know, can be stressful. Some learners find these structures useful, other learners find them essential.

The learning journey is just one way of communicating the pedagogical purpose of the activities that are to be used. Assigning purpose to each activity is an important way of supporting developing metacognition so that students become aware of the process they are embroiled in and begin to consider how they can control their thinking during it. It is therefore a great way of providing useful feedback to learners. Black and Wiliam's (1998) research indicates that good feedback should indicate where the students are, where they should be heading and how to get there. It is in this final step that sharing the process of learning helps students to reflect on their difficulties and move forward. Sometimes we need to see the content and process of learning together in order to work out the difficulties students have when learning our subjects.

To construct a learning journey, figure out what the key ideas and key activities are within either a lesson or a series of lessons, and then sequence them in a way that allows the content and classroom processes to become more visible to the students. I prefer a combination of images, key words and key questions that last over a few lessons. This helps me to provide continuity between lessons and a sense of progress for the students.

What is adolescence?

Another place we might find a relevant context is where the knowledge from the classroom can be applied or used outside of it: we may relate it to work, to careers, to events reported in the media or to aspects of the students' own lives. Doing this serves two noble purposes: firstly – and, in truth, this is the main reason for doing so – it helps to place the knowledge to be learned in a wider context in order to direct students towards identifying relevant experiences and prior knowledge they may have. The second is a more ethereal idea: that we can broaden their education so that it encompasses aspects of what Ofsted (2018: 40) calls 'social, moral, emotional and cultural' education, although these might be more usefully viewed through the prism of High Tech High's Larry Rosenstock, who ruminated that adolescence is 'a chance to try on new roles and identities'.[3]

Knowledge should, at times, be presented as part of the functioning world, and the importance of its application, specifically to the young people you are teaching, means we should not allow opportunities for contextualisation to escape or pass us by. The spirit of Rosenstock's statement is that telling students the things they need to know is not necessarily the best method at this moment in time; moreover, it is about creating an experience in which students begin to see the world as a place full of useful and clever ideas. As grandiose as this sounds, it can be done simply. For instance, stating that this knowledge is used by fire fighters to keep themselves safe is not enough. Asking, 'Who might find knowledge of how heat travels useful in their work?' is better. Alternatively, 'Why might a fire fighter find knowledge of how heat travels useful?' works well too. This version of questioning leads students to seek

---

[3] See https://vimeo.com/10000408.

out the importance of, and the connections to, the ideas. Learning relies on what is already known, and even the most seemingly tenuous links may be the start a student needs to recognise the connection between old and new knowledge.

Scenario challenge: an exemplar method for using tasks to set the context

A nifty way of using tasks to set the context is by structuring the task in the same manner as the 'scenario challenge' I first encountered in Antioch University's Critical Skills Program.[4] It is a rich experience through which students can practise their skills of learning (in this instance, collaborating to organise big ideas) alongside the content being learned. We will start with an example before we go about unpacking how this version of learning is structured.

This example is taken from a Year 10 BTEC science course and comes at the end of the topic, therefore much of the content has already been studied. This activity not only allows the students to review the information while placing it within a big idea, but it also gives them the opportunity to practise a literacy skill. In this case, the students have to 'paragraph' information — by, first of all, reading broadly, then filtering how important each idea is, and then grouping and sequencing the ideas. Yet it is the opportunity the task gives us to apply the knowledge in a scenario that is perhaps the most interesting feature of this teaching strategy.

---

[4] See https://www.antioch.edu/new-england/resources/centers-institutes/antioch-center-school-renewal/critical-skills-program/.

Book editing challenge – genetic diseases

You are a group of genetic counsellors who have been asked to edit a science book that provides useful information for potential carriers of genetic diseases. Several authors have contributed work for you to choose from. Frankly, your publisher, Media Mogul Mead, thinks that some of the authors' work is good and some of it is utter hogwash. Your task is to produce a high quality book that provides useful and detailed scientific information.

Your duties as editors include:

1. Giving the book an appropriate title.

2. Designing a cover that will convey the book's chief messages.

3. Writing an *editorial* introduction that explains what the book will help people to learn.

4. Creating chapters of information. You may want to use the following:

    a. What are genetic diseases? How are they different to contagious diseases?

    b. What are genes? How do genes pass on information?

    c. Specific examples of diseases. What are the symptoms? Give at least two types.

    d. What are the genetics behind the diseases?

    e. What is gene therapy? How might it be helpful?

5. Write a glossary of all the key terms.

6. Write a further *personal* introduction explaining why certain information was used and not others.

These tasks are vital to your success and should not be the job of one editor, but should instead use the ideas and comments of all members of the group. Media Mogul Mead's success criteria, which you will be assessed on, include your ability to work functionally as a team, so make sure it happens!

Careful planning and organisation of your work will help you to complete this on time.

With your deadline less than two hours away at 2.45pm, you must act quickly and decisively to ensure that an accurate and readable book is completed by that time. You may find that skim-reading the information is a useful start point. (*Skimming* is used to obtain the gist (the overall sense) of a piece of text.)

Content knowledge:

- To be able to identify and describe two examples of inherited diseases.

- To be able to identify the mechanism through which these diseases are inherited.

- To be able to investigate and describe the effectiveness of gene therapy to prevent inherited diseases.

Skills content:

- Collaboration

- Decision making

- Being creative

- Skim-reading

- Planning and organising

The components of planning a scenario challenge, like the one outlined on pages 59–60, include:

- Devising a scenario in which the ideas you are studying can be located.

- Devising specific tasks to aid the studying of the main ideas.

- Devising the tasks that are required to complete the challenge, including some that entail discussion, and making sure the students encounter useful skills in the completion of the task.

This type of structure provides a context which also gives the students clues about how to learn what is most important in the particular topic at hand. In many ways, such challenges provide a similar (but smaller) version of the more holistic sense of 'educational experiences' and are a way of practising the skills and attitudes needed for these.

Interestingly, students readily distinguish between tasks that appear authentic and those that appear more artificially contextual. Students start by making connections to their own experiences or knowledge. This can be done superficially (e.g. by recognising key words), but this fails to present the information as relevant beyond the current scenario. Some students quickly spot the relevance from their previous experiences but do so in quite an undiscerning way, overlooking the differences in the two scenarios. Nuthall (1997) suggested that application of prior knowledge will not happen until students find a good match between their prior knowledge or experience and the new one. Furthermore, they will engage more readily with tasks that appear to have an 'immediacy of usefulness' (Dalby 2014: 75).

We must bear this in mind when designing tasks. The clues provided within the scenario challenge, such as the potential longer term context of the content (which will become useful if and when they decide to breed), is balanced in the example by the more immediate learning skills of (say) skim-reading. This combination of the long-term application of content with the short-term acquisition of a skill helps students to stay on task in a meaningful way.

Sequencing tasks

The craft of sequencing teaching activities is another hidden part of our peda-gogical content knowledge. Cleverly sequenced activities make teaching time more efficient and more effective, allowing students to dwell more on the content being studied and to interact with the information in numerous ways. The best way to do this, logically, is to work from simple to complex. The start point can be as easy as locating a familiar analogy or a key idea on which the rest of the session can be built. Whatever the first activity is, the knowledge must be *developed* through the subsequent activities. Although this seems intellectually straightforward, it is easy to come something of a cropper, resorting to segregating ideas for the sake of simplicity.

Consider this lesson sequence:

Activity 1:   Teacher describes the organs of the digestive system.

Activity 2:   Students label a diagram of the digestive system.

Activity 3:   Students complete a table including the different types of enzymes used in the digestive system.

Activity 4:   Students watch a demonstration of how diffusion is used by the small intestine to absorb nutrients.

Activity 5:   Students draw a diagram to show how diffusion is used by the small intestine to absorb nutrients.

This sequence of activities illustrates the classic 'race to cover the curriculum' version of teaching: clearly, it covers the knowledge the students need, but it does so in a way that doesn't properly acknowledge or cater for the interrelatedness of the content. It omits the need for students to integrate their ideas, for them to view the concepts through the prisms of different activities and does not let them seek the connections that will give their learning meaning and purpose. What we want to do is sequence activities so the students can dwell on the ideas inherent in them and can then organ-ise them in increasingly complex ways. This takes time.

A comparison of abridged courses and courses that permitted a deeper approach to the topics highlighted that, although multiple choice test scores were not affected, scores on longer written tests were markedly lower if students were solely in receipt of 'hit it and run' lesson sequences. Scores on longer written tests are held to be indicative of students' depth of knowledge and their ability to relate concepts to other concepts (Hattie and Yates 2013: 41). This tells us two things: firstly, that we must consider how we are going to assess student learning and, secondly, we must also give consideration to which of parts of the course we can identify as the ones where students require/deserve/would benefit from a deeper, more detailed look at things.

Thankfully, it does not take much to create a sequence that supports the linking of ideas. We do this by allowing one activity to become the context for another. A possible solution might look something like this:

Activity 1:   Teacher describes the organs of the digestive system.

Activity 2:   Students label a diagram of the digestive system.

Activity 3:   Students sequence the route of the food as it goes through the digestive system by creating a flow chart.

Activity 4:   Students annotate the flow chart showing where enzymes are made and used.

Activity 5:   Students watch a demonstration of how diffusion is used by the small intestine to absorb nutrients.

Activity 6:   Students annotate the flow chart to show where diffusion takes place.

Activity 7:   Students draw a diagram to show how diffusion is used by the small intestine to absorb nutrients.

The vocab grid and info grid – an example of activity sequencing

Some generic (non-subject-specific) strategies are useful in sequencing activities too. Consider the 'vocab grid' and the subsequent 'info grid'.

The vocab grid, developed by Osler and Flack (2008), is simply a table with a selection of well-chosen key words taken from a key piece of text that will help the students to understand a topic or concept.[5] The key words are selected using two guiding principles: firstly, the key terms must be integral to the understanding of the topic and, secondly, there should be a combination of the known and unknown. This encourages the students to engage with the activity. If the new words are solely technical terms, students may potentially find it too difficult to make a start.

Before the students read the article, they are asked to define, exemplify or explain these key terms. This requires them to take a risk in attempting what is, in essence, really quite difficult. It is hard to define something that is new to you. It is certainly worth pointing out the structure of the lesson to the students: that they will be required to think, read and then finally reflect and define. However, we are not necessarily after the right answer here, but more of an investment of interest so that when the students come to read the article they are sensitised to the key words. For instance, the key terms for a text on digestion may be:

---

[5] Jo Osler and Jill Flack's *Whose Learning Is It? Developing Children As Active and Responsible Learners* is a truly wonderful text.

Key term	First try	Second try
Bile		
Surface area		
Membrane		
Molecule		
Enzyme		
Digest		

Of course, the article needs to be carefully selected so that it contextualises the words without defining them, so the students get to think about their meaning and not just copy the definition from the text into the table.

Having completed their first try, the students read through the text and can discuss what the words mean with some context to go on. As they begin to make their second tries, it is a good idea to point out some useful notation that goes with the vocab grid. If the original try of a word is entirely incorrect, then the student needs to add their latest thinking in the second try box. However, if the idea is partially correct, a small arrow should be drawn between the top of the first and second try boxes before adding the new ideas. If the first try is spot on then a large arrow between the first and second try boxes should be drawn. This explicitly shows where prior knowledge is being used and changed.

In SOLO taxonomy terms, the vocab grid is very much a unistructural and multistructural activity through which the students learn the very basic elements of the topic. It is a breakdown of the key elements of the concepts being studied. It therefore follows that an ideal activity would set about joining these ideas back up again. The designers of this procedure, Osler and Flack (2008), also designed a strategy called an info grid: it requires the students to join up several of the key terms in the original vocab grid and place them into a context (in SOLO terms, this is very much relational). In the example below, the students have just completed a vocab grid on key terms to do with digestion. Many of these key terms then appear in a connected form in the next activity.

Questions	Key ideas	Importance	Reminds me of ...
How do the organs work together to prepare molecules small enough to be absorbed?	• The teeth in the mouth increase surface area. • Bile increases the surface area of fat droplets. • Large surface area allows enzymes to work quickly on large molecules. • Small molecules are absorbed in the small intestine.	• Each organ plays a part; therefore the sequence is important. • Without small molecules, nutrients would not be absorbed and we would get ill. • Surface area is important for absorption.	• A chain gang breaking up stones. • We did an experiment about surface area and dissolving: the experiment showed that dissolving happens quicker if there is a large surface area.

The questions[6] are answered in the 'key ideas' section in bullet point form, so the grid itself does part of the work for the students in terms of beginning to join the ideas together. The columns labelled 'Importance' and 'Reminds me of ...' are more problematic as these require the students to seek connections beyond what they are currently studying to find the bigger contextual picture. These columns are flexible and, in this example, could easily have been titled in a more content orientated manner – for example, 'Important organs' and 'Important processes'.

Osler and Flack make it clear that, if students are aware of the two procedures and the relationship between them, then they will learn how to become critical consumers of the pedagogy on offer, which is one of the key means through which they might develop their metacognitive knowledge.[7] For the purposes of developing context, the

---

[6] These don't exclusively have to be questions; titles related to a big idea work just as well. In fact, you do not need to have four columns either. Students will find useful connections and context in fewer columns than this. Let the content and your students' needs decide what you do here.

[7] '[W]hat individuals know about themselves and about others in terms of their understanding of how learning works for them (and others) can take a variety of forms' (Beadle 2013: 94): for instance, knowledge about when it is time to use this strategy or that strategy, or knowledge about how much knowledge they have about a particular area.

two tasks provide context for one another, with the students (after they have done it a few times and been debriefed) understanding that foregrounding the accuracy and quality of their work when completing the vocab grid will help them to complete the info grid. Students learn to recognise the usefulness and relevance of the initial task because the info grid has provided the context through which the stuff in the vocab grid can be seen in a more connected, holistic manner.

Planning to make connections

Many moons ago, my then head teacher, Derek Wise,[8] and his erstwhile deputy, Mark Lovatt,[9] spent their summer visiting schools in New Zealand. My memory of this stems from one video clip Mark was keen to show me on his return. Mark is a big character, in every sense: big hearted, possessed of a substantial intellect and an equally fulsome personality. Yet it is the chastised quality of his voice that I remember most as he muttered, 'Er ... okay ...' as the diminutive tornado of an eight-year-old girl dragged him across her classroom. Be in no doubt: it was *her* classroom. All Mark had done was say 'Hello' and then asked her what she was doing. Her response was detailed. She explained that she was currently using a 'Double Bubble Map' to help her compare two ideas, and that she had chosen this from a selection of 'thinking maps' that helped her to think in a variety of different ways. At this point, she grabbed Mark's arm and took him towards a classroom display that had the all different maps on show.

Remarkably, this metacognitive marvel was aware that, not only can we think in different ways, but also how she could vary her thinking when confronted with different types of ideas. And she had the confidence to choose and then defend those choices. She left quite an impression. The tools that gave her access to these exceptional competencies were the range of maps originally developed by David Hyerle (he calls them

---

8   Derek was the ultimate outward looking educator – spending many summer holidays trekking the globe looking for the best practice to bring back. He is still an inspiration and is sadly missed. Derek transformed Cramlington High School over the 20 or so years he was there. He was awarded a CBE for services to education in 2008. He died in 2010.
9   I have worked with Mark for the majority of my career.

Thinking Maps) which help learners to control how they think about different ideas.[10] There are numerous varieties: maps to help define the context, to find similarities and differences in conceptual objects for comparison, to look at relationships between ideas, to sequence and order ideas, to analyse causes and effects, to classify ideas, to spot analogies, to describe and to collate.

Constructive alignment

Constructive alignment is a term defined by Australian psychologist and father of SOLO taxonomy, John Biggs (2003). Constructive alignment involves the purposeful alignment of the teaching activities with the intended learning outcomes – a simple enough idea. By understanding what knowledge we want our students to demonstrate in their assessments, we are better able to design instructions that will match what our original intentions were. This seems obvious to the point of being simplistic, but the magpie in us can all too often pull us in the direction of being rather more interested in the technique or strategy rather than how it interacts with a particular piece of knowledge. Therefore, the idea of constructive alignment should be a key part of our armoury of pedagogical content knowledge.

SOLO taxonomy helpfully defines what student understanding might look like at each of its levels. As we are interested in connecting ideas, it is worthwhile pausing briefly to consider how knowledge may be used if its usage is to be classified as 'relational'. To be relational, student knowledge must be coherent, integrated, linked and holistic. Relationships between concepts will differ: some may be a sequence, others might share several features while remaining different, some might be a cause and effect. All of them will be part of a bigger whole. Once we have identified the nature of the concept to be studied, it becomes possible to align tasks and scaffolds to enable our students to think and learn the concepts in the necessary manner. This requires the teacher to think in verbs.

When talking to teachers about thinking in verbs, there is a temptation to reach glibly for a diagram of Bloom's taxonomy in order to construct lessons in which

---

[10] The website www.thinkingmaps.org is a great resource for the maps and their use.

we work with 'higher order' verbs, thinking that we are making progress; whereas, actually, what we should be doing is allowing the knowledge itself to determine the verbs used. Ask yourself appropriately detailed questions: if the students are learning about the causes of volcanic eruption, do the activities make the cause or the effect the big idea to be learned? Will making a poster on the causes focus on the build-up of lava or on the pressure caused by that build-up? If the students are learning to distinguish between the different 'life' stages, will defining each life stage help them to judge which way a volcano is acting? Will students need an activity that helps them to focus on the differences? Of course, sequencing the activities consciously has currency here too. Defining the life stages and *then* having a task that helps the students to compare them will ensure that they can indeed distinguish between them.

This is where Hyerle's Thinking Maps become useful, with each map offering a different way of processing the information so that the relationships between ideas become important to, and identifiable by, the students. Hyerle's maps (which include a sequencing tool, or flow chart; a classification tool, or whole-part map; a cause and effect map; and an analogy chart, or a bridging map) have been aligned to the SOLO taxonomy levels and to different ways of thinking to allow teachers and students to select appropriate tools to assist with scaffolding their thinking about the content being learned. Consequently, it is not the product that undertaking these tasks produces, but the process and the focus on how separate bits of knowledge interact that is of chief importance.

Even in the early stages of using these tools, when we are in the territory in which the teacher directs, Thinking Maps allow students to see complexities in simplified form. When the teacher shares the purpose clearly and then explains the reasons for selecting a tool – for instance, 'We are using the sequencing chart to make the process clear' – the students get to see how an expert *thinks through* the complexities of the content. It is important to remember that, as experts, we can take our own understanding of what might be quite difficult information for granted and, as a result, we have to actively remember to empathise with how difficult such information can be for novices grappling with it for the first time.

The table that follows provides examples of how the constructive alignment of teaching strategies to the nature of the content being learned can occur. These tasks won't work on their own and require expert guidance from the teacher: firstly, in how to select the correct maps and how to use them, and, secondly, in how to refine their use in increasingly complex learning situations. The aim of this instruction is to help our students to use these ways of organising their thinking so they can see the connections between the ideas in what they are learning.

Type of thinking	Maps
Cause and effect	Multi-Flow Map Ishikawa (fishbone) diagram
Sequencing	Flow Map
Classifying	Tree Map Affinity diagrams
Describing	Bubble Map
Comparing	Double Bubble Map Venn diagrams
Linking whole to parts	Whole-part map

The concept map: a task that exemplifies making connections

Concept maps are a representation of meaning.

Novak and Gowin (1984: 15)

Concept maps, for me, are mental schemas made visible. They depict the key ideas in any topic and show the connections between them. Overall, they give the big picture, normally with the big ideas (generalisations or important concepts) at the top and connected ideas branching off them. Key words and terms are written in boxes, and explanations and reasons are written on connecting lines between the concepts. It is not enough to make the connection; the connection must be explained and have a narrative attached. For their originators, Joseph Novak and Bob Gowin, academics at Cornell University, they are, 'Intended to tap into a learner's cognitive structure and to externalise what they know' (1984: 40). They should ideally have a hierarchical structure because 'New information is often relatable to and subsumable under more general, more inclusive concepts' (Novak and Gowin 1984: 97). This is reminiscent of Nuthall's findings on student learning: that effective activities are built around posing big questions or problems.

Concept maps are particularly useful over a sequence of lessons during which they can be added to or amended. They are also potentially very effective as an assessment task because of their capacity to represent the uniqueness of student learning, showing both valid and invalid ideas. If used at regular intervals throughout a topic they will expose what is commonly understood and what is missing in terms of both concepts and connections between concepts, thereby allowing teachers to modify their teaching in response.

However, our focus here is to help our students make the connections in the first place; forgetting that these student representations of learning are unique will only impoverish their use. There is a clear balance to be struck between the connections that are 'correct' and the student version of this. Consequently, teacher feedback and structure are important and need to be undertaken with care. A framework with blanks to fill in may well seem to be an expedient way of getting the right answer, but it can stop the students from interacting as freely with the information as they might. The following procedure is a way of achieving a balance.

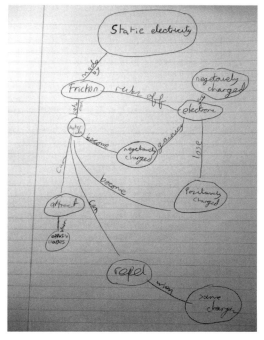

To set up a concept mapping task:

1. Give the students the key words or terms (when they get better at concept mapping they can provide these words themselves).

2. Select two key terms and model an example of making connections between them by pointedly writing what the connection is on the line between them on the whiteboard.

3. Bigger and more important ideas should go towards the top of the concept map (although it can also be laid out in a non-hierarchical way).

4. Let the students explore the connections between the remaining concepts one pair at a time – double check that they are adding reasons for the connections (they won't be).

5. Point out that some pairs of terms may have more than one connection, and some connections should be represented by an arrow if one causes another.

6. After a while, stop the class and draw lines between the selected items that represent the minimum number of connections that you, as an expert, expect. Then ask the students to add explanations to these connections.

7. Allow the students to check and amend their concept maps so that the connections in point 6 also appear in their work. Explanations and reasons should also be added to these connections.

8. Provide feedback, emphasising the importance of the connections the students have missed and potentially deepening the connections if they have been made too simply for your liking.

Building connections – preparing to write

The tools we have viewed so far have been focused on students processing ideas, not necessarily on communicating them. In reality, we need to construct opportunities for each. Learning to write academically incorporates both. Simple structures such as point-evidence-explain are helpful for students to organise their ideas.

Smart teachers, like Damien Clark, help students to prepare for writing as historians by using simple scaffolds which the students can use to prepare to write coherently and in detail.[11]

Title: Describe how the Vikings raided Lindisfarne

Paragraph 1: 'Terrifying tactics'

Point sentence: The Vikings attacked Lindisfarne by using terrifying tactics.

Evidence	What was the effect of this?	Why did they do it in this way?
For example ... *For instance ...* *Evidence for this was that ...*	*This meant that ...*	*Because ...*
The Vikings were fearless.	The people being attacked realised that the Vikings would be very hard to beat. Consequently, they became all the more frightened.	The Vikings were fearless: they were happy to die fighting because they believed that they could go to Valhalla (their version of heaven) if they died in battle.

---

[11] Damien is head of humanities at Cramlington Learning Village and blogs too infrequently at http://invisiblelearning.blogspot.com.

Evidence	What was the effect of this?	Why did they do it in this way?
They used terrifying violence.	People would be all the more afraid of them and would give up, giving the Vikings what they wished more easily.	They were ruthless, they would either kill anyone they came across or take them as slaves. They did not spare the lives of women or children.
They burned buildings.	So that they could get inside them more easily. Also, this would cause panic which would spread.	Because of this, no one would be organised to fight back.
They used swords, battleaxes and knives.	They appeared stronger and more brutal than the English.	The Vikings' weapons were passed down over generations, and they were still in fine condition. However, if the swords went rusty they were buried with their owner.
They didn't just kill men; they killed women and children too.	They did this to show the village that they would spare no one.	They spared no one, they were thought of as ruthless and strong, therefore gaining the respect of other Vikings and the fear of the villagers.

This type of planning structure helps the students to connect different ideas:

- The students are working towards one big idea (how the Vikings raided Lindisfarne).

- The idea of one main idea per paragraph has been taught (in the example, it is 'terrifying tactics' and, in subsequent ones, how the Vikings travelled and why they chose Lindisfarne).

- The idea of using a point or topic sentence to introduce the idea has been taught.

- The table makes it easier for the students to link supporting ideas to the main one.

- The table helps the students to make connections between cause and effect as well as giving them a structure and stimulus with which to explain these.

- The table includes helpful language that models how we might write about these ideas – for example, 'This means that …'

- Students do the content thinking before they take on the sizeable task of writing coherently on the subject.

Summary

In this chapter, we have been interested in how to help students make connections between the concepts studied. We have looked at this through creating contexts, exploring how different bits of knowledge are connected and linking cause and effect. In the spirit of this section, the summary also appears as an Ishikawa fishbone diagram.

These approaches are applicable to all subjects, although the types of connections sought will differ from topic to topic. This requires a lot of teacher thought and preparation, and we would not expect to do this for every concept or topic that we teach. Savvy teachers target this kind of effort on the most important and most difficult aspects of their subjects (the threshold concepts). This is the focus of the final chapter of our exploration of pedagogical content knowledge in relation to how a subject is learned.

How is Your Subject Learned?

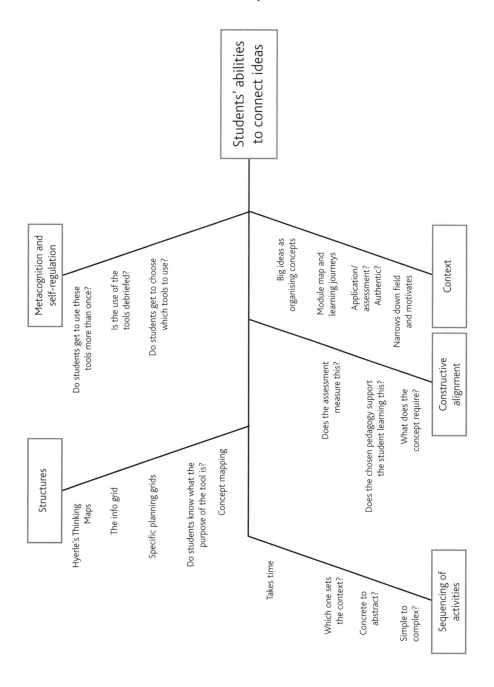

Students' abilities to connect ideas

Metacognition and self-regulation
- Do students get to use these tools more than once?
- Is the use of the tools debriefed?
- Do students get to choose which tools to use?

Context
- Big ideas as organising concepts
- Module map and learning journeys
- Application/ assessment? Authentic?
- Narrows down field and motivates

Structures
- Hyerle's Thinking Maps
- The info grid
- Specific planning grids
- Do students know what the purpose of the tool is?
- Concept mapping

Constructive alignment
- Does the assessment measure this?
- Does the chosen pedagogy support the student learning this?
- What does the concept require?

Sequencing of activities
- Takes time
- Which one sets the context?
- Concrete to abstract?
- Simple to complex?

CHAPTER 3

Using Pedagogical Content Knowledge to Plan to Teach Difficult and Important Knowledge

One of the most important planning questions to ask about the content to be learned is, 'Where is the hard stuff?' and 'What makes it hard?' Identifying the characteristics of difficult content makes us better equipped to anticipate it and plan for its impact on student learning. Two areas of interrelated research seem particularly useful in getting past the simplistic knee-jerk of 'Learners think this topic is boring' or 'There is a lot to learn in this bit.' The idea of threshold concepts, which were defined by Meyer and Land (2003), and of 'difficult knowledge', described by Perkins (2009), helps us to be more specific about why certain bits of content are difficult to learn.

Planning to go through threshold concepts

By definition, threshold concepts are 'troublesome' knowledge: they require mental and/or emotional effort to pass through the threshold of understanding them. Their difficulty will often stem from their counter-intuitive or complex nature, and they often lead students into a state of confusion before they are able to fully understand them. The term 'liminality' is applied to this state of being in-between two places (to be 'in limbo' means being somewhere between heaven and hell). Teaching, on the surface, appears to be a straightforward and linear process of understandable cause and effect: you teach, they learn. Meyer and Land's description of learning as being a liminal process jars with this idea: as students go from confusion to insight they pass backwards and forwards over these thresholds. If we consider Nuthall's 'multiple exposures' rule (where for something to be learned, we need to interact with the idea(s) on four separate occasions) then the idea of learning, forgetting and then learning it again, neatly integrates with the idea of threshold concepts (Nuthall 2007: 63).

A key feature of threshold concepts is that they integrate or pull together other ideas, and integration is often considered to be a feature that is interwoven into their transformative and irreversible nature. Threshold concepts should change how you think about something, and this, in turn, should lead to you not being able to change your mind (back again) about it. Threshold concepts, much like the mental image of a naked Michael Gove on holiday in a nudist resort in Lanzarote, are hard to un-see. Two other features are regularly added to the definition of threshold concepts: they are bounded within a context and, as we have seen, they are troublesome. Threshold concepts (conveniently and confusingly) are themselves threshold concepts, allowing us to grapple with our own understanding. (Interestingly, Ray Land now considers 'learning thresholds' to be a preferable term to threshold concepts.[1])

Threshold concepts are highly subject specific and are very much part of our wider pedagogical content knowledge. Teachers can use threshold concepts to aid thinking about the dynamics of teaching and learning in their subjects, as was the original idea, but they also reveal quite a bit about how students are currently schooled. The zeitgeist in many education systems appears to be geared around covering broad(er) curricula, teaching to gain a pass, students studying numerous courses, an onerous emphasis on pace and demonstrating that learning has 'occurred' within short time frames. This inevitably leads to the teaching of only superficial understandings, whereas to gain a thorough level of understanding of a subject requires the exact opposite; to fully understand a subject we must understand its threshold concepts. Land himself acknowledges that 'certain aspects that we would regard as important parts of education – deliberation and contemplation, for instance – seem to belong, historically, to a cloistered age, a slower time, as perhaps does something as

---

[1] Ray Land is one of the pioneers of threshold concepts. He is currently professor of higher education at Durham University and director of Durham's Centre for Academic Practice. He, along with Erik Meyer, during the Enhancing Teaching-Learning Environments in Undergraduate Courses project, recognised that a characteristic of strong teaching and learning environments was that certain concepts were held by discipline experts to be central to the mastery of their subject. These concepts became known as threshold concepts.

intellectually abstract and interesting as acknowledging the notion of the liminality of learning' (quoted in Rhem 2013).

If we go back to the crude concept mapping strategy detailed earlier, in which we mapped out the big ideas of a topic to check the sequence, the threshold concepts (or at least concepts with the demeanour of threshold concepts) stand out because of how integrative they are, and we can see this by the sheer number of connections they have with other ideas.

Threshold concepts are considered to be central to the mastery of our subjects and are at the heart of pedagogical content knowledge. They have three useful characteristics:

1. They challenge our intuitions.[2] For example, a student may consider the mass of a growing seed to have been absorbed from the soil around them; whereas, in fact, the increase in mass is explainable by the accumulation of organic compounds made by photosynthesising. An understanding of photosynthesis would therefore constitute a threshold concept.

2. They tend to be memorable but remain modifiable. This allows the concept to be accepted and then refined in the light of new theories or evidence. Good cooks know this and will spend time perfecting their base stocks; once prepared, the stock can be turned into soups, sauces, curries, risottos and so on. For me, being taught that atoms (or particles) are made from other things provides a good example. Mr Stonehouse described the Christmas pudding model to do this. Picture a Christmas pudding with the raisins evenly distributed throughout. The raisins represent the smaller divisions of matter that we cannot see. Although an incorrect model, it taught me about the idea that atoms are made from other 'stuff' — something I have never forgotten. It changed how I viewed the world.

3. Like the first domino in a chain, they tend to knock into other bits of understanding. Threshold concepts are the stuff you need to know before you know other stuff and therefore have been described as 'transformative' by Meyer and Land. This is best shown with a concept map adapted from *The*

---

[2] Reminding us of another aspect of pedagogical content knowledge: student misconceptions.

Atlas of Scientific Literacy which shows the possible developmental pathways of students' understanding, the relationships between concepts, how concepts inform a range of scientific fields and how concepts of increasing complexity are developed from more simple understandings.[3] It is intentionally not 'levelled' for assessment as its purpose is rather more worthy than informing any management function.

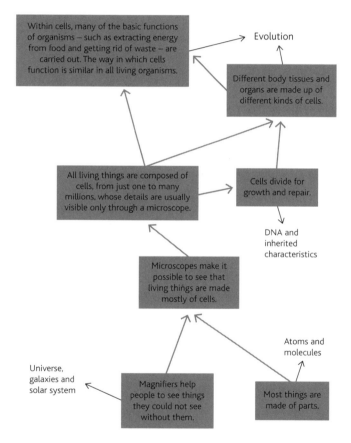

Source: Adapted from American Association for the Advancement of Science (2013)

---

[3] *The Atlas of Scientific Literacy*, produced by the American Association for the Advancement of Science (AAAS), is a joyous bit of research for science (and maths) educators. Every domain needs one of these. See http://www.project2061.org/publications/atlas/.

4. We put the concepts in boxes and locate the basic ones – on which the rest of the knowledge will be built – at the bottom. In the science example, students can see that cells are the basic unit of structure (because they can see them). What then follows about cells acting as the basic unit of function must be inferred from other observations. The unboxed text shows the other concepts that are linked to, but are not within, the current module of study.

In summary, threshold concepts are integrative, transformative, irreversible, troublesome, memorable and modifiable.

Thresholds are not the only difficult kind of knowledge that we have to teach. David Perkins (2009: 79–108) has done more than most in giving teachers working definitions of what he accurately calls the 'hard parts', giving us the opportunity to anticipate them in our planning and to try to understand why they do not make immediate sense to our learners. He defines these barriers to student understanding as ritual knowledge, inert knowledge, foreign knowledge, tacit knowledge, skilled knowledge and conceptually difficult knowledge.

Ritual knowledge

Ritual knowledge can be routine and rather meaningless or surface knowledge. Often, it is the manifestation of a coping strategy and may have little to do with the actual content. Occasionally, ritual knowledge can be useful, such as memorising that 8 x 5 = 40, but this does not equate to mathematical learning (Rohrer and Taylor 2007). But the ritualisation of knowledge through teaching strategies, such as student recall of facts in an initiation/response question and answer session, makes it difficult for students to transfer and use this kind of knowledge elsewhere. Dan Meyer, an American educator of note, describes this situation beautifully in his TED Talk, 'Math Class Needs a Makeover' (2010). He identifies five signs that students have poor maths reasoning skills:

1. A lack of initiative.

2. A lack of perseverance.

3.   A lack of retention.

4.   An aversion to word problems.

5.   An eagerness for formula.

All of which can be directly linked to teaching for ritual knowledge. Meyer asks us to ponder the clues that many maths questions contain and compare this to any worthwhile problem we may ever have had to solve. Life and learning are not as straightforward as the following problem might suggest:

> A filament of a light bulb has a resistance of 3 ohms and a current of 2 amps running through it. Use the formula $V = I \times R$ to calculate the voltage it works at.

To answer this, all you need to do is ritualistically substitute the numbers into the formula. But being able to do this tells us very little about how good a physicist or mathematician you are.

Inert knowledge

Inert knowledge is knowledge we have but do not use often. We have to go through a process of deliberately retrieving it, and to do this the right cues need to be present. Inert knowledge is a good way of explaining why transferring knowledge from one context to another is difficult. It often manifests when we are directly asked about it but it rarely emerges in more open-ended tasks. It is not uncommon for us to spot this in 'stuck' students who cannot work something out: when we ask a direct question they will (more often than not) know the answer. This knowledge is isolated and difficult to retrieve. This only adds to the importance of threshold concepts and their integrative quality – helping to join ideas together between contexts.

Foreign knowledge

Foreign (or alien) knowledge is knowledge that is difficult because it doesn't appear to fit with our current understanding, the current context, our beliefs or our cultural norms.[4] Let's take the example of the YouTube clip of astronaut Chris Hadfield demonstrating the unique skill set of how to brush your teeth in space, which involves Chris leaving his microphone, his toothbrush and globules of water just hanging in space.[5] This jars with our expected notions of what objects do. Here in Gateshead, if I held up my toothbrush and then let go, it would fall to the floor because gravity would act upon it. The laws of physics are the same in space and on earth, but the behaviour of the objects seems different because the context is different, and the behaviour is therefore alien to us. Objects in space seem to follow Newton's first law of motion (which states that an object will continue to do what it is doing until another force acts upon it). On earth, they do not because of forces such as gravity or friction. This alien or foreign knowledge gives us conflicting perspectives that make learning this bit of physics difficult because we will never get to experience it if we are not an astronaut.[6]

The same reasoning can be applied to the study of history. It is easy enough for us to view events through modern attitudes and social norms, but it does not necessarily develop a full understanding because historical attitudes and moralities can be wildly different to our own. It can be difficult for us to imagine the complexity that the context of the time forces on our understanding.

Tacit knowledge

Tacit knowledge is difficult to share with other people by verbalising it or by writing it down. Perkins (2009) considers it a highly functional, intuitive response to complex situations that can be troublesome to formal learning in several ways. As experts, our understanding is/should be deep and highly connected, but this renders it surprisingly difficult to teach because the quantity of interacting ideas becomes unwieldy. As a

---

[4] This should remind us of the problems learners face with incorrect prior knowledge.
[5] See https://www.youtube.com/watch?v=3bCoGC532p8.
[6] Being a space cadet does not count. Sorry.

new teacher, I struggled to teach the ecology parts of the A level biology course. This left me befuddled as this was the bulk of what I studied in my university days, and I knew this stuff upside-down and back to front. I found my students looking at the minutiae, while I was getting holistic and wondering why they weren't following me. Tacit knowledge embraces know-how; as Martin Said — erstwhile music teacher and now head of XP School Doncaster — puts it, it is knowledge that is 'caught rather than taught',[7] and includes the kind of things we learn by watching and mimicking before hanging formal knowledge on them.

Skilled knowledge

How to ride a bike:

1. Stand astride the bike.

2. Mount the seat while gripping the hand grips.

3. Place your right foot on the corresponding pedal and push off from the floor with your left foot.

4. When moving, put your left foot on the corresponding pedal and begin to rotate both pedals.

5. Balance on the two wheels as you move forwards.

6. Steer using the handlebars and break using the levers attached to the handlebars.

7. Pull a wheelie to impress passers-by.

Rather unbelievably, there are numerous websites that outline the process of riding a bike. Any of us who have learned to ride a bike will understand that, despite it

---

[7] A gentleman, a scholar and a teacher of quality. Read his blog at http://teachingandlearningmusic. blogspot.com and the exploits of his students and school at http://www.xpschool.org.

being quite easy on a procedural basis, learning to stay upright can hurt. It is skilled knowledge. Perkins (2009) identifies the troublesome aspect of any skilled knowledge residing not in having an idea of what to do but in the difficulty of actually doing it. Anyone learning an instrument or playing a sport understands this difficulty instantly, but academic knowledge can fall foul of this too. For instance, I kind of know how to conjugate Spanish verbs but I'm far from fluent. To develop skilled knowledge we need dedicated, deliberate practice.

Conceptually difficult knowledge

Many factors can go towards contributing to conceptual difficulty, as shown in the diagram below. Knowledge which can be described by any of the conditions on the left-hand side is easier to learn than if found on the right-hand side (based on Perkins 2009: 79–108).

This diagram begins to explain the loss of many of my teacher hours. At the time of writing, I had just spent many hours marking student reports on the reproductive system, finding that around 90% of them had failed to describe the role of the menstrual cycle accurately. I was expecting better and had taught them to give a two-pronged answer: that the menstrual cycle coordinates both the release of the egg and the preparation of the uterus lining. However, my students mostly gave me only one of these two things.

Let's look at the reasons why in a little more detail. The understanding I was after was about a simultaneous event rather than a sequential one; it was also a dynamic (changing) process rather than a static (non-changing) situation. This is akin to throwing two darts at two separate moving dartboards; of course, they found this difficult.

As it happens, the task the students were working on was designed to be drafted, and my teacher marking was to be the catch-all for these situations. However, I wish I had realised the nature of the beast before I taught it. I could have planned to make this aspect more front and centre. Luckily, not all knowledge that we want (or need) our students to learn is difficult. What Perkins' ideas allow us to do is to identify what is so that we support student learning in more effective ways.

What can teachers do to plan for difficult and important knowledge?

1. Value thresholds and difficult knowledge

The most important thing we can do is to see the idea of threshold concepts as vital guiding principles of our subject teaching. They help us to identify where scaffolds and assessments are needed in order to help the students learn difficult or threshold concepts. These are the moments in our lessons when we have to slow down in order to go faster. Threshold concepts are valuable for our students in terms of grasping our subjects and transforming how they view the way the world works.

2. Identify the threshold and difficult concepts

The next task is to identify the threshold concepts in your subject. A great start point for this is University College London's subject collection.[8] The experience and knowledge of our subject colleagues can be an invaluable source too. Asking the right questions also helps:

Nature of knowledge	Questions to ask
Integrative	What is the big idea being learned and how do the smaller ideas relate to it?
Foreign or alien knowledge	Are any of the ideas being learned counter-intuitive? Do any of these ideas conflict with previously learned ideas?
Transformative	What am I teaching that will lead to other knowledge?
Difficult through complexity (abstract, simultaneous, many rules, non-linear)	What ideas are simple and what ideas are complicated? Is there a logical order in which students should learn these ideas?
Ritual	Can any of the ideas become ritual knowledge? Is that where I want the student understanding to be or am I expecting more? How can I teach and not ritualise these ideas?
Inert and tacit	What might students already know that they might not readily link to this new knowledge? What is the tacit knowledge hidden in what is being taught?

---

8 See https://www.ee.ucl.ac.uk/~mflanaga/thresholds.html#gen.

3. Focus assessment on threshold and difficult concepts

Although it seems obvious that we should focus our assessment and feedback on the concepts we know our students find difficult, this constructive alignment is often overridden by the need to mark students' 'work' (note the distinction here: we mark work as opposed to marking (or feeding back on) learning). If the tasks are aligned to difficult content, this is not a problem; but it does require careful planning to ensure this, and vigilance over what is important.

4. Use implicit feedback

Threshold and difficult concepts, like misconceptions, benefit from tasks with lots of implicit feedback built into them. These strategies ensure that students are constantly provided with feedback as to how well they understand the new concept(s). To achieve this, we must again consider classroom dialogue. In some regard, the activities (or the classroom dialogue) must be self-correcting. In a world where around 80% of the feedback students receive comes from each other and in the region of 80% of this incorrect, the role of the teacher becomes essential in ensuring that the information shared is actually accurate (Hattie 2009: 4).[9] This doesn't mean that we become the sole arbiters of 'correct' in the classroom, and we must accept that students will – whether we want them to or not – provide explicit or implicit feedback to one another.

The type of classroom I wish to develop is one where the students talk about the ideas being studied and feel confident enough to correct one another. I am growing to accept Nuthall's assertion that students learn as much from their peers as they do from their teachers, and that these exchanges are not threats to our role or to student success but are opportunities we must exploit – the waves of the surf we must ride. There are many strategies that help to ensure the correct message is heard. Some of these involve the teacher, some don't, but both rely on the timing of the

---

[9] This research is attributed to Graham Nuthall's *The Hidden Lives of Learners* (2007) but I'm unable to find it in my copy. I first read about his work (and this statistic) in John Hattie's *Visible Learning* (2009). Although I am now doubtful of the figure, it was still a wonderful bit of serendipity to discover Nuthall's work.

feedback to avoid the knowledge becoming merely rote. Strategies such as think-pair-share or assertive questioning are useful here. When tackling a known difficulty, think-pair-share can be used by following these steps:

1. The teacher briefly outlines the procedure.

2. The teacher poses a question or problem for the students to respond to.

3. The students should be given a chance to collate their own ideas and check through their notes. The time given must meet the context but should be too short to fully bring together all the information. This phase acts as a reminder of what is expected to be known.

4. The students pair up to discuss their ideas. I have a preference for controlling the 'who' part in any student grouping and have developed a habit of changing these frequently. The student discussion is the start of the implicit feedback. However, dominant students, ill-prepared students and complicit laziness can all conspire so that students will be inclined to accept the first idea one of them comes up with. Paired discussion helps to negate this, as will the teacher's method of selecting the students, but prompts and teaching may be necessary to develop these conversation skills. A simple classroom display with conversation starters may be just the ticket as a prompt for dialogue:

    *   I agree/disagree with ... because ...

    *   I infer that ... because ...

    *   I noticed that ...

    *   I wonder if ...

    *   Do you think that ...?

    *   I was confused by/when ...

    *   For me, the important idea is ...

5. The teacher selects the student who responds on behalf of the pair. This is the lever to ensure student involvement in the paired discussions. They must be engaged in 'getting it', and knowing that they may be asked is often enough

to ensure that students join in the conversation. Consistency of approach matters here. It is essential that the correct answer is emphasised.

6.   The teacher now takes several student responses, seeking justification, agreement or disagreement before agreeing the correct answer. These whole class discussions will be rich in implicit feedback too.

Methods like this are easy enough to apply during the course of a lesson, and the discussions are best served by a 'what students know–what teachers know–what students recognise' sequence. For instance, we might pair the students to check a piece of work and make suggestions to improve it, then the teacher might give a model response before encouraging further suggested improvements. Teachers should be mobile during these student exchanges, identifying who requires further support on this concept and who is ready to move on. Students then return to discuss what has improved in their work. Again, a procedural approach will ensure that, although the first run-through may not provide the smoothest teaching, subsequent attempts at it will be enhanced as the teacher has cued expectations about involvement.

It is difficult to separate the cultural aspects of this pedagogy from the technique itself. It is therefore necessary to prepare a classroom environment that is conducive to openness and risk taking by the students. Although this sounds simple, it can be difficult to perfect and we need to plan for it. Firstly, we must establish a 'learning focused' classroom where it is OK not to know things yet. This means being careful with our own language and with the language used by our students. It also means that we share the process of learning with them so that there is no secret teacher business. A safe environment is necessary, where incorrect responses are welcomed (or at least seen as useful to learning) as a way of increasing classroom discussion.

The safety of the classroom will also extend to peer relationships: students are constantly comparing themselves and their knowledge to that of others in the class. A teacher asking a question and accepting the first hand that goes up can be a complicit signal to other students that they can stop thinking. But students find not putting their hands up difficult when they think they know the answer, and will do so even after you have directed a question at another student, which inadvertently carries the message that 'I know and you don't'. It is not an over-exaggeration to say that many hands up when one person is struggling with an answer is threatening, and

I wonder how many times in a day individual students find themselves in situations where others know things they don't and this is explicitly obvious to everyone.

We are really after the direct opposite of this: we want to see other people's ideas as helpful to our own learning, and student mistakes are ready-made teaching points. We need to ask questions to help students learn, but we need to be clear about why we are questioning at each moment. How we question is important, as is who we ask. Do we give the students a chance to think before and after their responses? How do we respond to correct and incorrect responses?

5. Plan opportunities to act on the feedback

The nature of difficult or important content warrants us allowing sufficient time for the students to dwell on these ideas. But we can't magic up additional time to do this, so we should look for opportunities within tasks rather than between them. Consider a question sheet with (an arbitrary) ten problems on the same concept. Marking student work after five questions grants the teacher a chance to support learning during the period in which they are encountering difficulty and allows the students to act on the advice while actually in the act of learning.

Although this is apparently simple, the confusion between performance and learning is problematic. How often do we ask students to practise with content? In all honesty, if a student has completed five problems on one concept, it is likely that I would attempt to move them along in the name of 'progress'. However, if the task has isolated the difficult content and the students are likely to make mistakes, then practising with the opportunity of receiving feedback on that practice is essential. Practice needs to occur in many contexts so that students are more likely to transfer the new skills or information to new situations – which begs the question, is five questions enough? The simple answer is no. A set of practice problems would only constitute one exposure to this concept, but multiple exposures are needed for learning to happen; never mind the need for space between exposures and for the enhanced learning that can occur when concepts are interleaved (Bjork and Bjork 2011).

6. Ensure that these concepts have multiple exposures

Nuthall's (2007) 'four exposure rule' has become something of a mantra for teachers in recent times and is often used in a rather bludgeoning and unintelligent manner, devoid of the subtlety that his research suggested.[10] Here, I present Nuthall's categorisation of the types or extent of the exposure, not as a planning tool but as a way of analysing the information we present to students before we define how many exposures to it they might need.

It is worth noting the methods used by Nuthall in his research. The methodology was for teachers and researchers to identify, firstly, what the students were going to learn in a module: the learning intentions. An 'outcome test' was then designed in order to find out what the students knew and what they didn't know before they were taught the module. The teachers then set about teaching the topic and the researchers recorded everything that took place (and I mean everything: the teachers were wired for sound, student desks had microphones, photographic evidence of student work and classroom display was collected). They even habituated the students to the presence of the researchers in lessons so they could record human interactions without interfering with normal classroom conditions. What the researchers actually recorded was the students' interaction with information rather than a mere exposure to it. For learning to occur, students must interact with information, not just be present when a teacher says it or gives them a book containing that information.

The students were then retested using the same outcome test as had been used prior to the teaching of the module. The researchers were then able to work out exactly what had been learned (and what hadn't). Following this, the students were interviewed about what had been learned and how they had learned it. The researchers classified each exposure the students had experienced by its size and use. They then went on to piece this jigsaw of evidence together, looking at what was needed for learning to take place and, incredibly, managed to devise 'rules' that were able to predict learning to a degree that was assessed as up to 88% accurate based on the frequency and type of exposure students had experienced (Nuthall 2007: 126).

---

[10] If students interact with the same concept four times, the concept will be retained in long-term memory.

The crux of Nuthall's insight came from identifying the interactions the students had with the information available and whether it was complete. By this, Nuthall meant that in order to have learned, the students must have interacted with the exact and accessible information, whether through teaching or through activities. It may be that a picture or diagram was studied, or something was read, or they discussed a concept with their teacher. What was important was that they engaged with the content. When the students did this on four occasions, he noticed that he was able to predict accurately that learning would occur.

However, part of Nuthall's genius was that he identified that students do not always get, or do not always interact with, the full set of required information. At times, teachers chunk information into more manageable pieces, we implicitly use terminology when explaining concepts, and we mark student work and provide feedback that focuses on specific parts of the work. Partial information is not a flaw in a teacher's approach; it is a necessary reality in supporting learning. This may be information that can be used to lead students to make inferences and deductions. The partial information works in different ways: sometimes it provides a context for the learning and potential sources of useful prior knowledge, and sometimes we give information that will allow the students to work out what the concept is in a more direct way. This may be considered background information: it may involve giving the students definitions, thinking through concepts with analogies, using examples and non-examples or displaying visual information through posters on the wall. It still results in student learning.

Nuthall deduced that if a student interacts with the full set of information three times and has one additional interaction with partial information, learning will still occur – this being four exposures in total. However, if a student interacts with the full set of information only once or twice then they will need to interact with four partial sets of information. It is prudent at this point to remember that this research was an attempt to measure the predictability of learning occurring based on how students engage with the content, but it still provides some useful planning suggestions. For learning to take place, students must:

- Interact with a full explanation of a concept at least once.

- Interact with the information on at least four separate occasions.

And that:

- The more often they interact with the full picture, the better for their learning.

- Breaking down concepts is not always the best strategy because more exposures will be needed for learning to occur for each of the smaller parts and then for the big idea we intend to teach.

- Related information can be deduced, collated and learned from many pieces of information.

- We have to remember that, no matter how much we manage knowledge, we are entirely reliant on students engaging with it!

Nuthall (2007: 127) said: 'Provided a student is able to piece together, in working memory, the equivalent of three complete definitions or descriptions of a concept, that new concept will be constructed as part of the student's long term memory.' This makes it essential for teachers to be aware of what a full set of information may look like. This is difficult to achieve for every fact and idea you want the students to learn. Ergo, I do not think this is a planning tool, but a key piece of pedagogical content knowledge that will help us to plan better teaching sequences.

To make it manageable, it might be sensible for us to focus on the most important aspects of our subjects, such as threshold concepts and the ideas that students find difficult. The planning questions it raises about such concepts are:

- How many times do students get to interact with the concept?

- What does the information look like for the students? Is it a full set of information?

- Are the students likely to learn as a result of these exposures?

In extremis it may look something like this example from a lesson about electrical circuits. (THIS IS NOT A LESSON PLAN!)

The learning intentions were as follows:[11]

1. To understand that complete circuits are needed for currents to move and circuits to function.

2. To recognise series and parallel circuits.

3. To define 'current' as the movement of charged particles through a circuit that is not 'used up'.

4. To understand that movement of current is unidirectional.

5. To describe how current behaves in a series circuit.

Activity Predict-observe-explain (POE): bulb challenge	Intentions targeted	Nuthall predictor classification
Teacher–student discussion	1 and 3	ALF – hands-on task PSI – prior knowledge WOI – implicit use of key language
Draw bulb on board showing how the circuit is connected	1	WOI – deduction
Teacher explanation and discussion	1 and 3	PSI – corrections of ideas WOI – implicit use of language
Bike chain model of current with teacher explanation	3 and 4	FSI – definition and analogy

---

[11] These are broken down to make it easier to track but, of course, they are all connected.

Activity Predict-observe-explain (POE): bulb challenge	Intentions targeted	Nuthall predictor classification
Teacher questions: What would happen to the current if I turned this switch off? What would happen if I removed this cable (on an interactive animation)? How fast does current move?	1 and 3	WOI – implicit use of a concept to teach another BI – examples
Marching model of current in series and parallel circuits	1, 2, 3, 4 and 5	ALF – for current in circuits FSI – unidirectional flow acted out WOI – implicit use of a concept to teach another; can deduce circuits from this BI – analogy
Teacher question: If I was a switch in this circuit, how would you act? Answer: As charged particles moving around as current through the circuit in one direction.	1 and 4	WOI – using a concept to teach another
POE based on animated model/simulation	1, 2, 3, 4 and 5	FSI – from teacher explanation PSI – from prior knowledge BI – example

Activity Predict-observe-explain (POE): bulb challenge	Intentions targeted	Nuthall predictor classification
Practical – build this circuit	1, 2 and 5	PSI – from prior knowledge BI – example ALP – practical to see behaviour of current
Same two steps but with two bulbs	1, 2 and 5	PSI – from prior knowledge BI – example ALP – practical to see behaviour of current
Review task: What is the rule for the current in a series circuit?	1, 2 and 3	PSI – from notes and lesson discussion

Key: ALF – activity that leads to a full set of information, ALP – activity that leads to a partial set of information, BI – background information, FSI – full set of information, PSI – partial set of information, WOI – working out information.

If we track a single intention (4 – to understand that movement of current is unidirectional), it is easy to see that this concept will feature in its entirety three times during the lesson. Firstly, when the predict-observe-explain bulb challenge culminates in defining current and again during the teaching of the bike chain model (with the bike chain model being the first full exposure to the information). A quick look at a student's notes show that he, at least, has engaged with the ideas.

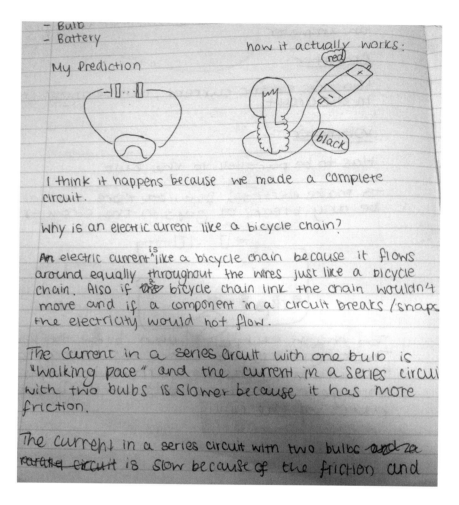

- Bulb
- Battery

My Prediction

how it actually works:
(red)
(black)

I think it happens because we made a complete circuit.

Why is an electric current like a bicycle chain?

An electric current *is* like a bicycle chain because it flows around equally throughout the wires just like a bicycle chain. Also if the bicycle chain link the chain wouldn't move and if a component in a circuit breaks/snaps the electricity would not flow.

The current in a series circuit with one bulb is "walking pace" and the current in a series circui with two bulbs is slower because it has more friction.

The current in a series circuit with two bulbs and za parallel circuit is slow because of the friction and

The remainder of the lesson gives the class two further opportunities to interact with this idea, one of which provides a chance to expose a misconception. The 'marching model' asks students to act out the current in a circuit drawn on the classroom floor. Keeping the instruction deliberately vague here helps to reveal student thinking. The students tend to gather on top of the battery symbol, thereby indicating that they think the current is stored there and jumps out when the circuit is switched on. The second (and pertinent) part of this reveals that they have not fully grasped that current moves in one direction only as, on the instruction, 'The circuit is now complete;

you can start being current,' the students inevitably start moving in both directions. For me, it is important to allow this mistake to happen to reinforce the concepts. This will form another full set of information (FSI) for this concept. If you are not keeping score, that totals three so far.

The final exposure comes from an online simulator that the students use to help predict what the current will be in a real circuit: in the image below, the electrons that make up the current are represented as little black dots moving in one direction around the circuit. Although this is not referred to specifically, it does provide background information (BI) to reinforce this concept. This makes the magical four exposures. As in at least three of them the students have interacted with a full set of information, the learning should have taken place – provided the students have engaged with the ideas.

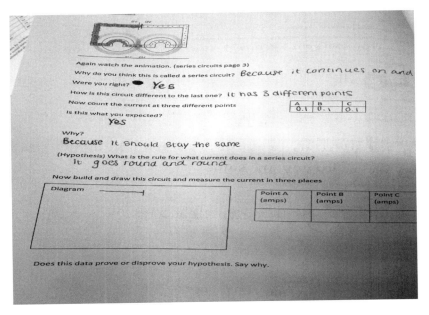

Again, the work shows that the student has interacted properly with these ideas. But it also reveals that they are interacting with other concepts. To deal with this, our planning must incorporate better isolation of ideas and spacing out of exposures over a longer time.

7. Isolate it to practise; reassemble it to a create a big picture

It will not have slipped your notice that the types of ideas that tend to be seen as more difficult (see page 85) also have more connections than the simpler ideas. This echoes with Willingham's (2009: 74) definition of 'deep knowledge': that more ideas are known and are 'richly interconnected'. With reference to this, we need to help our students learn the 'whole' of an area or subject, not just the constituent parts. It behoves us, therefore, to create opportunities to reassemble the broken-down practice parts in tasks that pull the pieces back together.

Of course, a teacher's ability to break down knowledge into chunks or individual concepts is an essential part of our planning of learning, not so that we can attempt to measure learning (though this is a convenient illusion for some) but in order for us to identify what the troublesome knowledge is — or, as Perkins puts it, the 'hard parts'. If we can do this, then we can plan lessons that will be all the more effective as they will allow the students to practise these hard parts. However, it could be argued that this practice is not as effective as helping students to identify the hard parts within the bigger picture; the learning remains whole because the hard parts are essential components of a larger question or problem. Practising the difficult parts therefore becomes 'deliberate practice' Ericsson (1993).

Listen to this wild boast: *I am a terrible guitar player.*

I am quite proud of having risen to the ranks of terrible guitar player as I am already vastly better than I ever imagined I might be after three years of disturbing the peace of Gateshead. I have made progress from being someone who *plays with* a guitar to someone who can *play* guitar. I can now get a tune of sorts from a stringed instrument and just about play a song from start to finish. I have achieved this by playing songs that I like, repeatedly, from start to finish. In short, I have practised. Deliberately. I have learned how to place my fingers in the once seemingly random arrangement of a chord. In fact, several chords, including barre chords! I have done this not by practice but by *deliberate practice*. I have spent time (clearly not enough), practising changing from chord to chord, G to C and C to G, over and over again. This is the part that I (still) find difficult: I recognise that I will only be able to play the songs I like if I can make these chord changes with some kind of grace, and so I have taken time out to purposefully practise this skill. This small constituent challenge is a part of the bigger challenge of playing a tune, which is a further small part of playing a guitar. Placing the smaller parts within the context of a bigger problem is not in any way a luxury. It is essential. You can't play a full song without mastering the difficult bits (the hard parts).

I have also done something a little more subtle. I have also chosen to learn songs that I don't necessarily like because they include chords that I need to learn in order to play the songs that I do like. Endless repetition is tedious and could lead to me becoming demotivated; although we understand that motivation does not necessarily equate to learning, it cannot happen without it. We can be super-motivated and still not learn a great deal. YouTube guitar teachers know this and use other songs as études, like composers of old. There are many video tutorials out there that start with, 'Hey guys, this song is great for those shifts from open chords to a barre chord.' So, I practise with songs that allow me to use these chords in different tunes to the ones I really want to learn. This is a chance to deconstruct the chords and the changes, and then to restructure the 'performance' of my chosen song.[12] The fact that I can now say, 'I can play the guitar,' means that I can read a guitar tab and work out how to time the strumming and chord changes for this new tune. Learning has become durable and it has become applicable.

Deliberate practice requires the following:

- A bigger problem that can be broken down into smaller ones.

- An understanding of the task at hand which allows investment into a conscious and focused effort.

- An element of choice or control over what is practised.

- A chance to deconstruct and restructure learning.

And this kind of practice can be planned into lesson and curriculum design.

---

[12] Here I do not mean performance in terms of the 'stage' version of the idea; more in the Robert Bjorkian sense that it has not necessarily been learned.

8. Spacing out practice

Spacing out the practice serves two functions: it increases the likelihood that the knowledge will be retained and it helps teachers to overcome the confusion between performance and learning.

Performance is categorised by its short-lived nature and the difficulty in transferring it to new situations, whereas learning tends be long term and transferable. Simple mechanisms such as removing the assessment of a concept from the lesson it is taught in and placing it in a subsequent lesson helps to combat the problem of short-term performance parading as learning. I have got into the habit of saying, 'I may test you on this next lesson or even in the lesson after that ...' to make the point that I am interested in my students learning ideas, not what they can recall 20 minutes after I've told them.

Think back to the problem of ritualised knowledge, where the problems we pose can be solved by substituting the information into the formula. If we assess learning during the same lesson, all the prompts and cues a student needs are going to be present, and therefore they are likely to be able to 'demonstrate' that they can perform the task. But emphatically this *does not* demonstrate that they have actually learned the concept taught, since the process of forgetting kicks in simultaneously with the learning. It is quite possible that by the next lesson (or even by the end of the current lesson), your students will have no information at all about what they know and what they still need to be working on.

The spacing of learning exposures (or opportunities to practise) makes retrieving the information more of an effort and therefore creates longer lasting memories. Students need time to adjust to a new regime that involves spaced practice, but their responses to realising that they actually know stuff can be enchanting. Spaced practice is difficult for teachers too, and so we will revisit it in Chapter 6 when we look at planning with memory in mind, alongside its happy bedfellow interleaving. (We are thereby exploring the likelihood that spacing is a potential threshold concept for teachers.) If spacing is the temporal distribution of problems, then interleaving is the order in which the problems are intertwined. Both these methods lead to 'large gains in test performance' (Rohrer and Taylor 2007: 482) and enhance 'memory, problem solving and transfer of learning to new contexts' (Kang 2016: 12), which seems particularly pertinent when dealing with misconceptions and difficult concepts.

Overlearning – or the strategy of massing practice directly after something has been understood – is, on the whole, beneficial to student learning and can improve subsequent test performance, but caution must be exercised. Consider this study on massed practice in a mathematics classroom: student exam performance was compared between students who completed three practice problems against those who completed nine. Surprisingly, in spite of the three-fold increase in practice, there was no improvement in short-term (one week later) or long-term (four weeks later) test performance (Rohrer and Taylor 2007: 482). In reality, what matters is the timing of the practice: 'practice … spaced out over time generally leads to superior learning' compared to having the practice accumulated straight after the initial learning experience (Kang 2016: 13). This is known as the spacing effect.

A particular difficulty for teachers is the fact that massed practice has a real short-term benefit: your students will appear to get it, so we will assume that our job is done and that we can move on. Teachers must learn to look beyond the here and now and consider what the students' learning will look like in the future. This is compounded by the fact that teachers who switch to spaced practice may, at first, have students who know less, because massed practice appears to be more effective than spaced practice in the short term. But spaced practice produces more durable long-term learning (Kang 2016).

In addition, pinning down the lag between practice sessions is tricky, with no optimal delay having been identified or prescribed. Two main factors determine this: the timing to the final test and the difficulty of the material being studied. If the test is one week away then a one day gap appears to be optimal. For teachers, this may be simply frivolous information because the timings of interactions with their students (lessons) is ultimately at the whim of a timetabler. However, it should be pointed out that students may find this useful when revising and preparing for exams. If the test is a year away then a gap of two months is suggested as optimal. This is of much more use to teachers when designing curricula. However, clouding the usefulness of these suggestions is that these timings are derived from studies that include a single revision of the study material (Kang 2016).

Bearing in mind that we are considering the teaching of problematic content, where there are misconceptions and difficult concepts, then multiple exposures would be most beneficial. By focusing on planning in detail we can make this manageable.

In order to cover these concepts over the course of a year, it may be worthwhile considering an 'expanding schedule' where the retrieval of material is delayed by an increasing amount each time. Early retrieval attempts ensure a high rate of retrieval success and, since retrieval slows forgetting, subsequent retrieval opportunities can be pushed farther apart in time to ensure that practice continues to be effortful and not trivial (Kang 2016: 14).

We have two options when considering how to manage these opportunities to revisit, retrieve and remind students of important content. We might consider the big ideas and threshold concepts and build the curriculum around these, but the simpler mechanism may be to consider how we devise and use low stakes tests and quizzes. These are, by design, tests that do not bring any grading or judgement – they are simply there to enhance learning. This is not to say that teachers cannot learn from these tests and use them to inform their teaching and lesson planning, but the students themselves do not have the burden of having a grade tossed at them. They benefit from being cumulative so that previous topics are included. They also benefit from being frequent: students expect to be tested, and this increases the likelihood that they will revise prior to lessons. They appear to have a positive influence on attendance too (Smith 2016).

A weekly quiz, lasting 10–15 minutes, might look like this:[13]

---

[13] This is based on an idea in a Learning Scientists podcast on spaced practice at: http://www.learning scientists.org/learning-scientistspodcast/2017/10/4/episode-4-spaced-practice.

Questions	When this content was taught	Why?	Example
1–3	Last lesson	Reminder of key ideas. Ideas that will be built on in this lesson.	What is the pH of the stomach? Name the acid produced here. Name the enzymes produced in the stomach.
4	Last week	Spaced practice of key ideas allowing for later subsequent retrieval.	What is the purpose of digestion?
5	Last month/ last topic	Spaced (extending schedule) practice of key ideas allowing for later subsequent retrieval.	What is the difference between a series and parallel circuit?
6	Several months ago Or A key idea/ threshold concept that joins the current and a previous topic	Spaced (extending schedule) practice of key ideas allowing for later subsequent retrieval. Or Spaced practice to encourage transfer of learning and support learning of threshold/ difficult concepts.	What is a pluripotent stem cell? Where are they found? Or What is diffusion, and how/where does it occur in the digestive system?

9. The role of metacognition and reflection

Planning detailed lessons that take account of every nuance of learning is, of course, fine in theory but, in all honesty, what students need are opportunities to grapple with concepts, and they will only do this when they have skills that are sufficient for them to do so.

The Expeditionary Learning design principles include one titled 'solitude and reflection' which summarises this need quite eloquently: 'Students and teachers need time alone to explore their own thoughts, make their own connections, and create their own ideas. They also need to exchange their reflections with other students and with adults.'[14]

Students need time and opportunities to reflect on their learning (and its processes), both as individuals and in groups, to help them dwell on each difficult and important concept. Simple questions can help here:

- What have you found out?

- What fact has led you to learn more facts?

- What has been the most useful thing learned in developing your understanding?

- What have you learned that you did not know before?

- What facts can you now link together?

- What is the most important fact you have learned?

- Did anyone find out a similar thing?

- Did anyone find out something different?

- Do you still think you are right?

---

[14] See https://eleducation.org/resources/design-principles.

- What questions do you still want to ask about the concept?

- What have you seen? What does it tell you?

Basic structures such as 'I used to think ... Now I think ...' also help students to draw the main ideas together and identify what has been learned. The examples below are taken from a Year 8 geography class who had been studying volcanoes.

How's a volcano like a person's head?

The mouth is the main vent and the nose is the secondary vent.

I used to think that more regular volcanoes were more dangerous than dormant ones.
But I have seen that what I thought was false.
Now I know that dormant ones are more dangerous than active ones.

you burp, this can be compared to a volcano erupting.

I used to think that all volcanoes were the same.
But now I have heard that they vary in destructive power, and size and the amount of lava or bombs or pyroclastic flow that they produce.
Now I know that every volcano is different and needs to be analysed to see if the volcano is dormant, active or extinct and if it should be is very dangerous and the villages around need evacuating.

Questions to debrief the process may include:

- What tools have been useful? How?

- What were your most useful questions?

- How did you go about reading the information?

- Did you think of the questions first or did you allow the information to guide you?

- What was the most helpful way of learning this?

- How did you interact with the information?

- What conversations helped you to learn today?

- Identify the moment when you realised you had learned something/corrected your previous ideas.

- Did anyone double check their work, see something missing and go back to correct it? How often did you reflect?

- How did you attempt to join ideas together?

- How (often) did you use the success criteria?

- What strategies in this lesson have been helpful?

Summary

Planning lessons is so much more than just creating structures and frameworks. Good planning involves us employing our pedagogical content knowledge; it dances at the intersection of our knowledge of:

- Our subjects.

- How our subjects are learned: the common misconceptions, threshold concepts and difficult ideas.

- How students learn.

- How (or whether) specific teaching strategies work.

This makes pedagogical content knowledge rich and deep. In some regards it might appear relatively surface level, but it is really a lifetime's worth of learning for us as professionals and is best figured out together.

The following pedagogical content knowledge extraction tool may help you to mine the recesses of your mind to extract the nuances of just how we might go about doing our jobs as well as our students might want us to.[15] It is based on the framework developed by John Loughran, Amanda Berry and Pamela Mulhall in *Understanding and Developing Science Teachers' Pedagogical Content Knowledge* (2012), though it's not just for science teachers. Many of my colleagues across all areas of the curriculum have found it to be a useful prompt for thinking about their teaching and a way of pulling ideas together before they plan lesson sequences. It is not a checklist and there is no need to use each question – choose which prompts are most useful to you, to your students and to the content. Although the example that follows includes many questions that appear to be helpful, it is best targeted at areas where important difficult concepts or misconceptions lie.

Aspect of pedagogical content knowledge
What is the concept to be learned? (a single concept works best for clarity)
What should students know before learning this?
What might they already know?
What misconceptions might they have?
How will you find out about student ideas?

[15] Or you may consider it a list of questions …

Aspect of pedagogical content knowledge
What will they find difficult? Why will it be difficult?
How can this be made easier to learn? Is this idea so important that you will deliberately manage the number of exposures over coming lessons?
How will you represent this knowledge so that it is unambiguous to students? • Analogies/models • Symbols • Language • Sequence • Diagrams
Why is this knowledge important? Is this one of the main concepts of your subject?
Where is this knowledge going? How might it be used in future learning?
How will teaching and tasks/activities help the students to engage with this idea? Why have you chosen these activities?
What caution do you need to exercise? How might you teach a misconception?
What else might influence student thinking on this? How might they know what they know?

The following table reveals the richness of teacher pedagogical content knowledge. You may recognise some of it, especially in terms of concepts you have taught previously. Undoubtedly, there will be some discrepancies between what is in the example and what you know. This is a good thing. It is not the right or wrong of things that matters here but the breadth of knowledge. Pedagogical content knowledge is unique to our own experience(s), knowledge and context: by attempting to make it concrete and share it, all of our students benefit. It is therefore the perfect tool for starting to plan collaborative schemes of learning, modules or topics.

Exemplar use of the pedagogical content knowledge tool

Aspect of pedagogical content knowledge	Science	Maths	MFL	Health and social care
What is the concept to be learned? (a single concept works best for clarity)	How dissolving takes place (Year 7 beginner science).	How to calculate the percentage of amounts (Year 7 beginner maths).	Verb conjugation in the present tense in French (Year 7).	Behaviour theory (according to psychology)(Year 12).
What should students know before learning this?	Particle model will help students to understand how this process takes place. Key terms: solvent, solute, solution.	Strategies for finding a half, a quarter, a fifth and a tenth. Dividing by 10 and 100 (or multiplying by 0.1 and 0.01). Common equivalent fractions, decimals and percentages, e.g. 40% = ²/₅. What a percentage is (complements to 100).	That conjugation is the interaction of a subject pronoun and an infinitive verb, and is shown by changes in verb endings relating to the subject. Key terms: infinitive, verb, subject, pronoun.	What affects the way we behave? What a theory is. Key terms: self-esteem, self-concept, cognitive.
What might they already know?	Lots of examples of things that dissolve and things that are dissolved.	Where to find percentages in everyday contexts (e.g. % extra free on food packaging, 50% off discounts and results on an assessment).	A verb is a doing word.	The work of Bandura and Pavlov: how we learn our behaviours/ habits.
What misconceptions might they have?	That the material being dissolved disappears when in solution. Students find the change of state of the material being dissolved confusing. Often they think of it as melting. This is exacerbated by the fact that both are increased by heating the materials.	Students are stumped when faced with percentages over 100% (e.g. 150% profit). Students often assume that if 10% is one-tenth, then 17% is one-seventeenth.	That a verb is just a doing word – it is more than an action. That there is a relationship between the subject and the verb ending.	That a theory is always based on facts. That it can be applied to everyone. That only psychologists use the theories. That everyone is in control of their own behaviour.

Aspect of pedagogical content knowledge	Science	Maths	MFL	Health and social care
How will you find out about student ideas?	Ask them to predict the volume of liquid produced when mixing 100ml of water with 100ml of ethanol. Do they know that particles can be different sizes in different materials? How aware are they of the size of the spaces between particles in a liquid?	First, ask students to estimate what they think 82% of £82 would be. What does estimate mean? How big is 82%? How did they arrive at their estimate?	Cut up exemplar sentences in English to examine the relationship between subject + infinitive = change (conjugation) (e.g. He ... to play the guitar).	Show the class the video clip and ask the students why the children copy the adults? Ask for examples of when they have learned to do something. Can learned behaviour be unlearned? How? How do you know if a theory is true? How is it used in education?
What will they find difficult? Why will it be difficult?	Visualising what is happening to the particles when in solution. Distinguishing the key terms due to similarity. When materials dissolve they look, on the surface, like they have disappeared.	82% is an unfamiliar percentage to work with. Finding a percentage of an amount more than a half is also unusual. The problem can be tackled in a variety of ways. The difficulty is increased by the fact that the 100% value is actually £82. Solutions will be to two decimal places.	To learn the different endings and the way they are applied to the infinitive stem. Identifying the infinitive groups ir/er/re is unfamiliar to English speakers. Also, matching subjects to verb endings is often subliminal in mother tongue.	The key terms are difficult as they are not part of students' common everyday language. Positive/negative reinforcement and punishment, modelling and vicarious reinforcement, conditioned/unconditioned stimulus and response, neutral stimulus, behaviour modification, family therapy. How to apply it to the health and social care sector through behaviour modification strategies.

Aspect of pedagogical content knowledge	Science	Maths	MFL	Health and social care
How can this be made easier to learn? Is this idea so important that you will deliberately manage the number of exposures over coming lessons?	Rice and pea model will help visualisation. Multiple exposures to the terminology over several weeks. Work from concrete (examples) to the abstract (particle model). I will have a Venn diagram activity (on standby) for this lesson for when we study changes of state to distinguish between dissolving and melting.	Using a number line to visualise where 82% is. Name the 100% value £82. Use a bubble map with 100% (£82) in the centre. Students write as many percentages as they feel confident with around the bubble, alongside annotations. Decimal equivalents will be referenced as students will be working with decimal multipliers when calculating compound interest.	Build up the structure over time. Examine the role of a subject pronoun (pro + in place of noun = thing) (i.e. Chris, *je*, *tu* and *il* can all refer to the same thing). Look at finding infinitives using the dictionary. Explore with mini whiteboards the impact of subjects and endings. Recognise first before applying.	Visualisation through role play. Video to explain Bandura's theory – Bobo doll. Examples of how it is used in school: reward charts. Relate to *Nanny 911* timeout, routines, etc. Students are given the consultation structure and complete an interaction case study.
How will you represent this knowledge so that it is unambiguous to students? Analogies/ models Symbols Language Sequence Diagrams	Rice and pea model. Concept map of key terms. Discuss examples of solutes, solvents and solutions before defining them.	Bubble map is then extended to a concept map. Which pieces of information from the bubble map can we use to contribute to our solution? Do you have everything you need? What connections can you make? Flow chart – breaking down how to calculate 82%. Compare and contrast methodologies using a comparison alley (peer assess).	Flow chart of choices and questions which mimic the thought process of conjugating.	Artist easel technique, role play, matching activity for key words, interaction case study, discussion of real life examples/experience.

How is Your Subject Learned?

Aspect of pedagogical content knowledge	Science	Maths	MFL	Health and social care
Why is this knowledge important? Is this one of the main concepts of your subject?	Two-thirds of the earth's surface is a solution. Living things rely on solutions for transport and function. Lots of complex science is based on this.	Confidence with percentages is essential in business (percentage profit), analysis (percentage change), shopping (understanding offers), mortgages and credit card APR.	Core part of grammatical understanding – in this case in one tense, but will create solid foundations for tense change.	Part of the Unit 12 examination on human behaviour, and is one of four theories they need to learn. In all of their future roles, they may well use this approach without knowing it.
Where is this knowledge going? How might it be used in future learning?	Students will soon learn about the factors that affect the rate of dissolving. Students will use this knowledge to separate soluble and insoluble substances (i.e. it is a property). Later, students will study ideas about concentration, osmosis and rates of reaction.	Calculations involving compound interest and depreciation will be studied by students later in Key Stage 3/ start of Key Stage 4. This, in turn, will lead into reverse percentages (working backwards).	Students will become familiar with the key terms (subject, conjugation, etc.) which are repeated in every tense, and the concept of conjugating.	They need to: Define what a theory is. Explain the basic principles of the behavioural approach. Compare three different views on the theory. Apply the theory to the health and social care environment. Know the thoughts of key players in the theory (Skinner, Bandura, Turnpike).

Aspect of pedagogical content knowledge	Science	Maths	MFL	Health and social care
How will teaching and tasks/ activities help the students to engage with this idea? Why have you chosen these activities?	Rice and pea model makes what is happening accessible and is a reference point. As does the simple summary: solute + solvent = solution. A brief practical on dissolving (and its subsequent write-up) allows for plenty of application of new language and ideas.	Video footage from regional news about the local football team being sponsored by a pay day loans company. People arguing for or against. Local news and football team are popular within the community (buy-in). Opportunity to talk about percentages in a real life context, revealing that a lack of understanding can have a significantly negative effect on social well-being. The ethical implications of not understanding the maths (e.g. APR, interest rate and projected payback amount). Emotional buy-in creates classroom discourse and engagement.	Build from recognition and understanding in English sentences, chunking down of the language units and exploring their functions. Building up the mental map of the process. Application and practice. To help learners place new learning in a familiar context, chunk down concepts, build up conceptual framework and apply in 'safe' practice.	
What caution do you need to exercise? How might you teach a misconception?	Care must be taken when talking about the rate of dissolving. Using terms such as 'fastest' are misleading, but will be part of everyday student language. Important for the knowledge to be applied in different situations so it does not become 'inert'. Practicals will help with this.	When moving on to more complex percentages involving decimals, that 25% as a decimal is 0.25, but 0.25% is a quarter of one per cent (and not 25%). Use of real life examples to address these issues. Start with the percentages students feel comfortable with.	The concept of irregular verbs – bring this up early as a reference (lots of English examples to draw on) and look at regular conjugations in order to develop a conceptual framework; then challenge it with irregular conjugation patterns.	

How is Your Subject Learned?

Aspect of pedagogical content knowledge	Science	Maths	MFL	Health and social care
What else might influence student thinking on this? How might they know what they know?	Lots of TV adverts proclaim fast action when they mean 'in a short period of time'. Kitchen/cooking experiences may provide some useful start points. Reminding them of the taste of seawater will remind them that solutes do not disappear.	Check out supermarket deals. If a packet of biscuits has 25% extra, then the packet is bigger than the original (not a quarter of its size).	Level of English literacy. This approach depends on an understanding (albeit non-explicit) of conjugation in English. Also, the idea that a verb is a doing word needs to be dispelled.	Television, their own experience, having already covered the topic in psychology modules.
Contributed by	*Me*	*David Gray at Cramlington Learning Village*	*Chris Harte at John Monash Science School, Australia*	*Tricia Wright at Cramlington Learning Village*

Aspect of pedagogical content knowledge	Music	PE	History/ social studies	English	Geography
What is the concept to be learned? (a single concept works best for clarity)	How diatonic triads are built in the key of C (Year 8).	How to retain possession in basketball (Year 8 invasion games principles).	How does propaganda work? (Year 9/GCSE)	How to use an apostrophe for possession and contraction (Year 7).	Formation of spits, bars and tombolos (Year 11).
What should students know before learning this?	What a chord is, characteristics of the scale of C major (esp. when applied to keyboard – white notes only), the difference in sound between a major and minor chord. Key terms: triad, diatonic, root, third, fifth, major, minor.	The choice of recognised passes. Key terms: chest pass, bounce pass, shoulder pass.	Some knowledge of the specific topic/ period is helpful to contextualise propaganda. Some knowledge of the concept of stereotypes/ caricatures can be helpful. Key terms: claim, message, provenance, purpose.	That they are essential forms of punctuation.	Students should understand the processes of erosion, deposition and longshore drift.
What might they already know?	There is such a thing as the key of C, not just a C major scale. Chords can sound wrong or unusual when placed alongside one another in a sequence.	The difference between the types of passes.	Many visual poster examples – often from First World War, recruitment into armed forces. They might know that governments are often involved in the production of propaganda. Examples of persuasive writing and techniques.	If they aren't used, meaning is not usually hindered.	Students might know examples of spits such as Holy Island.

How is Your Subject Learned?

Aspect of pedagogical content knowledge	Music	PE	History/ social studies	English	Geography
What misconceptions might they have?	All chords have three notes. A seventh chord has seven notes. Chord is spelled cord. Chords are only played with the left hand (keyboard players esp. as opposed to piano players). Orchestras don't play chords as many instruments are single note instruments. During: all chords are just play one, miss one …	That dribbling is better than passing, that you have to rush a pass or that a long pass is the best option. Many students pass the ball high and long when under pressure.	That propaganda is/ was always effective – that the audience simply accepted it or was not aware of its true purpose. That propaganda is obvious and can be spotted easily. Propaganda is created by one 'side' against another (not yet recognising black propaganda).	That they are used with every word that ends in 's'.	Students may think that a longshore is a continuous process along a shore or that a bar, spit and tombolo are the result of different processes.
How will you find out about student ideas?	Ask how many students have played chords before. Show them a C chord on the keyboard and then a B half diminished. Ask: what is different?	Set up a game of three vs. one 'keepball'. How do players without the ball help to retain possession?	Use modern advertising examples to discuss how aware they are, as an audience, of the messages and techniques used to target reaction. Use widely known images like Uncle Sam, John Bull and political cartoons of contemporary figures to explore thinking about caricatures and stereotyping.	Give them 10 common words that use an apostrophe either correctly or incorrectly. Ask them to correct those that need it and explain why they have or haven't corrected them.	Ask students to think about how sand moves along a beach and what can stop the movement of sand across a beach.

Aspect of pedagogical content knowledge	Music	PE	History/ social studies	English	Geography
What will they find difficult? Why will it be difficult?	Getting their fingers in the right places (e.g. using 1, 3, 5 on piano/keyboard instruments or making the appropriate shapes with the left hand on guitar). New muscle memory. Relating the chords to the scale. It will be hard to keep tabs on the different numbering systems (e.g. fingers, root–third-fifth, chord I, chord II, tonic, supertonic). The concept that there is no zero in music.	Passing early if their teammate hasn't created an angle for the pass. They might resort to passing over the head of the closing defender.	Detecting the hidden messages of propaganda. Use of cultural symbols (Russia = bear, Germany = eagle, Britain = lion). Use of analogies (comparing Germans in First World War to King Kong) that often rely on specific knowledge. Understanding the effect of the propaganda on the audience. Relating propaganda to specific events from a period of study as opposed to wider issues. Unfamiliar word choices.	Plural apostrophes for possession. How to show possession for words that are already plural, such as *children's* where the apostrophe would normally be placed after the 's' if the word followed a regular pattern (e.g. *the rabbits' hutch* – hutch belonging to several rabbits).	Visualising the longshore drift movement and the role of an object in preventing it. The role of the second wind causing the hook of the spit. Students may struggle to distinguish between a spit, a bar and a tombolo.

How is Your Subject Learned?

Aspect of pedagogical content knowledge	Music	PE	History/ social studies	English	Geography
How can this be made easier to learn? Is this idea so important that you will deliberately manage the number of exposures over coming lessons?	It can be easier to show another example to reinforce the diatonic relationship between scale and chords (e.g. F or G diatonic chords). Easier to work on keyboards first (even if student is a guitarist) to appreciate linearity.	Restrict the movement of the defender to allow him/her to stay in a specific zone.	Use a variety of types of propaganda (film, poster, writing, speech, cartoons). Multiple exposures over key stage. Use examples aimed at a variety of audiences (adult, child, enemy, ally) and from a variety of contexts and historical periods. Build a definition or common checklist as students are exposed to a variety of examples, which can be added to, modified and refined.	Practice! Students could design their own model of apostrophe use. (A comic strip approach has worked in the past, particularly if the misuse of the apostrophe results in humour – more memorable!)	Animated images showing the key processes in action. Use of key words for students who struggle to recall these words from the introduction lessons. Use of real life examples (from across Northumberland where possible).
How will you represent this knowledge so that it is unambiguous to students? Analogies/ models Symbols Language Sequence Diagrams	Exemplify through finger charts, notation and taking unnecessary notes away from chromatic glockenspiels. Model of a tree to think about meaning of the 'root' of a chord. Use fingers to talk about the lack of zero in music (i.e. move up two notes for an interval of a third – not three).	Use demonstration or diagram to show requirements of the drill. Provide key teaching points regarding role of attacking team. Show angles of movement.	Give many examples of the features of propaganda. Model with students how to analyse propaganda and relate it to historical context (create annotated examples). Create generalisations together around the question: how does propaganda work?	See above – comic strip. Students could then act this out so the memory is reinforced. Those who grasp it quickly can act as experts, taking over from the teacher.	Step-by-step diagram. List of key words that must be included.

Aspect of pedagogical content knowledge	Music	PE	History/ social studies	English	Geography
Why is this knowledge important? Is this one of the main concepts of your subject?	Chord families are the first step for many for composing, esp. four chord tricks. Chords are fundamental to western harmonic theory.	It stops the ball being intercepted in possession and gives more options for a pass. Lots of invasion game principles are based on this.	Knowledge of the different types of propaganda are essential to understanding the purpose of authors/ sources used in history. Propaganda is a recurring theme in many aspects of historical study and informs students' understanding of more subtle sources where the author's intention is not immediately obvious. Allows discussion of the unhelpful term 'bias' and emphasises focus on interpretations.	It will be picked up in all key assessments and GCSE exams. It gives writing a 'lazy' representation and therefore wouldn't look good in a professional or formal document.	It is a major depositional landform that involves numerous coastal processes. Due to rising sea levels and increasing coastal flooding, it is important to understand the role various processes play in shaping our coast.
Where is this knowledge going? How might it be used in future learning?	Leads into being able to say why chords are major or minor. Gives a reference point against which chromaticism can be contrasted. Tonality and cadences.	It will be added to dribbling and shooting as the game moves from closed practice to conditioned games.	Students often learn about the political control of states and international relations between states. Within this there is frequent reference to competing ideologies.	It eventually becomes habit. Students are then in a position to tutor/monitor others.	Students will continue to learn about other depositional and erosional landforms. This can be used when introducing managing coastal erosion by the use of groynes.

Aspect of pedagogical content knowledge	Music	PE	History/ social studies	English	Geography
How will teaching and tasks/ activities help the students to engage with this idea? Why have you chosen these activities?	Building chords can lead to aural discovery of tacit knowledge (e.g. V–I sounds like a full stop, complete, end of a symphony). 'Ah! So this is how they do it.'	It is a competitive situation, but it also allows the players to think about their choice of pass and what they should do when they have released the ball.	Use concrete examples such as modern adverts and modern political cartoons to introduce idea of ridiculing/ lampooning. Use of strictly visual examples (First World War recruitment, Nazi election campaign, Tudor portrait) as they are intrinsically interesting and easier to decode. Use 'enemy' propaganda with students – helps them to see that the defining features can be universal. Use analysis structures commonly used with sources such as 'circles of inference'. This is used early in Key Stage 3 as a basic framework to introduce students to 'questioning' or interrogating sources. The 3Cs (content, context, comment). Analysis tool brings together a variety of ways to investigate a source. Pupils create their own piece of propaganda (poster or speech) with 'hidden' messages and a specific audience in mind.	Once the key concepts are embedded, it needs to be monitored in context – as part of a whole piece of writing. A group of students or one student per table could be designated the 'apostrophe police'.	Use of step-by-step diagrams and images will help engagement. Students who prefer writing can take the role of 'Sam the Sand' and describe how he ends up as a spit.

Aspect of pedagogical content knowledge	Music	PE	History/ social studies	English	Geography
What caution do you need to exercise? How might you teach a misconception?	Do not allow students to think of the 'play one–miss one' pattern as being related to keys on the keyboard but to notes in the scale. Show what happens if you just go with the first idea. Use best judgement when deciding which fingers to allow students to use – the ideal is to use 1, 3, 5 – but access to the sound is also important.	Giving too much or too little space. Stopping the students from introducing novel responses. Care must be taken with ability grouping.	Caution needs to be taken when using more challenging examples, particularly with propaganda whose source is not from the usual perspective (e.g. How did the Germans view the First World War?). You can teach a misconception about the source of propaganda by using examples of black propaganda or propaganda which has been influenced by pseudoscience (e.g. physiognomy or phrenology used to 'prove' social Darwinism).	See above – irregular plurals (*children's*). Students should become familiar with other irregular plurals, so they are then able to apply the same skill to the pattern.	Ensure students are aware that spits are not just associated with river estuaries. Introduce students to an example at a river estuary but also at a bay.

How is Your Subject Learned?

Aspect of pedagogical content knowledge	Music	PE	History/ social studies	English	Geography
What else might influence student thinking on this? How might they know what they know?	Hearing practice rooms and recognising chords, but regarding this as something only the 'musos' can do.	Watching videos of others and of themselves. Seeing the impact in games so they can predict the value of retaining possession without resorting to dribbling.	Modern media coverage and influential debates such as immigration/ Islamophobia have strong influences on pupils' general knowledge, so we can use these as a reference point (especially with the features of propaganda list of criteria).	The way we verbalise contracted forms (*I'm, don't, they're* – missing letter in written form). This connection needs to be made with the way we write them. Similarly, the way we verbalise possessive forms (e.g. *Tom's work* vs. *Toms' work* when there is more than one Tom). We cannot hear this but we can make it clear in writing with a plural apostrophe.	Students may have a basic understanding from primary schools. Students living close to important coastal environments may already have some knowledge.
Contributed by	*Martin Said at XP School Doncaster*	*Paul Steanson at Cramlington Learning Village*	*Damien Clark at Cramlington Learning Village*	*David Bell at Cramlington Learning Village*	*Natalie Sateri at Cramlington Learning Village*

PART II
Pedagogical Content Knowledge: Expert Teaching and Learning

CHAPTER 4

The Art of Teacher Communication: Planning What to Say and How to Say It

Good teaching is good explanation.

Calfee (1986: 1)

What is teacher talk for?

Much of the visible art of teaching comes from the moments when we open our mouths. With between 10% and 30% of lesson time being spent explaining, we must be confident that this is time well spent and that our explanations are effective (Brophy and Good 1986). Explaining is teaching and so, in defining what teacher talk is, in some ways we define teaching. Assigning purpose to why we talk is the first planning step, with each purpose taking on a different set of qualities. Talking about content may seem like the predominant substance of teacher talk, but this may just be a small part of what we do with our craft, where we rely heavily on 'keen levels of intelligence and interpersonal sensitivity' (Hattie and Yates 2013: 109).

As a result, teacher talk is a mix of content explanation with talk of motivation, emotions, strategy, instructional guidance, questioning and feedback. As befitting something that is aimed at developing the understanding of other people, teacher talk is far from a simple construct. We speak for different purposes or through different modes for the same purpose and, more often than not, we speak to integrate the different approaches of the classroom (Department for Education and Skills 2004; Odora 2014). Establishing why we are going to speak helps to keep us purposeful. The first part of this chapter aims to define the purposes of teacher talk.

Context setting

Teacher talk can help students to make sense of new information by establishing a context for the learning about to take place. This may be done by setting objectives, reminding them of previous experiences or useful knowledge they may have or by defining the constraints of a problem. By their nature, explanations require problems to be explained and so part of the skill of teaching comes in the framing of circumstances and relationships in which the knowledge is or will be useful (Brown and Armstrong 1984).[1] The problem could be viewed simply as something the learner does not know or has a misunderstanding about. Equally, it could be more esoteric and wrapped up in a problem – for instance, explaining why atoms are neutral or why Hitler invaded Poland.

Engaging and maintaining interest

Student engagement – and let's not forget that the maintenance of interest occurs at four different levels: in the subject, in the lesson, about the concept and in a task. Although they are not of equal value to learning, all of these may need to be attended to at some point as we seek to enable learners to take 'an intelligent interest in the lesson, to grasp the purpose of what is being done, and to develop their own insight and understanding of how to do it' (Odora 2014: 71).

Representing new information

Representations of new ideas and concepts are defined by Wragg and Brown (2001) as instructional explanations where the teacher provides the meaning of principles through examples and summaries. This is usefully thought of as a combination of describing the factual and the conceptual, and explaining cause and effect or why things happen.[2] Representation can take a variety of different forms: verbal or

---

[1] And, yes, I am aware this is somewhat tautological.
[2] These may be considered to be the different forms of knowledge (Krathwohl 2002).

non-verbal, an analogy, a physical or mathematical model, illustrated in pictures or diagrams, defined by examples or non-examples, in writing or video. The content being taught determines our choices, although there is a need for us to have multiple representations at our disposal to ensure we can be flexible and responsive to student needs. Multimedia applications can play a big role in making new information meaningful for students, with the combination of words and images leading to 'strong learning' (Hattie and Yates 2013: 115).

Emphasising the important

Within busy classrooms, when dealing with complex knowledge and the myriad of interactions that take place while learning, it is easy for students to become distracted from the big ideas. Part of our craft is not only to manage the complexity but also to return and make important the key ideas within each lesson. We do this through our phrasing, with our plenaries, by slowing down, by asking rhetorical questions and by setting problems and challenges. At times, it is our ability to cut through the complexity by interpreting or classifying an issue or a problem, by identifying what (or when something) is important or by specifying the central meaning of a term or statement that helps our students and grants understanding (Brown and Atkins 1997).

Differentiation

Differentiation has one clear purpose: to grant access to the ideas to all students. We modify what we say to different students by adjusting the complexity of the explanation, the rate at which new ideas are introduced and the size (or the chunk) of the information given to each student. At times, we make the complex simple, while at others the exact opposite is true, and we make the seemingly easy into something counter-intuitive and thought provoking.

Building a narrative

Narratives can exist within the content, within the process of learning or within a lesson sequence. Teachers can craft the story of a lesson by setting problems and dilemmas, sequencing the introducing and revisiting of ideas in tasks and by focusing teaching on the connection between the ideas. Storytelling and anecdotes are also useful narrative tools but caution must be applied because, although they can enhance retention, the memories tend to be less accurate (Thorndyke 1977; Kulkofsky 2008).

All of which gives me an excuse to tell my favourite story: I use it to help me introduce a lesson on pulse and measuring heart rate. It involves a dear childhood friend, Richard, who was on his way to dental school when he had an opportunity to become a hero.

One morning, fresh and bright, Richard was travelling towards Newcastle University on a Metro train. The train was crowded and he was unable to find a seat, so he was standing in the doorway. The train set off but, moments later, a woman who had been standing next to Richard collapsed and started fitting. Now, if this had been me as a 19-year-old, I would have panicked and looked for someone else to take responsibility. But not Richard, who had extensive first aid training. He just helped.

Instinctively, he told his fellow passengers, in no uncertain terms, to 'get out of the way'. He then protected the woman's head from the floor, door and posts of the train vestibule, shepherding her as she convulsed. Before the train had reached the next station, Richard had commanded two older passengers to help him. One was told to pull the emergency alarm, and the other, in the days before mobile phones, was told to get onto the platform and use the station intercom enquiry button to get an ambulance.

Once the woman had stopped fitting, Richard placed her in the recovery position and checked her breathing, only to find she wasn't and that she was apparently dead. He then checked for a pulse, placing his first two fingers – you should never use your thumb to test for a pulse since it has its own – on her carotid artery, just to the side of the Adam's apple. (I demonstrate this and it is always fascinating to see students copy me doing it.) Alas, no pulse. Once more he checks for breathing but again finds no sign. Richard does not panic – I guess it is one of the benefits of knowing stuff – and he checks for a pulse in the radial artery on the outer third of the wrist (again I demonstrate). Once again, nothing. The seconds tick by. He checks the carotid and radial arteries again. Nothing.

In silence, I stare at the class with dead eyes.

He begins to ponder the necessity of cardiopulmonary resuscitation (CPR). He has practised on a dummy and is confident enough, but he also knows that it is best not to perform CPR unless it is entirely necessary. What he wants most of all is to find a pulse and to know the woman is fine. Cool as a cucumber, Richard knows that the best place to find a pulse is in the largest artery that runs close to the surface of the body – the femoral artery that supplies the legs with blood. Richard knows it runs through the groin. At that moment he notices that the woman is wearing a skirt.

He feels the eyes of gawkers on him and, for the first time, feels a little pressure. But he knows he has to find a pulse. A small bead of sweat trickles down his forehead.

I ask rhetorically, 'What do you think he did?' At this point, I raise my hand above my head and tentatively begin to lower it. The students gasp, cringe and giggle in equal measure.

'That's right,' I say, slowly raising my hand, 'he checks the carotid for a final time' – again demonstrating exactly where the fingers should be placed. This grants a great opportunity for me to play the innocent card (which is a real engager for many students) who are relieved for Richard.

Thankfully, he found a pulse and the woman slowly regained consciousness.

'Now, the first thing I would like you to do is to find your own pulse. You have a choice of three places to try; actually, scratch that, you have a choice between the carotid and the radial artery. You may find it easier in one of these two places …'

The lesson begins.

Sharing procedural knowledge

At times, it is know-how rather than knowledge that makes the difference when working through a problem or completing a task. Teachers may give specific instructions, or a general way of working, or a metacognitive way of thinking about the content, or maybe how to retain the knowledge (e.g. through the use of mnemonics), but it is often more effective to allow the students to work out at least some of the instructions for themselves.[3]

Nuthall's fourth premise states that 'effective activities are managed by the students themselves'; with experience, they can learn to 'manage their own learning'. This therefore becomes a 'parallel goal' of an effective learning activity (Nuthall 2007: 38). In addition, we can reveal some of our procedural thinking when modelling expert thinking: explaining why you do things in a certain order and why you don't do certain things, giving air to the decisions you make when working in your subject specialism. It is this disciplinary thinking that gives 'legitimacy' to new ideas and provides some of the context for interpreting new ideas (Odora 2014: 73).

Guiding students to generate
the knowledge themselves

Teacher talk can be designed to stimulate and guide student thinking so that they generate the knowledge themselves. We can do this by drawing out the responses of the learners through open questions and through encouraging long responses. Brown (2006: 207) described these as 'imaginative explanations'. Although this slows down learning at first, it greatly aids the long-term retention of information. Experimentally, Richland et al. (2005: 1851) showed this by testing the recall of word pairs, where the pair 'bread and butt__' was recalled better than 'bread and butter'. A miserly 13% of the word pairs were recalled by 'read only' students; a more comforting 43% were recalled by students when they had to generate the answers themselves. This is not an advert for fill-the-gap exercises, but an

---

[3] See the exceedingly useful principles for effective learning at the Project for Enhancing Effective Learning website: www.peelweb.org.

illustration of the potency of having students deduce the correct information from a stimulus rather than spoon-feeding them.

Summaries and plenaries

Both lesson summaries and plenaries are used to aid retention of knowledge. A teacher summary seeks to make the complex simple: an act that can only be done when students have developed some understanding. Summaries tend to focus solely on the content, identifying and emphasising key points. Plenaries have a more student and process orientated focus and may review what students do and do not know and how they know it (or don't).

Stimulating student thinking

Classroom dialogue stimulates both student thinking and recall. However, the purpose of this dialogue is often lost as the archetypal tool for this, the question and answer session, is too often conflated with an assessment of student knowledge and understanding. Assessing 30 students on a complex area through a dynamic, teacher directed conversation is hardly likely to give reliable information that informs us of what to do next. As such, a question and answer session may be better considered as being just another exposure to the information, a chance to think, discuss and develop student understanding. Dylan Wiliam elegantly challenges teachers to get away from ping-ponging questions around the classroom like some bizarre form of performance art (Wiliam 2009a). Instead, he suggests to pose a question, pause, ask another student to evaluate the answer child 1 gave and ask a third for an explanation of how and why that is right or wrong. In essence, he suggests we dwell on each important idea.

Building and maintaining relationships within the classroom

Relationships are, of course, a (if not *the*) key component of a successful classroom culture. And these, of course (again) are not only between the teacher and the class but between the students themselves. Successful classroom cultures are ripe with high expectations, helpful attitudes and values. Creating such relationships may be as simple as modelling the behaviour we want from our students by pointedly saying, 'Thank you' ad infinitum; or we might be more ambitious, attempting to create a culture that develops, for instance, an academically aspirational outlook from students This goes way beyond crass and intellectually reductive emotive affirmations such as, 'Yes you can', and requires a consistent approach to designing challenging activities and promoting certain beliefs about intelligence in a manner that can only be communicated by actions that are beyond what we say. Students who believe they can be successful through effort and with support from their teacher, and who have knowledge of a variety of strategies, will perform better than those who don't. The same can be said for students who feel a sense of belonging, who feel that the school values them and has purpose for them. Such beliefs can be communicated verbally, and we need to think about the content of the messages we regularly give students about what they should expect from school.

Elsewhere, our relationship building may manifest in responses to behaviour. However, we shouldn't define our classroom culture entirely on how we react to poor behaviour because inculcating good learning behaviours is rather more than not having an ability to stop bad behaviour. It also means encouraging habits and behaviours that allow young people to flourish. We can plan to create a classroom climate that we know will help our students to be successful, and having a 'script' helps teachers to tackle problems more effectively than we might be able to do on impulse. A script leads to consistently communicating the invaluable notions of fairness and equality – values that even the most truculent begrudgingly appreciate.[4]

---

[4] A very helpful podcast on behaviour interventions can be found on the Pivotal Education website: http://pivotaleducation.com/scripted-behaviour-interventions-pp1/.

Providing models of formal communication

As a Geordie, I have my own sense of grammar, punktuation [*sic*] and spellin [*sic*]. Regional dialects are great for this this; however, I am (almost) able to communicate in standard English too and have the ability to punctuate my speech with more sophisticated markers than the word 'like'. We may be the only exemplars of formal language that students will ever experience and, beyond this, we also exemplify how to articulate complex ideas within our subjects. We must therefore consider how we give reasons and opinions and how we engage in conversation, rhetoric and debate.

Inputs and outputs

Clearly, each of the distinct purposes of teacher talk do not, and should not, have equal weighting in value for student learning, but they all matter all of the time. The teacher is the number one resource in any classroom: we know the content, we know how the content is best learned, we know how learning happens, we know how to engineer feedback, we attend to well-being, we role model behaviour, we exemplify specialist thinking. For students, we are perceived to *be* our subjects. However, none of this automatically means that if we say something, it is learned. This is not just a case of poor explanations not leading to learning (although this is true), but that good ones do not necessarily register immediately and nor are they automatically assimilated into a student's understanding. Although listening is far from a passive process, encouraging great amounts of thinking, it does not tend to lead to great amounts of learning without structure or without planned interaction with prior knowledge and practice (Hattie and Yates 2013: 49). This seems obvious on paper, detached from the moments in our classrooms when we plaintively cry, 'But, I just told you ...' What is apposite here is to define and value the differences between inputs and outputs.

The problem teachers face when dealing with this is desirability; our knowledge, the correct knowledge, is what we want our students to have. However, this ambition can cause us to forget that the vastness of the difference in the depth and quality of knowledge that we possess, as subject experts, can never be fully communicated. We simply see things in a more holistic, joined up and detailed way. The temptation to delude ourselves by telling students just 'the facts' is therefore pretty strong. But this approach is not always comprehensible or hugely helpful for learners.

Learning is a result of so much more than just what we tell our students. Explanation is not only about explaining the reality of a phenomenon or event. We also talk so that learning can take place. Indeed, a useful definition of a teacher explanation may be 'an *attempt* to provide understanding of a problem to others' (Brown and Armstrong 1984: 122; my emphasis). As teachers, we control the flow of information, the form it takes, the type and the number of interactions, the intensity of student engagement and many factors besides. Our lesson structures help to manage the exposures, and no matter if the structure we choose is teacher centred or student centred, the students will at some point rely on our ability to represent the knowledge being learned.

Talking about content has two distinct yet connected purposes. Firstly, it exists to help the students understand the content and, secondly, to help students retain or *learn* this understanding. Each of these requires subtly different strategies – for instance, talking to aid understanding is mainly about how we represent the ideas so they can be understood, while talking to aid retention is more about how we summarise key learning points.

How do teachers represent knowledge?

Representing knowledge is not the same as telling students about the content. It is the craft of structuring the ideas to be learned so that they are understandable, learnable and, most importantly, result in a correctly functioning representation of that knowledge in the mind of another person. Sometimes we do this by being entirely focused on the content; at others we must focus almost entirely on how to learn that content. Often, we dance between the two. We take into consideration the students in front of us, the content to be learned, the intentions of the lesson and the tasks, and what we expect as an end point for our students.

The idea of representing knowledge may seem like a psychological nuance when trying to teach little Bob to calculate the Hardy–Weinberg equation, but it is deeply practical. Our ability to choose or design appropriate representations gets better with our teaching experience (Hogan et al. 2003) (it therefore is part of our pedagogical content knowledge). Our representations will take different forms which are often used in combination; whether they are verbal explanations, visual illustrations, practical demonstrations or examples, a teacher has a panoply of choices in the act of teaching. A major difficulty teachers face is one of superficial appropriateness due to a lack of appreciation of the complexity of the content. Beginner teachers are (apparently) prone to this: overloading students by introducing new representations alongside new content and using representations in isolation (Turner 2008). What is clear is that we do not speak enough about how we represent ideas (Turner 2009). Considering that this is one of the few classroom practices that is most easily observable, this is surprising.

The content itself is the dominant force behind how we represent ideas to students; so much so that some subjects may need their own categories of representation to define these (e.g. mathematics revolves around numeric, algebraic and geometrical representations). All teachers require multiple ways of communicating an idea or concept because this is a way of ensuring flexibility and improving responsiveness to student needs (Brophy and Alleman 1991). Indeed, students organise their learning better when they are shown images and are involved in explanations so that they retrieve knowledge more efficiently (Sheehan 2008). All in all, representations help to bridge the gap between the concrete and the abstract, and this enhances the explanations of our subjects (Shulman 1987). We do this in the act of choosing and designing visual representations, analogies and examples. So how do we do this well?

Choosing visual representations

Visual representations or illustrations can foster an understanding that words alone can't manage (Cook 2011: 175). The many kinds of possible illustrations complement our verbal explanations in helping us to convey a lot of information to students. There are a myriad of ways to show students information non-linguistically – ranging from symbols to graphic organisers, to computer simulations, to hand drawn sketches and diagrams – although not all illustrations are equally helpful to student understanding (Marzano 2010). Images are the most common supplement to teacher talk, and rightly so: if an idea is shared both verbally and with an image, the likelihood of the idea being retained is better (Fadel 2008). As with verbal communication, illustrations have to be 'read', and therefore the ability to interpret and highlight salient factors within the illustrations becomes a key part of teacher talk (Cook 2011: 176).

Five types of illustration have been defined (see Mayer and Gallini 1990; Carney and Levin 2002):

Type of illustration	Definition	Examples
Decoration	Images that are not directly related to the content.	A picture of Windsor Castle when talking about the monarchy.
Representational	Show one useful element.	A drawing of the tissues of a leaf. A diagram showing the layers of the earth.
Organisational	Show the relationships within the content.	A timeline of the events during the Cold War. A table to compare and contrast plant and animal cells.
Explanation/ interpretational	Show how the system works.	An illustrated sequence of words and pictures that show how to perform a task. A weather map.
Transformational	Images that make the material more memorable.	A labelled diagram of an avocado representing the proportional sizes of the layers of the earth.

Strong learning occurs when words and images are combined (Hattie and Yates 2013: 115). It is the combination of a well-selected image with decent labelling and a honed teacher explanation that helps to ensure that students begin to understand the new information being shared. Considering the ubiquity of the slide show presentation as the interface of choice (or of management diktat) between teacher planning and student experience, we must give great thought to how the ideas and concepts are represented. It is the capacity of the slide show to be a repository for a teacher's whole lesson that makes them attractive: everything can be sequenced so the lesson will flow (allegedly). However, in this large scale lesson slide show, a teacher can get lost while searching for appropriate and quality images for the students to interact with. We must therefore think about what makes a quality image.

The humble weather map is a neat example of what we want to do with the images in our lessons. It has a range of iconic symbols to represent different weather and deals with complex and interacting relationships by simplifying the information in a way that still makes it useful. Interestingly, meteorologists are considered expert decision makers – partly because of the huge computational capability at their fingertips but mostly because they are acutely aware of the limitations of forecasting. It is no surprise that the long-term forecast they provide is only for seven days, and they have long argued that five days is a more accurate option. Significantly, weather forecasters do not just refer to the accuracy of the forecast, instead preferring to talk about 'forecast goodness' – a blend of accuracy and public value: ultimately, their information needs to be actionable. The public needs to be able to use the information they provide; as such, they are not there solely to provide scientific accuracy.

The reality of weather is more than a simple mind can comprehend – air pressure, temperature and humidity all interact – and so all this complexity is reduced down to a few numbers for temperature and perhaps wind speed, some arrows to show wind direction and a symbol of a cloud or a cloud with lightning that gives us not only the gist of the weather but also enough information to decide if we need to take an umbrella with us or not.[5] We can learn a lot from weathercasters by being thoughtful about what we can and cannot communicate clearly, by focusing on the key ideas hidden in the mass of data and by simplifying our message when needed. Like a weathercast, our information must be useful and must also be actionable by our students as they develop their own understanding.

---

[5] For more on this see the interview with Phaedra Daipha, assistant professor of sociology at Rutgers University, speaking on BBC Radio 4's *Thinking Allowed*: http://www.bbc.co.uk/programmes/b06zttbs.

What does research tell us about choosing useful visual representations?

Images are a great way of drawing students into a lesson, increasing their curiosity and empathy, helping to lead towards clarity, creating a context for learning, elaborating on or highlighting specific aspects of an idea, even of responding to student questions and comments and often providing an alternative explanation when needed.[6] It should be noted that students perform worse on retention tests when images are merely entertaining or decorative, which seems like a classic case of engaging students in tasks rather than concepts. Images that have been designed to improve motivation and interest in topics have also been shown to be ineffective (Cook 2011: 176). Although novel images are great for drawing student attention, they suffer when used too frequently.

Selecting images that have a suitable level of complexity not only gains students' attention but also holds it rather better than a more simple image.[7] Additionally, images that show how a system works lead to cognitive interest (rather than emotional interest) and are therefore more useful when we are attempting to develop students' understanding (Seguin 1989). However, caution must be exercised: images that are too elaborate can be problematic as they may be too difficult to read or might be interpreted in too many different ways by the students to support the ideas being taught. As always here, we must consider what our students already know and what they can do, and we must maintain the development of student understanding as the central factor behind our image choice.

Visual representations might be best used when teaching more complex ideas since our visual system is better at dealing with complexity than our linguistic system is (Lemke 1998: 110). When ideas are complex, seeking an image to simplify them is a useful technique: illustrations can help to highlight differences between ideas and spatial relationships and can help us to isolate individual components of a broader idea or concept. However, not all forms of image lead to the same degree of understanding. Illustrations that are too realistic tend to provide ancillary information that can obscure the central idea we are trying to communicate. In terms

---

[6] See https://www.dur.ac.uk/education/research/current_research/maths/visual_rep/.

[7] See http://www.comet.ucar.edu/presentations/illustra/illustrations/illustrations_new.htm.

of developing understanding, simple line drawings can often be the best solution at an early stage and may form a decent basic representation of knowledge before we move on to more complicated and realistic representations as the students' knowledge grows (Dwyer 1970: 236).

Pictures can also help students to organise written information so that it is better remembered, especially for poor readers who can transform the information into a 'mnemonic prompt'. Although providing a picture may help factual recall, it can diminish the student's ability to describe the overall purpose of a text. It seems that the location of the image also makes a difference: a picture that comes after the text may improve the comprehension of the information in the text better than a picture placed before it (Wilson et al. 1981).

This leaves us with the following planning questions that can help when selecting images to support learning (adapted from Carney and Levin 2002):

- Why do I need an image? To help students organise information? To clarify complex ideas? To provide contextual information? To draw student attention towards an idea?

- Does the image help to set the best context for learning? Is the image believable or familiar?

- Are the images congruent and supportive of the text or information?

- For complex ideas, can a graphic be used rather than a photograph?

- Does the image isolate the cause and effect of the idea?

- How will the teacher interact with the image?

- Will the students interact with the image? If not, how might they?

- How can the image be simplified?

- How can colour be used to emphasise the differences, to direct attention or aid retention?

Remember that even professionally designed pictures and illustrations may not perfectly convey what you want. Be selective.

Constructing analogies

Analogies are at the heart of cognition (Hofstadter 2001). They are a natural method of, or conduit for, thought, and they are a way in which we attempt to communicate new meaning. Analogies work by making connections between what is already known and what is to be learned. They provide concrete models for the abstract, reveal how processes work and can be used to deepen understanding of content. Be aware, however, that poorly chosen or constructed analogies can lead to misunderstanding and can actually secure misconceptions in students' minds (Brown and Salter 2010).

There are things that we can work out on the hoof as we respond to the ebb and flow of a lesson, but analogies should not be one of them – especially when we consider the key role students place on them for remembering content. Through both their familiarity and their ability to raise curiosity, analogies can help to motivate students into meaningful interactions with the ideas. This is perhaps because an analogy is expressed in familiar language: one study suggested that science students are four times more likely to engage with new ideas expressed in familiar language rather than in new technical language (Orgill and Bodner 2004). Importantly, analogies can help students to identify the misconceptions they currently hold about the concepts.

Analogies are best used with challenging and difficult concepts, although the concepts should not be so complex as to be overwhelming, of course. The only way to judge this is to discern first what the students already know. Although analogies can be a good way of introducing new ideas, it is best to avoid them with concepts that are already known: analogies are a poor method for reviewing content. They have particular value with concepts that are difficult to visualise, as with matters of scale where something is either too large or too small to be easily visualised.

Since analogies are to be interacted with and are not just a 'tool for telling', it is well worth listening to what the students say are the key facets of an effective analogy in class. Orgill and Bodner's (2004: 26–28) research suggests that the best analogies:

- Are simple.

- Are easy to remember.

- Have familiar analogous concepts.

- Have a clear purpose.

Students also add that when teachers use analogies to teach they should:

- Try them out first.

- Build from the familiar to the new and abstract.

- Point out the limitations of each analogy.

- Explain the relationship between the analogy and the taught concepts.

- Support with a visual.

- Avoid using analogies too often.

From this, it becomes clear that our planning of analogies should match the relationship between the respective parts of the analogy and the taught concept, it should identify the limitations of the analogy and it should also have a 'meta' element, where we teach students what an analogy is and the limitations of their use (Brown and Salter 2010: 167).

An additional complication with using analogies is that students sometimes struggle to separate the analogy from reality and end up using it mechanistically. A pet hate of mine is when I see teaching materials which say that 'mitochondria are the power plant of the cell'.[8] As an analogy it is OK but students rarely get beyond this, and therefore never get to the actual content they need to learn – that the mitochondria

---

[8] Incidentally, this is the fourth top suggestion on a Google search of the word 'mitochondria' and is surprisingly common.

are the site of respiration. This example shows clearly how a poorly implemented analogy can limit student understanding (Ugur et al. 2012: 211).

To avoid these potential problems, when choosing an analogy during planning we can check their suitability by asking the following questions:

- Does the analogy have any misleading properties?

- Does it emphasise what is important?

- Are any important properties missing?

- Does the analogy use any common language that may confuse the students? (For instance, 'energy' is very problematic when teaching science.)

- Does the analogy teach more about the analogy than the content?

- Is the analogy more focused on descriptive aspects rather than mechanisms and relationships?

The following teaching strategy uses these ideas to teach students to use analogies well. As with all procedures, each step of the method has an important pedagogical purpose.

Teaching with analogies and WASPS

An apology here for throwing in another acronym for a teaching strategy, especially one that is neither crude nor remotely funny. I long to create the FART tool, but for now we are stuck with a horde of wasps. The procedure is as follows:[9]

1. *What?* An initial introduction of the content to be learned by the students.

---

[9] This has been adapted from http://www.csun.edu/science/books/sourcebook/chapters/10-analogies/teaching-analogies.html.

2. *Analogies*. The teacher shares the analogy to model the thinking required for the rest of the concepts. The students should then attempt to generate multiple analogies for each concept (where they are able to do so). If possible, provide prompts that will help them to produce both generative analogies (which explain how things work) and communicative analogies (which describe how things are) because this encourages the students to think about the content in different ways.

3. *Strengths*. The students identify the strengths of each of the analogies while the teacher circulates, prompting, questioning and, above all, assessing the students' understanding of the content. It may be necessary to stop the class in order to share and challenge ideas.

4. *Problems*. The students identify any weaknesses in the analogies. It may be necessary to stop the class again in order to share and challenge ideas.

5. *Summary*. Finally, the students produce a summary of what they now understand about the content from the analogies.

The strengths and problems part of the process is an acknowledgment of the fact that analogies can be incorrect or can have severe limitations. It is useful for the students to know that analogies and models have bounds as this gives each individual analogy its own purpose and helps to avoid misconceptions. A useful prompt is to ask the students to consider what the limitations of the analogy are or what it does not explain. As this encourages criticism of the concept, it should lead to further analysis and reflection on the content knowledge.

It is often difficult to see student misconceptions because assessment methods tend towards the black and white: you're either right or you're wrong. But learning is not that simple. Thankfully, analogies work in both directions: helping students see abstract ideas in a more concrete way and also presenting an opportunity for teachers to see a student's conceptual understanding. It is therefore important to communicate the value that each student generated analogy possesses. Even wrong analogies provide formative information for both student and teacher alike.

Another advantage of student generated analogies is that they are in student language and can therefore be a powerful tool for peer teaching. Even in the most formal of settings 'spontaneous peer talk' is a significant method through which students learn: it is estimated that between 6.5% and 27% of the items learned in a module are through spontaneous peer talk (Nuthall 2007: 87). Students understand student speak and their ideas resonate with their peers. The challenge for the teacher is to ensure that incorrect ideas are tackled through immediate feedback. Obviously, teacher movement and willingness to stop the class to discuss errors as they arise are key to this, as is the final step: summarising the class's findings. A teacher led summary at the end can blend students' ideas and correct answers, and this is a key part of the procedure.

The example below is used to teach the anatomy of the kidney with A level biology students.

What?	Analogy	Strengths	Problems
In the urinary system	*Reminds me of ...* *Is a bit like ...* *Is analogous to ...* *Works a bit like a ...*	*Which parts of the analogy are most relevant?*	*Weaknesses, omissions, wrong relationships, least relevant parts*
Glomerulus	Reminds me of a knot of string. Works a bit like a tangled hose that stops the flow of water, building up the pressure so it jets off when untangled.	The blood vessels are highly folded and twisted. The job of the glomerulus is to increase pressure to filter out filtrate from the blood.	A knot would stop blood flow. The capillaries are not sealed like a folded hose. Unlike the water, the filtrate leaves through the sides of the capillaries. Nothing is filtered in a tangled hose.

What? *In the urinary system*	Analogy *Reminds me of ...* *Is a bit like ...* *Is analogous to ...* *Works a bit like a ...*	Strengths *Which parts of the analogy are most relevant?*	Problems *Weaknesses, omissions, wrong relationships, least relevant parts*
Vasa recta	Is a bit like the net around a piece of meat.	That it surrounds the outside of an object.	The vasa recta absorbs blood whereas the net does not. It is not joined up to the glomerulus.
Filtrate	Is a bit like filtered material: in a coffee filter, the coffee grounds are left behind and the coffee liquid is free to move.	The blood is filtered, so the liquid part is separated from blood cells.	The filtrate stays within tubes. The filtrate and cells are mixed again. Coffee and coffee grounds remain separate.
Loop of Henle	Is a bit like the meat in the net. Is a bit like a contraflow system on a motorway. Cars go in opposite directions.	Helps describe the position of the vasa recta. The flow up and down the loop is in opposite directions.	This does not explain why the filtrate gets more concentrated on the way down. It does not explain why the water leaves the loop and heads back into the vasa recta.

What?	Analogy	Strengths	Problems
In the urinary system	*Reminds me of …* *Is a bit like …* *Is analogous to …* *Works a bit like a …*	*Which parts of the analogy are most relevant?*	*Weaknesses, omissions, wrong relationships, least relevant parts*
Podocytes	Look like a bit like a bunch of starfish. Works a bit like a colander to filter.	The shapes mean that there are little gaps between the cells. More like a colander than a sieve, with more solid than holes.	Gives no sense of scale. What will be filtered? What will stay inside the blood vessel?
Summary	The parts of the nephron work together to filter blood using the high pressure glomerulus. The podocyte's star shape leaves gaps for it to pass. It is then reabsorbed by the vasa recta which surrounds the loop of Henle. The loop of Henle helps to get rid of excess water and returns water to the blood cells in the vasa recta.		

Choosing examples

Examples have two distinct pedagogical roles. Firstly, they are inductive, making clear either a general characteristic of a concept or a specific instance of it: they embody the concept being taught and, in doing so, make the abstract more concrete and understandable. Their second function is more illustrative: they provide practice with, and eventually assessment of, the concept. Choosing the 'best' example to use for the specific circumstances you are in is reliant on your own pedagogical content knowledge (Suffian and Rahman 2010).

Good examples encourage purposeful discussions and thinking from students while other less accurate examples can also play a role in making clear the distinction between critical and non-critical features of a concept, helping students to gain a rich conceptual understanding (Zaslavsky 2014: 119). We need to be aware, however, that there are also instances where poor example choice can lead to misunderstanding.

Let me exemplify this with an apocryphal tale:

> Once upon a time there was a class of Year 4 students who were studying lines of symmetry. Oh, how they enjoyed it when they painted butterflies, looked at faces with mirrors and plotted shapes and letters on squared paper using coordinates. Their teacher's face was permanently etched with a paroxysm of joy. 'My word,' she exclaimed, 'they've really got it!' To test them, she asked them all to spot the line of symmetry in the letter 'E'. Imagine her surprise and profound consternation when every single child in the class failed to spot it. After much reflection, they realised that the examples chosen to teach with had lines of symmetry solely in the vertical axis and the students had simply copied this. Oh, how silly everyone felt!

Our choices matter. Applying pedagogical content knowledge in our planning is essential when using examples to bridge the gap between knowing something for oneself and being able to help others know it for themselves (Huckstep et al. 2003).

Poor example choice can lead to students being distracted from the concept being studied. For instance, a maths teacher teaching subtraction by decomposition using the column format would choose $72 - 48$ as an example over $72 - 44$. When subtracting $72 - 44$, the students will eventually subtract 4 from 12. This would result in some students resorting to finger counting and 'counting on', rather than practising the method being learned. Another problem of poor example choice can lead to key features being obscured, making it less easy for students to see the reality of things.

A classic example comes from when young students are learning to tell the time at a quarter past and a quarter to the hour. Of all the times we could choose, quarter past three and quarter to nine are the most problematic because, on an analogue clock, the hands obscure each other. For clarity's sake, all other alternatives are preferable.

A similar example appears in science when introducing students to using an element's valency (or the number of chemical bonds each element can form) to work out chemical formulae. Choosing methane (CH_4) as an example is much clearer than carbon dioxide (CO_2). To understand the carbon dioxide formula, you have to introduce another idea – that chemicals can form double chemical bonds. This increases the number of ideas the students have to handle at once and makes it more difficult for them to see that carbon has a valency of 4. It is clear that pedagogical content knowledge is manifest in all these examples.

How to use examples well

Examples should be sequenced from simple to complex and from examples to non-examples (Petty and Jansson 1987). They are a fantastic classroom tool for guiding students towards uncovering the rules behind a concept. This is easily accomplished by providing them with a wide variety of examples so they can unpick common elements. The contrary can be used to help turn the concept concrete, with the students generating examples from a set of rules or concepts.

Displaying several examples at the same time encourages the students to recall the key characteristics of the concept. For instance, consider some common garden birds: chaffinch, bullfinch, greenfinch and goldfinch. They are all obviously finches because of their roundish heads and triangular beaks. If you then saw a brambling (a less familiar bird) you would be able to identify it as being a finch because of these features.

A classroom example can be seen in the strategy I use to introduce the terms solute, solvent and solution in my own science lessons. A table with the columns 'solute', 'solvent' and 'solution' is displayed (I always display them in this order as it eventually helps the students to understand the concepts). The students are asked to suggest examples of solutes, solvents and solutions. I write correct examples into the table and respond verbally to any incorrect answers using the new key term for clarity: 'No! That is not a solvent' and so on. At first, the students are hesitant and unsure what these words mean, but with each subsequent correct answer they begin to generate the rules themselves. They get to the point where they can spot the similarity between sugar and salt as solutes through further prompting along the lines of, 'Any more kitchen examples?' and 'Can anyone think of a bathroom example?'

It is important for students to start with what they are familiar with before getting them to extend their thinking. With several teacher confirmed examples on the board, I then ask the students to define what the key words mean – an act they now find surprisingly easy. At this stage, after the students have outlined their definitions, I always throw in the non-example of chalk, just to ensure that they are not using surface reasons to define the new terms. (Chalk, like sugar and salt, is a white powder, but it is not soluble.) The strategy of giving multiple examples at once is easily translated into other subjects – for example, giving students four poems to be classified as examples and non-examples of First World War poetry. Giving them the poems separately allows the students to discard the key features in favour of the specific characteristics in front of them.

Examples and non-examples can also be paired so that distinct differences can be held in the students' working memory. For instance, when teaching the primary colours of light, I introduce the idea of a colour filter – a material that absorbs light so that only one colour of light is able to pass through it. A red filter will transmit red light onto the screen, a green filter green light and so on. Next, they are shown the how the primary colours of light mix to produce the secondary colours of light: red and green produce yellow, red and blue produce magenta, blue and green produce cyan. The two ideas – primary colours of light mix together to form secondary colours and filters transmit only one colour light – are easily enough understood by all.

However, when two differently coloured filters are placed in line, student knowledge becomes homogenised. They cannot predict that a shadow will form as each filter will absorb a different part of the light spectrum, meaning that the whole spectrum is absorbed. When asked what we will see if we place a green and red filter together over the projector, they all say yellow (a secondary colour of light will form). The two ideas are not yet distinct for them. It is not until I show them what happens in reality that I hear an audible groan telling me that they now get it. All subsequent examples are then readily explained. It is interesting to note that the students seem to be organising their knowledge around colours and not around the phenomena. It is the juxtaposition of the examples illustrating the two opposite phenomena that makes their central features clear and understandable.

For a chapter entitled 'Planning What to Say and How to Say It', there has been precious little on how teachers verbally explain concepts to students. So far, we've focused on the visual aids, analogies and examples we can use to supplement, augment, complement and, at times, be an enactment of the things we say. But, pivotally, we must also consider how teachers explain things.

How do great teachers explain things well?

Explanations are complex: they require students to interact with you and the content. It is therefore not something that can be readily planned for. This is a skill that we learn over the years and is very much part of our pedagogical content knowledge, so much of what follows is focused on what we can plan and organise.

The first step to improving our capacity as an explainer is awareness, which enables us to target our development in our planning and practice and through reflection. To assist in this process, Hargie and Dickson (2003) suggest a P5 approach:

1. Pre-assessment of the explainees' knowledge

2. Planning

3. Preparation

4. Presentation

5. Post-mortem

I would humbly suggest that, despite the clear logic of this sequence, teachers rarely do much more than the planning, preparation and presentation of teacher talk – and, even then, the planning is more likely to be about the lesson structure or activity rather than our explanations. Spending a moment considering student understanding is often outweighed by what the content demands, so reflecting and dissecting our performance too often seems like an unnecessary luxury. However, this is how we learn to perform the explanations better next time. This is how we perfect our craft as teachers. Pedagogical content knowledge is at the heart of these skills (and, indeed, is how we can set about learning them), and it is accompanied handsomely by the expert behaviours of teachers.

Fortunately, what is said in a classroom is one of the few concrete manifestations of a teacher's skill set that can be observed. This makes learning how to do it that bit easier since observation and observational and correlational studies can help us here. Not everything a teacher does can be seen, so it is worthwhile pausing to consider what can be seen, and among the observable skills are what expert teachers do when speaking to their students. The term 'expert teacher' can be problematic because there is no guarantee that an experienced teacher is any better qualitatively than a complete novice, as experience does not always correlate with a rich view of what teaching entails. But what we can say is that teachers' learning inside and outside of the classroom is key to the transformation towards being 'expert' (Pitkäniemi 2010).

To circumvent this problem, studies use one of three ways of defining expertise: they either compare experienced teachers to novice teachers, they compare teachers who get the best results to peers who do less well or they use surveys of student perspectives. I have included all of these in this book's definition of an expert. This is not to provide an absolute definition but to act as a reflective tool with which to view your own expertise.

In short, expert teachers have more pedagogical content knowledge about how the content is best learned and they select better explanations and activities than novices do. Pedagogical content knowledge also improves their capacity to improvise and respond to learning as it takes place. Experts are more skilled at managing the tension between the needs of the students and the necessary complexity of the content by using what they say to engage students' thinking and by structuring the information in the most helpful way. Expert teachers also communicate with greater clarity and highlight key messages within the content.

In the following five sections, we will examine how the behaviours of expert teachers can help us to plan what we say when we are teaching and learn how to improve our ability to teach.

1. Expert teachers have more pedagogical content knowledge

Expert teachers have more elaborate, complex and interconnected knowledge schemata that are more easily accessed.

Borko and Livingston (1989: 475)

As we have already seen, pedagogical content knowledge is our professional knowledge. Lee Shulman, the originator of pedagogical content knowledge, defined it as the characteristic that separates someone with content knowledge (who may well be a novice as a teacher) from the teacher who can represent ideas, 'so that the unknowing can come to know, those without understanding can comprehend and discern, and the unskilled can become adept' (Shulman 1987: 7). Changing our professional focus from *what* is to be learned to *how* it is learned may not be impossibly intricate in itself, but it is accreted impossibly slowly and can feel somehow secondary to our subject knowledge. Collaborative planning, research and reflection are all ways in which we can accelerate its acquisition.

Expert teachers are better at spotting patterns in knowledge and do so with more accuracy

Interestingly, in spite of an expert teacher's greater ability in spotting patterns (with more accuracy to boot) in their domains, they tend to solve the problem of teaching more slowly. Far from being a bunch of lumbering dunderheads, their time is spent examining the problem more deeply so that they devise richer, more student friendly representations of the ideas to be taught (Berliner 2004: 13). Experts use this knowledge to plan – properly. Spotting sequences, connections and potential difficulties in learning the knowledge happens as part of the planning process.

Expert teachers are more selective about the choices made to teach

What is abundantly clear from the research is that our talk should be dominated by considerations of language. Expert teachers make twice as many decisions relating to language and 'focus significantly more on content than on classroom processes' (Tsui 2003: 35). This is not as clear cut as just talking solely about your subject. Expert teachers are better at considering the audience and using responses and questions as springboards for further teaching while still keeping the lesson on track. The breadth of student 'understanding' can lead teachers to navigate several interesting yet unrelated cul-de-sacs. Expert teachers are more able to separate important from irrelevant information (Corno 1981: 364). Again, subtlety pervades this understanding: sometimes the cul-de-sac is merely an interesting dead end, whereas other instances will require you to go over relevant background knowledge again. Thankfully, the incredible short-term memory of expert teachers helps to keep track of what is important and what is not (Hattie and Yates 2013: 85).

2. Expert teachers are better at balancing student and content centredness

Understand that there are three factors in making a great explanation.

Brown and Armstrong (1984: 121)

At the heart of this is an understanding that every good explanation has important constituents: an explainer, a problem to be explained and some explainees (otherwise known as students). For each explanation, we must consider the problem the content itself presents as well as the knowledge and skills of the students so that the input is pitched correctly. We must display sensitivity both to the elements of the explanation the task itself demands and to the social situation of each teaching problem ('How do I teach X and Y to Bob?'). In considering both, we break down the problem the explanation presents so that the solution can be strategised about and planned.

To plan explanations, the following sequence seems prudent (adapted from Brown 2006):

1. Analyse topics into main parts or 'keys'.

2. Establish links between parts.

3. Determine rules (if any) involved.

4. Specify the kind or purpose of explanation required (context setting, interpreting, thinking, unpicking examples, describing, linking cause and effect, etc.).

5. Adapt plan according to learner characteristics.

It is here that our pedagogical content knowledge about how students learn specific concepts becomes invaluable, as we strive to balance the student and content centredness needed for great teaching. In other words, we need to understand our students' current knowledge, how the content is learned and how the two elements will interact. Task design and, importantly, our questioning is how we do this in practice.

While we must acknowledge that questions are conversations and that a degree of spontaneity is not only inevitable but is to be encouraged, it is essential to plan ahead so that you focus on the important aspects. Many of us will have already had to have the awkward birds and the bees chat with our own children. It may well be awkward for the child and for the parent. It is therefore easy to picture this well intended exchange to be a bit rushed and to garble as you try to get it over as quickly and painlessly as possible. It is inevitable that you will miss something important. Likewise as busy classroom life events take over (maybe not to the nervous magnitude of telling your child the joys of puberty and reproduction), key messages and thinking can be missed without careful planning.

Expert teachers are better at considering student understanding

We know that prior knowledge is highly influential on new learning, with the implication that teachers must pepper their explanations with stimulation that helps the students to recall and remember key knowledge regularly during a lesson. New information that cannot be related to prior knowledge is quickly lost, while understanding stems directly from a student being able to connect what is new to their prior knowledge (Hattie and Yates 2013: 115). For each episode of learning, the prior knowledge is necessarily specific so that the right idea is accessible to the working memory, thereby helping students make connections to the new concept.

As ever, subtlety pervades our understanding: students recognising ideas is different to students remembering them. The act of remembering is more difficult but makes the mind more active and therefore more likely to learn (Hattie and Yates 2013: 116). Tasks that help or force students to recall are preferable to reminders.

Expert teachers are better at judging the required pace of input (Kyriacou 1997: 103)

The notion of pace is a fraught one in education, often bastardised by observers who think that going through activities quickly equates to a kind of *joie de vivre* in the learning taking place. In reality, what is probably happening is a highly structured performance in which there is little valuable thinking, which is likely to be accompanied by unchallenging activities and expectations. Real learning takes time, therefore pace can be slow (though it can be faster). The content should determine the appropriate pace.

One way we can control the flow of ideas our students are presented with is by not speaking for too long. It is impossible to set a steadfast rule, although the possibly short attention span of students should be considered. Fifteen minutes has been mooted as a cut-off time to teach an idea, but I prefer to work with the rule of thumb of a student's age +/−2 minutes. At times I speak for longer; at others I speak for less.

As we will see in Chapter 5, there are a variety of ways of chunking up the ideas to be taught to accommodate the differences in the working memory of students and the amount of knowledge they have within the topic. It is not inconceivable that those students who know more or have better working memories should be given bigger chunks of information, while those beginning to learn a topic or who have weaker working memories get smaller chunks. Other planning and teaching considerations for ensuring that students work with the optimal amount of new information involve identifying where to pause in explanations and when to include demonstrations, along with consideration of the timing and duration of activities.

Expert teachers are better at getting back on track

At first glance, the ability to create a student centred experience seems to rub up against the need to focus on what the content demands. However, this relationship can be treated as a useful tension during explanations that a teacher must manage. During class discussions, the teacher must work hard to 'keep the main thing the main thing' (Duffy 2009: ix). This is more difficult than we think: inexperienced teachers can be more likely to drift off topic or curtail useful discussions so that they cover what they have prepared in the lesson plan, regardless of the current state of student understanding. In short, they put their needs before the needs of the students (Tsui 2003: 25). The planning implications for this are simple: identify where the students may get lost or confused and consider what interesting things you may be tempted to mention that might actually get in the way of the important ideas.

An alternative solution is a fairly rigorous teaching script. This does not mean a word-for-word monologue; however, planning what the key ideas might sound like if they are clear and to the point, what order they should appear in and where the emphasis needs to be placed is a fairly serious thing to do. Emphasis can be achieved through the use of an example, illustration, diagram or discussion point. These scripts are often routines of explanations that we hone over the years and are clearly part of our pedagogical content knowledge. We will have refined these mental scripts having accumulated a series of reflections on what worked in previous attempts, watched colleagues in our department and identified potential distractors. Potential distractors might be an off-topic or barely linked anecdote, or even a helpful anecdote that would have worked better had it been timed more carefully. Alternatively, perhaps we simply provided too much information all at once. We perfect these mental scripts through the process of performing them and then improving the next performance.

Expert teachers show more enthusiasm and interest (Brophy 2008: 141)

Our ability to show enthusiasm for our subjects and for the act of teaching is generally appreciated by the students rather more than our seniority or even our ability is (Harden and Crosby 2000: 339). And this can be more of an act of self-discipline than an ability to act. To successfully convey our genuine love of what we know and what we do, we must banish phrases like, 'I know it's boring, but it's on the syllabus' or 'The sooner we start, the sooner we finish.' It is incumbent on us to be role models of inspiration and aspiration for our young people. We are adverts for being educated, for being rational and community minded. This must shine from us.

Beyond the quasi-moral aspects of teacher enthusiasm, there is evidence that teachers who display more enthusiasm obtain higher student achievement (Brophy and Good 1984: 49), although its main effects seem to result in more positive attitudes in students. Interestingly, a teacher's enthusiasm for teaching is a better predictor of student attainment than their enthusiasm for the content being taught, because teachers whose passion is for teaching tend to demonstrate more frequent helpful teaching behaviours, such as monitoring, social support and higher levels of cognitive challenge (Kunter et al. 2010: 477). I guess this is entirely predictable: if you enjoy being a teacher, the more committed you will be to student learning in the classroom.

Enthusiasm also manifests itself in expressiveness, use of praise and in the types of questions asked. Expressiveness is defined by Keller et al. (2013: 247) as:

- Varying the speed and tone of voice.

- Maintaining eye contact.

- Using gestures and lively facial expressions.

- Choosing highly descriptive and illustrative words.

- Actively seeking students' ideas and feelings.

- Maintaining 'drive' throughout the lesson.

In terms of planning, we need to look for opportunities to express our love for our profession, for learning, for the relationships of the classroom and for the very idea of schooling. We also need to think about how we communicate during the lesson and the impressions our behaviours give to our learners. My old head teacher, Derek Wise, was not a fan of the teacher's desk: he saw it as a barrier to proper interaction. Through the lens of teacher enthusiasm, I see his point. What impression does a teacher give about their profession if they set students away working and then write the 125 student reports that are due next week? Workload is a massive problem in schools, but the time with our students is precious and it is through our behaviours and style of communication during this time that we can increase our students' attention, motivation and recall of information (Frymier and Shulman 1995: 42). Don't skimp on the important stuff.

Expert teachers engage students and increase the relevance of the new information

Enthusiasm and relevance are key parts of the puzzle of student motivation. Students can be motivated by a teacher's enthusiasm but still not see the relevance of the material. Alternatively, they can be motivated by the relevance of the material but have a teacher who shows little immediate interest in them or the subject. Frymier and Shulman (1995: 41) suggest that making the content more relevant to students increases their motivation more than does mere enthusiasm.

Teachers have two chief choices when it comes to making the information relevant to students: (1) make it relevant to the lives and experiences of the students and (2) make the relevance of content clear to the students. The first way is much easier, and students will often be able to do this themselves without any external prompt from the teacher. It is easy to dismiss personal relevance as a gimmicky child centred teaching fad, but students who make a personal connection with the content are more likely to properly engage with it and less likely to resort to 'means end' or peripheral content just to get the task completed (Petty and Cacioppo 1986: 146).

The second way requires a broader understanding of the subject and therefore it is very much the job of the teacher to show this. In essence, we seek to make the new information 'interesting and worth knowing' (Roberson 2013: 1). The relevance of the content is every bit as important as learning it and is 'directly related to student engagement and motivation' (Martin and Dowson 2009: 330).

Frymier and Shulman (1995) suggest that teachers can do this by:

- Using examples to show the relevance of the content.

- Explaining the importance of the content.

- Linking the material to careers and real life.

- Linking to other content areas or other concepts in the topic. Threshold concepts may be particularly useful here.

- Asking students to apply the content to their own interests.

- Using our own experiences to show the importance of the content.

- Using student experience or knowledge to introduce new ideas.

- Linking to current events when teaching.

- Highlighting what students will be able to do.

- Using expert guest speakers.

Expert teachers are better at allowing ownership

The simplest and perhaps the most useful way of defining student ownership is for teachers to see it as sharing some of the intellectual control of the classroom. Lee et al. (2007: 122) describe the environment required before we can successfully place more control of learning into the hands of learners through the use of generative learning strategies. To support generative learning the classroom needs to be 'advisory' so that learners can be 'guided, rewarded and reinforced' as they 'manipulate information by moving text, graphics and media' while they develop 'their own understanding of the relationships' between the concepts. They are clear that they are not describing discovery learning but a 'student centric' classroom with 'specified activities for actively constructing meaning'.

The following section may seem at odds with the intent of a chapter about the craft of teacher talk, as in some ways it encourages us to say less, but, in truth, what we want is for the students to work out the content for themselves. It is, of course, a gross oversimplification to say that students should work out the answers themselves.[10] Teachers must carefully craft the stimuli that will motivate the students to engage with the material in a way that ensures that they think about the meaning of the material so learning can take place, but it has been shown definitively that eliciting self-explanation improves both student understanding and problem solving skills (Chi et al. 1994). In practical terms, this can be as simple as asking a student to self-explain after reading a short section of text.

But dwelling in an ugly manner among the benefits of generative learning (namely improved motivation and retention of knowledge) sits the teacher's arch nemesis: time. Generative learning inevitably slows the pace of instruction. It is worth chucking a whole load of apposite clichés in the direction of this fear since they all apply: 'haste makes waste', 'look before you leap', 'softly, softly, catchee monkey', 'measure twice, cut once', 'slow and steady wins the race', 'you reap what you sow'. Selection is key: the second principle of teaching from the Project for Enhancing Effective Learning states that we should, 'Look for occasions when students can work out part (or all) of the content or instructions.'[11] This is not always feasible but opportunities do exist, and using such opportunities during the process of teaching leads learners to construct meanings and develop a plan of action of how to learn (see Wittrock 1991; Chi et al. 1994; de Winstanley and Bjork 2004).

---

[10] Just as it is to say that the only way a teacher can share new information is by talking.

[11] See http://www.peelweb.org/index.cfm?resource=pip_principles_of_teaching for more on the principles of effective teaching.

Generative activities take many different forms, but ultimately they must lead students to make links between concepts and between their prior knowledge and the new information. You cannot generate knowledge when you have nothing to generate it from. There are two broad classes of generative activity: those that help students to interact with the content and those that provide structure to the process they use to learn or complete a task.

Wittrock's (1991) model of generative learning has four sequential and interacting parts: attention, motivation, knowledge and preconception. These are followed by the act of generation and give us an insight into the purposes of using generative learning as part of our teaching. We must first draw attention to the important detail, then help the students to find motivation for learning it, and then help them to connect to their prior knowledge before generation can happen.

Types of generative task

Five categories of generative learning activity have been defined, these being coding, organisation, conceptualisation, integration and translation (Lee et al. 2007.)

The simplest way of structuring this interaction is with *coding* tasks, which involve the students creating titles, attaching labels to content, underlining, note taking and answering comprehension questions inserted into the text.

We can also prompt the students to *organise* the content through writing summaries and outlines (it is useful to distinguish between summaries and outlines for task design purposes: summaries will consider all of the information, while outlines will mainly focus on the big idea being learned). Which version we use will depend on the stage the students are at in terms of learning the new content.

Paraphrasing tasks encourage *conceptualisation* of the content, while tasks that require the students to complete explanations help them to learn about where the content is applied. Activities like creating concept maps are useful for identifying important information.

Integration of new ideas with prior knowledge can be done directly – for instance, by asking 'How do the ideas from today's lesson relate to last lesson?', by checking lesson plans for opportunities for the students to integrate their information or, as we saw earlier in the chapter, by the students generating relevant examples and their own analogies.

In the final category of generative activity are *translation* tasks. These encourage the students to analyse and evaluate information. Admittedly, this may sound too close to the much derided Bloom's taxonomy (in brief, the idea of progression through a hierarchy is problematic since there is no scientific basis to it), but the level of thinking is not the point here. What we want is to structure tasks so the students get to interact with them with a degree of autonomy.

Translation tasks may ask the students to draw inferences or make predictions about what will happen next. This form of activity has more in common with how Hirschman and Bjork (1988) envision generative learning: students predict and infer further meaning from the content, and a series of cues are used – images, first letters of key words or rules for generation such as rhymes, associations, synonyms and antonyms – indeed, anything that encourages an actively produced response as opposed to a passively produced one, such as reading an answer. However, we must be wary that these techniques do not fall too much into cued recall, the limitations of which seem obvious during exam season. We can all name students who 'get' the content but struggle to perform in exams when the cues or their context is either removed or altered, leaving their memories to be found wanting.[12]

All in all, it may be better to consider *when* rather than *whether* you use generative strategies, since, as students are better at cued than free recall, they are best used when they have already met some of the material before. It is easy enough to plan a generative activity that encourages the students to recall key points from a previous session as a starter; it is far trickier to plan a way for them to work things out to generate an idea. This difficulty does not mean that you should avoid doing so, and nor should the fact that such practices are slower in terms of showing an impact. Every time a learner has to look up an answer or be told or shown a solution, rather than use the cue and clues available (along with their prior knowledge) to work out or generate a response, they are 'robbed of a powerful learning opportunity' (Bjork

---

[12] Dan Meyer's 2010 TED Talk describes this aspect of students reading classroom clues rather than thinking about the content: https://www.ted.com/talks/dan_meyer_math_curriculum_make over?language=en.

and Bjork 2011: 61). This act of retrieval is held to be an important memory modifier. This has been simply demonstrated by comparing the effect of teacher provided and student generated acrostics: psychology students who were at the time studying the subject of cranial nerves remembered more and for a longer period of time when they generated their own acrostic rather than using the teacher provided one (Putnam 2015).

Which strategies are useful and when?[13]

The chance to increase knowledge retention is probably the reason teachers should be interested in using more generative strategies. Strategies such as student generated notes help them to retain knowledge; writing summaries as part of the note taking task has even greater benefit. Weirdly, however, the reviewing of teacher created notes leads to better retention than reviewing learner generated ones. This apparent contradiction reminds us of the balance needed between allowing students to work out the content for themselves and the role teachers play in ensuring learning takes place (Hamaker 1986).

During reading comprehension, simple strategies such as underlining improve retention; students precising and summarising information also helps retention and improves understanding of the material. The teacher's role in this is vital as students fare better when teachers provide structure in the form of headings and adjunct questions that guide thinking and activity. Frequent questions placed within text encourage the students to reread and organise facts; problem solving questions focus their attention more, while questions that guide them to create their own notes are also positive for retention (Chi et al. 1994: 440). All question types benefit from requiring a response that can be acknowledged publicly, either in writing or verbally.

It is worth reminding ourselves of the importance of teacher expectations, especially during generative activities where students will, at times, perceive the onus for learning being placed solely on them. The messages teachers give, both consciously and subconsciously, about the difficulty and purpose of a task can influence student

---

[13] This question is an example of an adjunct question. These are questions added to a text to influence what is learned. They are therefore a generative (and useful) strategy.

learning – for instance, students who expect difficult assessments (i.e. essays, or extended writing in the parlance of our times) perform better than those who expect easy or multiple choice questions in tests that require recall of information.

Perhaps students who are expecting a multiple choice quiz feel that less effort is required to simply recognise information (although we should not dismiss the value of multiple choice questions both in terms of being useful diagnostically and for learning itself: Foos 1992). It is also extraordinary to note that even an incorrect pre-quiz multiple choice question benefits long-term learning success. It seems that grappling with the unknown primes us to be more aware of our ignorance and there-fore more attentive when a correct explanation comes along (Richland et al. 2009: 246). In designing our teaching and assessment, we must ensure that the students expect to work hard and to be challenged. In short, a blend is needed to aid learning and provide the motivation to persevere and study topics deeply to ensure learning takes place.

Student generated note taking can also help to transfer knowledge from one situ-ation to less familiar situations, and having students extract their own rules from a series of examples is a particularly helpful technique. To accommodate this, we can readily sequence teaching so the rules are not revealed until the students have grappled with the examples first. Careful selection of examples is needed to provide the structured thinking they need.

Illustrating what generative structures might look like at their simplest and at a more complex level will require the exemplification of two further techniques. The first is a simple way of ordering instruction: it involves the physical manipulation of objects (another helpful generative activity for retention) but serves to illustrate how genera-tive strategies do not have to be overly complex or long. The second, the Fox Thinking Tool, is a longer strategy (and potentially a lesson structure in itself).

Are those for keeps or just for lens?[14]

Rather than state the names of the two shapes of lens – 'This is a concave lens, chil-dren, and this is a concave lens' – the students were told, 'There are two shapes of

---

[14] An Eric Morecombe joke, when presented with a pair of new glasses.

lens. One is called convex and the other is called concave. Your first task is to work out which lens is which.' They all set off on a simple practical session and were asked to be ready to identify each lens. As the students worked, I circulated around the room discussing the qualities of each lens and why they thought what they did. The students quickly spotted that the concave lens 'caves in' and inferred that the other must be the convex lens. Interestingly, almost every response involved a student picking up the concave lens and then tracing their figure along the inside shape. This potential for physical interaction ensured the students had enough structure to work out the content.

The Fox Thinking Tool – an exemplar strategy for increasing student ownership

Developed by Pete Fox of the Critical Skills Programme, the Fox Thinking Tool uses adjunct questions at the end of a reading task to help students think convergently, arrive at important learning points and generate their own summary.[15] Following a class summary, questions are used to prompt divergent thinking – namely, applying the new knowledge from the reading task to new situations. Since this task is concerned with generating connections between concepts, I often ask for concept maps as a response.

To run this procedure, the students are placed in groups of four or five, and each individual student is given a different article to read about the topic being studied. Finding, editing and ensuring access to materials is a major part of the lesson preparation (the length of the article depends on the age of the students). They are then given a little time to read the article – say ten minutes or so – and then another five minutes to summarise it onto a template. Following this, a second template is provided onto which the students use a different filter to view the article. Some topics may require a numerical summary, others describe the difficulties and problems associated with the concept. Each topic will vary but its purpose is constant: to force the students to read and to think again. They are then given a further few minutes to summarise their thinking.

---

[15] For more information visit https://www.antioch.edu/new-england/resources/centers-institutes/ antioch-center-school-renewal/critical-skills-program/.

The shape and size of the template is important too. I draw a rough doughnut shape onto an A3 sheet of paper so that the outer circle touches the edges. The doughnut is divided into ten (for groups of five) or eight (for groups of four). I then cut it up and hand it out to the students. This task is a surprisingly good motivator: in the first lesson where I used this strategy, a student grabbed back the blank template he had presented to his group. Obviously embarrassed by his lack of contribution, he quickly wrote a few lines so that he had something to contribute. Limiting the size of the paper forces the students to be selective and encourages them to think convergently. The students then stick the doughnut back together and lay it on a large sheet of sugar paper. The students share what they have read and distil the key information by summarising all of the big ideas in the hole in the middle of the doughnut. Again, the size restriction forces them to make decisions and prioritise what is important from all of the group's reading. This convergent thinking helps the students to arrive at a definitive answer or summary.

This summary now provides the stimulus for their divergent thinking: they have an opportunity to apply this new information to new situations. I often ask the students to make concept maps to record detailed answers and records of their discussions. Normally, I provide two questions that use the information.

The next stage is for the teacher to record what each individual group has decided. This helps the class to dwell on the subject and ensures that facts and ideas are not missed; it also provides a student led way for the teacher to add information. It is at this stage that teacher input through modelling and explanation can be most useful: at the point when the students have begun to accumulate some of the prior knowledge required for learning, the interplay between helping them to work out the content and teaching it comes into play. The procedural structure, and the anticipation of what questions will help the students to organise and comprehend the new content, is very much the antithesis of the FOFO (f*@k off and find out) approach that phrases like 'let the students work out the content themselves' may foment. Record these ideas on a flip chart, making sure that every idea is included. From this list, we can check the students' learning and ask further questions to develop their ideas about the content.

The final stage sets up the divergent thinking, where the list becomes a useful resource for the students. Usually, one or two questions or problems are set which require the students to apply this knowledge. Even if this is just a mechanism to encourage the revisiting of key content, it is worthy – for instance, 'Why are plants important in the development of the earth's atmosphere?' or 'In what ways might history have been changed had the Spanish Armada defeated the English in 1588?'

Here are some examples:

Topic	Haber process (GCSE)	Artificial selection (GCSE)	Industrial enzymes (A level)
Source of information	Four different chemistry texts.	Two textbooks and two *Science* magazine articles.	Twelve individual journal articles. Students are given one each at the start.
Group size	4 or 5	4 or 5	4 or 5
First task	Write a summary of the information you have read.	Write a summary of the information you have read.	Write a summary of the information you have read.
Second task	Highlight the problems that had to be overcome in the Haber process.	State the pros and cons of using artificial selection.	List the uses and properties of enzymes.
First group task (convergent thinking)	Synthesise this information into the key points.	Synthesise this information into the key points.	Synthesise this information into the key points.
First review	Teacher compiles ideas from every individual on the board.	Teacher compiles ideas from every individual on the board.	Teacher compiles ideas from every individual on the board.

Topic	Haber process (GCSE)	Artificial selection (GCSE)	Industrial enzymes (A level)
Second group activity (divergent thinking)	Brainstorm the uses of ammonia and how the problems in its manufacture could be solved.	Brainstorm how to overcome the problems caused by inbreeding. How would you breed the perfect cow for a tropical island?	Do we make the best use of microbial enzymes? Why is it important that enzymes are specific in industrial processes?
Second review	Teacher compiles ideas from each group on the board.	Teacher compiles ideas from every individual on the board.	Students summarise their key points for the other groups.
Demonstrating new learning	Students complete a summary sheet from the notes and flip chart.	Students answer exam questions on this.	Students produce a set of notes on this topic. (Students given all articles.)

Student ownership of learning is a strange creature. It will happen regardless of the teacher's approach, whether it be a teacher led or student centric pedagogy. The largely unique nature of student learning tells us this, even in the same class, with the same teacher and the same resources (Nuthall 2007: 100). When you also add in the idea that 'much of what students do in the classroom is determined by social relationships' (Nuthall 2007: 37), then the craft of the classroom teacher becomes all about how we construct and influence the students' interactions with the content and each other.

Expert teachers are better at eliciting responses

Teacher questions serve different purposes: to aid retention, to induce thinking, to help the students to understand, for the teacher to understand what the students understand, for the teacher to understand the different qualities of student involvement. If the intention is to impart factual knowledge to 'novice' learners, then a greater proportion of lower cognitive questions seems to be most beneficial for learning. Frequent questions that require recall or identification focused on singular or simple facts are most helpful for this function. (Although the research directs its findings to younger students, I've expanded this interpretation to consider students who have little or no knowledge when starting a new topic. So, the decisions you make about your questioning may not be exclusively about who the questions are for but when in the teaching sequence they are intended to be used.) When questioning students who are beyond novice level, or those who have some relevant experience, then a combination of higher and lower order cognitive questions is more effective than the exclusive use of one level of questioning in terms of fostering learning (Cotton 2001).

In an average classroom (whatever this maybe), questions are split 60:20:20 between lower cognitive, higher cognitive and procedural questions. To increase attainment with classes that are beyond the novice stage, the percentage of higher order questions used must be 'considerably more' in terms of proportion (Cotton 2001: 5). Strangely, such vagueness is helpful in reminding us that a good explanation is made up of an explainer, a problem to be explained and a set of explainees. The proportion of questions must depend on who and what is being taught. The real danger here is in our own perceptions, with teachers asking students they perceive as being lower ability, slower or poorer learners fewer high order questions than those they perceive as being more able. Happily, Cotton's research also suggests that the increased use of higher order questions with students who are perceived as weak can lead to an improvement in teacher expectations. It is safe to say that the planning of our questions is essential.

For older and more knowledgeable students, or for those coming towards the end of a topic or module, using 50% or more higher order questions has many benefits for learning: improvement in student engagement in the content, increased motivation and ownership of their learning, improved understanding and command of topics, and increased quality and fluency of their work (Cotton 2001: 5).

Expert teachers are more patient in waiting (Black and Wiliam 1998)

Sometimes, when eliciting responses from students, it is what is not said, rather than what is said that can be the effective element. It must be added that this is not solely a teacher behaviour and must be the behaviour of every person in the room. 'Wait time' – or, preferably, 'think time', as this is the primary purpose – is the time given to students to recall or process information after a question has been asked or after a student has responded (Stahl 1994). Think time will not work if the teacher is trying to use it without advance warning and the students are shouting out answers and jostling to put their hands up. Students need to be trained to sit patiently while others think, and it is the teacher's role to bring in others at appropriate moments so that all feel as though they are contributing. At the heart of this is the understanding of why we are having the conversation with the class. If it is a performance of knowledge for someone else's benefit, where the questions and answers are ping-ponged back and forth like some bizarre ritual (Wiliam 2009a), then we, as teachers, need to think again. If it is a way of getting students to dwell on ideas for longer or bring ideas together, then time spent thinking or discussing in small groups is an important part of this. Students need training to do this and also to be taught the importance of the technique.

Think time has been shown to improve student achievement, aid retention of knowledge, increase the sophistication and length of student responses, increase the participation of all students in discussions (including unprompted contributions and questions) and generate more student ownership of the content and process of learning with less disruption and more interactions between students (McComas and Abraham 2004: 8). Nevertheless, not all students benefit from its use because this is influenced by teacher perception of student ability: weaker students (those who would probably benefit most from this technique) receive less time to think than those deemed more able. In terms of intentions, this is more an act of kindness than of malice: teachers probably don't want to embarrass those students who struggle to answer. The only way is to normalise the idea of thinking time so that students experience it so regularly as to become habituated to it: thinking and being patient becomes what we do. Until such time, teachers need to be vigilant of their own behaviour, and plan questions as well as methods of fairly distributing these, and teach their classes how to use this technique well.

The length of wait time is crucial: waiting over three seconds following a question and three seconds after a student response is beneficial to student learning (and improves teachers' behaviour). It has been noted that waiting this amount of time leads to teachers asking more high quality questions, including a greater number of higher level cognitive questions, and that these questions are based on a better understanding of student knowledge. Simply put, we listen more carefully and then respond more appropriately to student responses (Stahl 1994: 3).

Strategies such as think-pair-share are wonderful for preparing students to be involved in the thinking needed to contribute to a whole class discussion. It is fair game then to follow student responses with subsequent questions to pass the ideas between students in the manner of, 'Bob, do you agree?', 'Can you explain why?' or 'Can you give a different explanation?' to ensure that key ideas are dwelled on by students.

3. Expert teachers provide more structured explanations

Expert teachers are better at problematising teaching

> In general, supervision of teaching practice was primarily understood in terms of the application of methods rather than an opportunity for problematising and contextualising teaching.
>
> Akyeampong et al. (2000: 1)

In part, this facet of expert teaching explains my own objection to checklists and to providing ready-made, one-size-fits-all solutions and answers – so much so that this book is dedicated more to asking the right questions than to giving a range of solutions. Activities, teaching strategies and content are the basic structural units of teacher planning on a day-to-day basis, while learning objectives seem to be optimal when thought about on a much longer time scale (Tsui 2003: 26).

Educators need to be better at living in the grey areas, of not knowing an absolute answer. Richard Feynman, when speaking about his Nobel Prize, astutely said, 'It is not about the prize, I've already got the prize. The prize is the pleasure of finding the thing out, the kick in the discovery, the observation that other people use it [his work and ideas].'[16] For me, Feynman speaks of the planning process when he describes his scientific work as the 'pleasure of finding things out' and, like Feynman, teachers and their administrators (scratch that … especially their administrators) have to be able to live with the idea that there is not necessarily a right answer. In education, there is no one right way, albeit there are processes and approaches that (in some circumstances) may be more effective than others. We need to make the decision to enjoy the 'kick of discovery' while planning and to ask worthy questions about the processes and approaches that will work for the content and our students. In doing so, we will identify the problems that require solutions and further identify the problem that will contextualise the content for the students. After all, every explanation needs a problem to be explained.

Pedagogical content knowledge brings this to the fore, identifying the difficulties of learning the concepts at hand and how to choose the 'right' pedagogy to help the students. Before we can consider an appropriate plan or path we must first turn teaching into problems to be solved. Rather than saying, 'I am going to teach this particular topic in this way,' we must ask:

- What makes this topic difficult for students to learn?

- How can teaching be organised and structured to help them?

- How can I make this topic accessible to all?

- What am I going to do to help them remember this topic in the long run?

This is how we begin to problematise planning – by bringing in elements of curriculum design nearer in time to the act of teaching, not at the start of the year and not taken in its entirety off a shelf, either dusty or clean. Once we have done this, we

---

[16] Quote from a 1988 interview with Richard Feynman for *Horizon*: http://www.bbc.co.uk/programmes/p018dvyg. Go on, hunt this out – you will very much enjoy it.

can then reconcile the everyday problems of teaching. In doing so, we might think it sensible to consider the following:

- The variety of student knowledge, interests, motivation and ability.

- The availability of teaching materials.

- The syllabus.

- The timetable – when we see the students and for how long.

- External expectations of what teaching and learning look like.

- How long each task will take?

- How to provide feedback on learning. (Calderhead 1984)

Rightly, Calderhead (1993: 15) describes the lesson planning process as a 'Creative, interactive, problem-finding and problem-solving process'.

Before concluding this section, it is important to point out again that students also benefit from the context provided by a problem. Graham Nuthall's (2007: 37) third premise in *The Hidden Lives of Learners* states that 'Effective activities are built around big questions', where big ideas provide a semantic structure for learning to take place. Communicating the purpose and context of each task therefore becomes part of what we need to communicate.

Expert teachers are more likely to engage in longer term planning

Expert teachers engage in unit planning, daily planning, weekly planning, term planning and yearly planning. When doing so, they consider the sequence of the content to be covered, how one topic will support the next and approximate timings for each topic (Shanteau 1992). What teachers gain from longer term planning is a more precise view of the context which frames the direction the topic and module will take, which then becomes part of the explanation. This includes important connections, clearer purposes to teaching particular aspects of each topic, identification of where more time can be useful and where time can be 'saved'.

It is perhaps best to think of the act of long-term planning as an opportunity to reflect and to engage in 'conscious deliberation' about 'what normally works'. It is through this, in part, that expert teachers can become more efficient and automatic in their planning. Teachers who have high professional standards often reflect on their lessons and how they could improve them, whereas those who get stuck in a rut generally rely solely on what normally works. The success and failure of previous lessons and activities is a rich source of decision making, and this can only be enhanced by collaborating with colleagues, drawing on their experience and challenging them to help us in our search for better answers. By asking experts to think aloud, qualitatively rich accounts of an expert's reasoning processes become accessible (Shanteau 1992).

Expert teachers plan flexibly, enabling them to respond to context (Tsui 2003)

The following example describes a planning sequence which starts with a concept map that identifies big ideas and clarifies how the knowledge is interconnected.

Planning What to Say and How to Say It

Knowledge Map

α + β decay

Different Elements formed

Nuclear Equations

4 Types of Decay αβγn

Decay is a random process

Rate of decay measured in Bq

Must understand IDEA of average

Define radioisotope

What makes an atom nuclei unstable

LESSON FOCUS
Unstable atom nuclei give out radiation to become more stable through radioactive decay

rate = "per" unit time

Example speed m/s

Idea that Nature seeks stability

Laws of Thermodynamics

Balanced Formula Equations

Conservation of mass Law

"Things" falling and reacting

INITIAL FOCUS

What an isotope is

Atoms/Element are defined by their proton/atomic number

Model of the structure of an atom

Interpret mass and proton number

Radiation - waves carrying energy

How to use the periodic table and symbols

What an ion is.

vibrations cause waves

The Radius of a circle

MAP TO HIGHLIGHT PRIOR KNOWLEDGE AND LINKS BETWEEN CONCEPTS THAT CAN BE USED TO TEACH.

With the key ideas identified, it becomes easier for teachers to identify misconceptions and potential difficulties for forthcoming topics. This example utilises the pedagogical content knowledge framework used in Chapter 3. It also helps us to identify where and what the assessments need to be in order to best support student learning.

Module title: _____	Stuff for kids to learn						
Key ideas to be taught (threshold ideas, organising ideas, big ideas)	Idea 1	Idea 2	Idea 3	Idea 4	Idea 5	Idea 6	Idea 7
Potential misconceptions and difficulties in teaching (concept map of topic to show prior knowledge of these ideas)							
Methods and strategies to expose the misconceptions							
Teaching strategies to alleviate difficulties and misconceptions. How will you represent this idea? How will an explanation be built up?							
Assessment strategy/ tool to assess students' understanding of this concept. How do you know they know this?							

With the big ideas or key ideas identified, it is also easier to manage the number of exposures across a module or topic. This is yet another trait of expert teachers.

Expert teachers plan for multiple exposures to representations that aid student learning

This simple grid is again part of medium-term planning of the key ideas in a topic. It enables us to check that all the important ideas have had more than one exposure and to identify the specific prior knowledge needed for learning each session.

Lesson number	Idea 1	Idea 2	Idea 3	Idea 4
1.	✔			
2.	✔			
3.	Used to introduce idea 2	✔		
4.		✔	✔	
5.			✔	
6.	Used to introduce idea 4			✔
7. Review/ assessment lesson	✔	✔	✔	✔

Expert teachers are better at ordering goals, activities and tasks

It is often assumed that the best way to plan teaching is to create a logical sequence of: deciding the objectives, designing (or finding) the teaching materials that will help the students to learn, sequencing the use of materials and then teaching. Yet when experienced teachers plan, they appear at first to be more concerned with the flow of activities over a period of time (Tsui 2003). This appears to be a practical response to the complexity and speed of classroom life, and these decisions come about as a result of years of teaching experience. When controlled by the teacher, the combination of talk, topic and direction has a positive effect on student learning (Scott 2009: 8).

To plan these decisions more easily, we can consider the following questions:

- What will the students be doing for most of the time?

- What is the most suitable seating arrangement for this activity?

- Does this activity do what we need it to do for the content at hand?

- How will the teacher and support staff facilitate the activity?

- How will the transitions occur?

- What are my plans B and C if the students either struggle or zip through the activity?

Expert teachers are better at structuring explanations

It will come as no surprise that good explanations are seen as being both logically structured and interesting (Brown and Armstrong 1984: 123). It may be logical to construct an explanation as a hierarchy or a sequence, as a comparison of a thesis and antithesis, or to build it around a problem (Wragg and Brown 2001). As we have seen, explanations are often complemented by the use of analogies, images and examples.

Rothwell and Kazanas (1998: 197) propose nine approaches to sequencing instruction, each of which serves a different type of content knowledge and places each learning task into a context established by what goes before it:

1. Chronological sequencing

2. Topical sequencing

3. Whole-to-part sequencing

4. Part-to-whole sequencing

5. Known-to-unknown sequencing

6. Unknown-to-known sequencing

7. Step-by-step sequencing

8. Part-to-part-to-part sequencing

9. General to specific sequencing

Although certain content may appear to naturally fit one of the sequences, it may not be the model that best serves the learning of the content – especially if you aren't aware of all the other options. For years, I taught the topic of digestion by starting with the mouth and then working our way down through the digestive tract. The result of this was that however well the students could identify the organs, they still struggled to explain the big idea of what digestion is. It was not until I re-jigged the sequence of teaching from a part-to-part-to-part structure to a whole-to-part structure that my students started to become competent in both.

To begin an explanation effectively teachers may:

• Provide an overview or advance organiser.

• Outline objectives.

• Give a lesson outline with activity transitions.

- Identify and define new vocabulary.

- Seek to engage students.

Each of these methods seeks to involve students in the planning and organisation of the lesson, and this benefits achievement (Coker et al. 1980: 132). Good explanations also frame the concepts in interesting ways and focus the students' ears on important ideas which are connected, helping to engage them and provide understanding. This can actually be made easier when the students are helped to understand the problem before they are given solutions (Hattie and Yates 2013: 105). It can be useful to clarify students' understanding of the new knowledge before an explanation as this is a way of orientating their thinking towards understanding the new content. However, the old adage of starting on a joke is apparently not true for teaching as this may be a potential distractor. There is no such advice for starting on a song ...

Five features of explanations that can be planned for have been identified (adapted from Snyder 1991: 32; Brown and Manogue 2001: 238):

1. *Keys:* The core elements of an idea or concept. We can locate these by defining new terms and through the explicit use of language.

2. *Links:* Connections or relationships between keys. These may be constructed in a hierarchy, a sequence, a comparison or as problems.

3. *Framing:* Setting the lesson or ideas in context. Quasi-rhetorical questions and other such leading statements can draw students into an explanation or provide clues to useful prior knowledge or ways of thinking about the content.

4. *Focusing:* There are methods to draw students' attention to the keys and strategies which help them to make sense of new ideas – for example, media (videos, images, animations, etc.), class materials, gestures and changes to voice tone/volume. Verbal cueing – phrases such as, 'And here's the important bit' or a pause after a key point – also draws students' attention to the important parts of our inputs. We can also utilise repetition of key points throughout an explanation – we can paraphrase and summarise the information as we build a detailed picture.

5. *Examples:* These attempt to make ideas, concepts and principles concrete to the learner, helping them to organise and classify new information. Examples need to be clear, appropriate and concrete, and they should be provided in sufficient quantity. Expository examples are constructed to show all the features of the concept that we want a student to see. They aid the development of conceptual knowledge while also helping students to make the transition from knowing about something to being able to use this knowledge.

How well teachers identify the keys of the explanation is central to their ability to explain; more effective teachers use a greater number of keys. For research purposes, Brown and Armstrong (1984: 128) assigned each key a cognitive level (1 for the lowest and 5 for the highest), which I have retained in the table below, as they found that good explainers tended to make higher cognitive demands on their students. This does not mean that they always used, for example, level 4 type explanations; however, they did tend towards using a wide variety.

Cognitive level	Explanation – key types
1	Stating, defining, simple describing (e.g. what something is), classifying, designating
2	Comparing, descriptive explanation describing a process or structure in detail (e.g. how something works), interpretive (clarifies/exemplifies the meaning of things)
3	Reason giving, causes, motives
4	Conditional inferring (If ... then ...)
5	Evaluating

It is worth stating that the cognitive levels should not be seen as teaching outcomes but as a classification of some of the ways through which we try to attain student understanding. It is a combination of these keys which varies cognitive demand and causes students to link their understanding coherently: we work from easy versions of ideas to harder versions. Expert teachers give more reasons for each concept, make cause and effect distinct and clear, use more examples and use aids to teach from (Brown and Armstrong 1984: 132). It is important that the explanation is then well-summarised, using, 'for example, key statement, examples, qualification and restatement' as these make teacher explanations potent (Odora 2014: 74).

A simple organisational strategy is to focus on the main or big ideas of the lesson, allowing us to plan teacher talk around the sequence of: make a point, explain it, support it, conclude it (Hamm 2005). However, it is not the mere repetition of the key idea that leads to improved achievement. Within explanations, repeated information should be contiguous, preventing teacher talk from sounding like a random list of sentences (Smith and Sanders 1981). Consider the connectedness of these three teacher explanations of why a cooling liquid forms a solid.

The first is a direct explanation:

> When a liquid cools, its particles lose kinetic energy, allowing the particles to get close enough for the force of attraction to stick the particles together and form a solid.

The second uses the repetition of a key idea:

> When a liquid cools, its particles lose kinetic energy, allowing the particles to get closer. The particles in the liquid have lost kinetic energy. The particles can now get close enough for the force of attraction to stick the particles together and form a solid. The particles in a solid are stuck together because they are close enough for the force of attraction to work.

The final version appears in a table in order to emphasise where ideas are repeated, where old ideas fade out and where new ideas are introduced. The concepts are contiguous between the sentences so that related facts are clearly linked in each sentence.

Teacher explanation	What is happening?
When a liquid cools, its particles lose kinetic energy.	New idea introduced.

Teacher explanation	What is happening?
So the particles in a cooled liquid have less kinetic energy.	Repeat.
In other words, they are moving less.	Simplifying repeat before moving on.
Particles that are slower moving are closer together.	Redundancy used – moving less is equated to slower. Contiguous: particle movement linked to new idea of being closer together.
When particles are close, the force of attraction between them is strong enough to pull the particles together.	Contiguous: linking closeness and new idea of force of attraction. Emphasis on key language: this is the fourth sentence that uses the word 'particles'. (Can you tell that when my students come to explain changes of state, I want them to explain what the particles do?)
Remember – the force of attraction can only work when the particles are very close.	'Remember' is a prompt for prior knowledge. In all likelihood, my explanation on this topic would have started by saying what kinetic energy and the force of attraction are. Again, particles are mentioned.
If they are close enough and the particles are moving slow enough, then the particles can stick together.	Repeat elements of earlier sentences to get back on track. Contiguous with previous ideas.
So, when the particles of a material have a greater force of attraction than kinetic energy, the material will change state from a liquid to a solid.	Repeat, but contiguous to link particles, force of attraction, kinetic energy and the change of state.

In the first version, I am sure any 'sciencers' will read this and go, 'Yeah, that works. He's telling it like it is.' However, for 'non-sciencers' a second read-through probably helped you to get the gist. The same would be true for students if all the teacher did was to tell it like it is. In the second version, a repetition is added which, rather than being helpful, actually causes the meaning to be lost rather quickly. The ideas do not flow; there are no links between the explanation keys. The final version uses a large amount of redundancy to say the same thing in different ways. In addition, each sentence has a connection to previous sentences or ideas, serving to join them together.

So, which do I hope I sound like during my teaching? Well, all of them at differing points of a lesson or topic sequence. When the students have their heads around the complexities, the first one may be a useful summary statement. The second may be best used while the students are working it out to add emphasis to key parts. The final one is more likely to be beneficial during the initial teaching of a complex idea.

Finally, within the structure there must be dedicated time for a teacher to judge the students' understanding and time to then provide feedback in the light of this. Good explanations are not just explicit information about the content but are sensitive and responsive to the emerging student understanding (Duffy 2002: 34). This leaves us with several planning questions (Chilcoat 1989):

- What are the key parts of the explanations?

- What are the links within the content?

- How much do the students know before I start? How do I need to pitch this? Are there parts where I need to be purposefully simple and parts where introducing complexity will be engaging?

- How will the students preview information before I explain?

- What new vocabulary may need introducing?

- How will I engage the students in listening to this content? Will a rhetorical question help?

- What are the steps in explaining this content?

- Will this be the clearest and most logical way to explain?

- How will I assess the students while information is being given?

- What transitions between ideas will need signalling?

- How will the explanation be repetitive and contiguous?

- What key phrases will I need to do this?

- What examples and non-examples could illustrate the key features?

- What will need to be stressed to the students? When?

- Where will I pause?

- What content will I try to avoid to reduce potential digression and distraction?

- When during the explanation will the key ideas be reviewed?

Expert teachers use more rules, examples and links to cause, means and purpose

Well-structured explanations tend to follow a rule/example/rule pattern: the teacher states or defines a key point, then exemplifies it, before restating or paraphrasing the initial rule (Brown and Armstrong 1984: 146). Examples play an important role when principles are being taught and students are making sense of concepts. Starting with a definition or rule is best for students' first experience (I'm being purposefully vague here as this could be a teacher or student led activity); matched examples and non-examples then ensure that the 'rule' or feature under scrutiny becomes prominent. Students who do not see matched examples are at risk of over-generalising the concept. Students also benefit from seeing a divergent set of examples, where multiple features can be seen to different extents and combinations. Sequencing these from easy to hard is important. Students who do not see a range of examples are more likely to under-generalise the concept, making it more difficult for them to transfer the idea to new contexts.

As always, we must be alert to examples that may emphasise irrelevant attributes or risk teaching a misconception (Merrill 2008: 146). It is not just the content that may require explanation but also the links (see the section on keys beginning on page 182). These links help the students to identify the relationships between the content and may need explicit teaching in themselves. Planning therefore requires identification of these occasions. These may be when we need to explain why something occurs, how something occurs or the purpose/consequence of something.

Expert teachers are better at reviewing the main ideas

Decent explanations review information with purpose, so expert teachers avoid generalised questions such as, 'Do you know what I mean?', 'Got that?' or 'Any questions?' They also avoid asking too many surface review questions and mix the variety of questions to encourage deeper, more thoughtful responses from students. Brown and Armstrong (1984: 136) give the following examples from a lesson observation study that categorised the teacher questions as either high or low scoring. Both sets of questions were on the topic of ecological succession.

Question	Traits of potential student response
High scoring	
Which plants can grow straight onto the rock?	Although seemingly closed, this question contains a specific detail 'can grow onto the rock', thereby repeating a potential key point of the lesson. The question is directed towards the main idea: succession.
How do mosses replace lichens?	To answer this the students will need to make a series of connected statements. The question is directed towards the main idea: succession.

Question	Traits of potential student response
Which plants replace mosses?	This will be a simple response but, again, it is very specific. (The answer is ferns and grasses, by the way.) You can view it as a repeat of a key point linked to the previous question. The question is focused on the main idea: succession.
What is this process called?	A simple recall response, but in combination with the previous questions it does two things: firstly, it draws out a rule (or a bit of organising language) and, secondly, it varies the cognitive level. The answer to this question is a return to the main idea: succession.
Low scoring	
In what two ways can we group organisms?	Although this is an ecological question, it has little or nothing to do with the topic of the lesson.
Which organisms are producers/ consumers?	This is linked to the question above and not to ecological succession. It may be a review of a previous lesson but the focus should be on new information. The question is also one dimensional.
What do we call it when one community takes over from another?	Although superficially similar to the first of the high scoring questions, and while it is directed at the main idea, it still falls short in quality. Although this teacher has begun to review the actual topic, their questioning is still only superficial. If the teacher was looking for a one word response, then the definition of succession given by the teacher is too vague. It does not state what the community is and the phrase 'takes over' can be interpreted in several non-ecological ways.

The question is also overly complex with two question words, 'what' and 'when', in quick succession. This could be confusing for students. This question would have provoked a better response: 'What is succession?' |

Question	Traits of potential student response
How does ecological succession take place on a bare rock?	This is the best of a bad bunch, although if we were coming to the end of the lesson this is the one that would be missed out. The response to this could be a series of statements, but the content here requires more specific information. I would rephrase this as: 'How does ecological succession *start* on a bare rock?' There seems to be a conflict between the general idea of ecological succession and the exact process at its beginning.

Summaries must also be completed or finished to be effective, and here we run into the age old problem of teachers believing that a review comes at the end of a lesson rather than throughout its course, so we run out of lesson time and rush through an important opportunity to explain things – see the next point.

Expert teachers are better at summarising sub-parts in complex explanations

Explanations that provide information without checking on understanding are usually inefficient (Department for Education and Skills 2004: 12). It is therefore important that teachers review and summarise the smaller parts of an explanation as they go. This may be in the form of a task review, a teacher precis of the information so far or a student directed plenary.

Summarising may be of particular use in monitoring learning and understanding (Anderson and Hidi 1988). This is especially important when we remember that explanations 'unfold in unpredictable ways depending on how students restructure what teachers say' (Duffy 2002: 34). Getting back to the detail clarifies the progression of the explanation, the lesson and, ultimately, the student understanding of the content.

4. Expert teachers are better communicators

Explanations and explaining are distinct: explanations are the structure of how the content is shared, while explaining is a skill of communication. You can have a very well-structured explanation, but unless it is delivered with skill, panache and aplomb, it may well prove useless. Teaching, or more specifically the act of explaining, is a performance skill and, as such, our proficiency at it is dependent on practice that is usually distributed over extended periods of time (Hargie 2006).

However, this does not necessarily mean that the more you do it, the better you get. It is not practice we require but *deliberate practice*. To improve our ability to explain we need to target a particular aspect of the performance of teaching, plan for it, attempt it, get some feedback and reflect on it before we have another go. Part of our planning should also therefore consider what we ourselves need to learn about our craft. This appears luxurious in the thrust of classroom life but it is the crux of professional learning, and so the next section highlights areas we might want to consider deliberately practising so that our expert explanations are more fluent, less vague, use more signalling and deploy more deliberate redundancy.

Expert teachers are more clear, have greater fluency and are less vague when explaining (Titsworth 2010: 7)

Expert teachers have an almost unnerving ability to explain the complex with clarity, and this can contribute significantly to student achievement. Clear expression and explanation involves both presentation and structure, of which presenting is the more important skill since a well-structured lesson cannot on its own give the clarity needed for learning. Unsurprisingly, the need for teacher clarity grows in parallel with an increase in the complexity of the concept being taught, so a combination of clear expression and structure becomes all the more important when ideas are complex (Snyder 1991: 19). However, it can be difficult to define exactly what teacher clarity is because it is 'multidimensional' (Hiller 1971: 152).

Earlier in this chapter, we came across the five features of explanations that can be planned for: explanation keys (the main idea or core elements of an idea or concept); linking statements that reveal connections or relationships between keys; framing statements which either set the context of the lesson or place new ideas into context; focusing statements which are ways of drawing students' attention to the keys; and, finally, examples which can be planned to make concepts and principles concrete to the learner. These features provide a useful start point for improving the clarity of our explanations. Yet we must also understand that a teacher's ability to clearly explain is an 'adaptive process' because teachers and students 'negotiate meanings'. This means that a teacher's clarity is directly linked to their ability to assess a student's current understanding and to their responsiveness in ensuring that the student shares the teacher's understanding (Titsworth 2010: 5).

Expert teachers avoid vagueness (Smith and Land 1981)

Fluency comes from continuity, and discontinuity may be the result of including irrelevant or poorly timed relevant information during an explanation (Brophy and Good 1984: 85). 'Don't be vague' is a fairly vague expression, admittedly, but unclear language in explanations can have a substantial negative effect on student learning. Since teachers do not script every word they say, it is inevitable that some vagueness will sneak into our explanations. However, when teacher explanations are excessively vague (in excess of 7.2 vague terms per minute), then student achievement and perception of clarity in the lesson are negatively affected (Snyder 1991: 3).

Teacher clarity has three main impediments: lack of knowledge, lack of preparation and vague terminology. When a teacher lacks knowledge, they use a greater number of uncertain or vague terms and avoid full explanations (Hiller 1971). The key skill when we do know our stuff is the ability to translate this into how it might be best learned. Professional learning is crucial here, and each topic to be explained will develop over time if effort is made to learn how to do this: planning with others, observations, video and sound recording and reflection all help to hone our subject explanations.

Vagueness terms are best considered through the ears of a novice. We saw this earlier in this chapter in the section on structuring explanations. It is all too likely that terms we think are crystal clear are, in fact, reliant on learning a whole new set of rules. There are times when we will require students to think through an issue, and ambiguity or vagueness can be a boon to this. However, on occasions when there is a lack of resolution, vagueness can be problematic. Unintended vagueness is also a substantial threat to student understanding. The following table categorises vague terms and teacher errors made during presentations or explanations. This is presented not as a checklist to plan what to say but more as a way of focusing on where professional learning might be most useful. The signs are that even a narrow focus on one aspect of instructor vagueness can have a positive influence on teacher clarity (Smith 1982: 8):

Vagueness from what is said
(adapted from Smith 1982; Noghabi and Slawinski 2006; Titsworth 2010)

Vagueness terminology	Teachers may ...	Examples
Using approximation when setting definitions or quantities.	Lack specificity in what is communicated. Not set clear boundaries of where rules apply.	Other people, somewhere, under certain conditions, pretty much, nearly, almost, sort of. A bunch of, most of, a couple, some.
Bluffing phrase that make uncertain things sound certain.	Lack sufficient pedagogical content knowledge. Be ill-prepared for a complex explanation.	Actually, and so forth, anyway. As a matter of fact, of course.
When we describe possibility or when a negation evades a clear response.	Indicate a lack of clarity or lack of definite knowledge that may lead to reduced student confidence in the teacher.	Maybe, might, could be, chances are, perhaps. Not always, not quite, isn't necessarily.

Vagueness terminology	Teachers may ...	Examples
When a multiple ideas are needed at once.	Gloss over complexity.	Aspects, types, lots, factors, kinds. Generally, often, probably, ordinarily.
Accidental anaphora.	Use excessive pronouns rather than a direct reference to the content. This may make the explanation more difficult to follow.	I, she, he, the, the former, the latter, them.

During explanations, novice learners can be distracted by accidental teacher word mazes. Students get lost and miss the point we are trying to make in the twists and turns of what is said. This can be as simple as repeating a phrase, repeating a phrase, which can then disjoint, can then disjoint, the meaning of the sentence.[17] Likewise, pauses and vocal fillers can break the teacher's fluency in communicating a point clearly. Other turns of phrase may make the students doubt if something is real or if we know something is right; 'perhaps' and 'maybe' are prime examples and make students more likely to doubt the explanation. Much of this is a natural part of how we speak and a way of granting ourselves time to think of the next statement. Errors are also more common than we think with an average of four vagueness terms per minute of teacher talk (Smith 1982: 2). This seems to make an argument for teacher scripts, but since teaching is an interactive business, actor scripts are simply not an option. Among the things a script cannot help you to do are:

- Accommodate for student prior knowledge.

- Support the revisiting of the misconceptions that students still have from last week's lesson.

- Replace pedagogical content knowledge.

---

[17] Now we're partying!

- Tell you when you can speed up or slow down depending on the student.

- Help you to answer a curious child's weird yet still on topic question.

- Change how you teach the same lesson to different classes on a Monday morning and Friday afternoon.

- Re-explain the same concept in different ways.

I could go on, but I won't.

As Loughran et al. (2012: 2) point out, 'Although it is important to have some routines in teaching, when teaching becomes "routinized", elements of quality teaching (e.g. engagement, enjoyment and intellectual challenge) can be dramatically diminished; or worse, absent all together.' However, practising in order to reduce our *unintended* use of vagueness terms remains valuable. As Smith (1982: 1) concludes, 'Teachers can be trained to significantly reduce the frequencies of vagueness terms they use. Such training involves intense focus on vagueness terms per se and on preparation of lessons to eliminate vagueness terms. Interestingly, it appears that teachers can reduce mazes by simply presenting lessons and reviewing their presentations'.

Versions of vagueness in lessons
(adapted from Smith 1982; Noghabi and Slawinski 2006; Titsworth 2010)

Presentational vagueness	Teachers may ...	Examples
Re-covering	Lose track of where the explanation is heading.	Anyway, to cut a long story short, you know, do you understand?
Admission of error	Break fluency. Reduce student confidence.	I guess, I'm sorry, excuse the error, I don't know what's going on.

Presentational vagueness	Teachers may ...	Examples
Vocal fillers	Break fluency, making it more difficult to follow the ideas.	Erm, er, basically, OK?, look, right!, well.
Word mazes that confuse the meaning of your statements.	Make a false start to an explanation. Not make sense. Halt in speech.	Unconsciously repeating phrases.
Improper pacing occurs	Speak too quickly or not allow sufficient time for students to process information.	You realise in the last five minutes of the lesson that you have not explained something vital ...
Express our reservations	Lead to doubt about a point of view or fact. Lead to students being less likely to accept the information as helpful.	Apparently, appears, relatively, seems.

However much I might seek to deny it, I am not omnipotent and nor am I perfect. From time to time students say or ask something for which I have not got a ready explanation. Often this is a distraction technique to get away from the work but at other times it has relevance. As I want my students to be curious, I want to demonstrate how to work or find things out, I want to model becoming 'unstuck' and, as such, I welcome these questions. To cope in these situations I have a script. I always say something along the lines of, 'Great question' and follow this with, 'Mmm, I don't have a full answer to that' or, 'Let me get something to help me explain it.' Both ways allow me to figure something out in front of them or, if it is more complex, I say, 'Let me get back to you.' I then ensure that I provide the answer in the next lesson.

There are times when a teacher undoubtedly wants to be vague to induce the students to think. There are benefits to the fuzzy boundaries afforded by vague information, with students having to make their own connections and interpretations based on contextual information. In a way, this sounds quite a lot like the generation effect, and so, at times, teachers need to choose when to control the amount of new language being introduced. Vagueness can be used as a deliberate tool; it is unintended vagueness that is detrimental to student learning (Mishra 2011).

Expert teachers use more signalling

There are five ways in which we can effectively signal important information to students. In using these, we indicate new terminology, definitions, examples, connections or relationships. We also signal changes or transitions in information during our explanations. The five clarifying signals (adapted from Brown 2006; Titsworth 2010) are:

1. *Signposting* statements that set the structure and the direction of the explanation such as, 'I would like to now explain the seven biological steps that lead to a pregnancy' or, 'We've just seen that the ground-up sugar dissolves faster than the sugar cube. Now we want to explain why this happens.'

2. *Framing* statements signal the beginning of a subsection to a complex explanation such as, 'So those are the main causes of the Cuban Missile Crisis. Now let's look at how the events unfolded during the crisis.'

3. *Foci* statements draw attention to key ideas such as, 'So this is very important' or, 'Be careful not to confuse … with …'

4. *Linking* statements connect different parts of the explanation such as, 'This leads to …' or, 'So when this happens, it causes …'

5. A *written* cue can be simply noted on the whiteboard or found in a task sheet or on a PowerPoint slide to draw attention to exactly what the students are supposed to do.

In terms of planning, we need to identify the features of the content so that we can consider potential turns of phrase. This leads us to the following planning questions.

- How does each activity connect to the next? What information in one activity is useful in the next?

- What is the context for each activity or explanation?

- What are the main ideas? What are the potential difficulties?

- What are the 'chunks' of the explanation? How can these be connected?

Expert teachers use more deliberate redundancy in their explanations

'Redundancy is a feature of an information source which insures that the communication receiver is able to reconstruct a message that has somehow suffered from transmission interference or deletion, and so interpret it satisfactorily' (Wit and Gillette 1999: 3, citing Nubold and Turner 1987: 33–34). For teachers, redundancy is less about linguistic features and more about us as the information source 'repeating, and reviewing general rules and key concepts' (Muijs and Reynolds 2011: 41). Redundancy has been shown to increase achievement when it is used to 'a certain degree' and is well structured. Good structure is a sequence that gives an overview, signals transitions, calls attention to the main idea, summarises the sub-parts and reviews at the end (Brophy 1986: 248).

According to Wit and Gillete (1999), six purposes of redundancy have been identified and they all resonate with (even my science) teaching at some point or other:

1. Enhancing comprehensibility

2. Resolving ambiguity

3. Isolating a feature

4. Contrasting elements

5. Emphasising or intensifying

6. Creating 'poetic' effect

This leads to some useful planning prompts:

- What are the main points?

- What are the sub-parts?

- How often does the main point arise?

- What parts may necessitate support to be understood or comprehended?

- What parts need emphasising?

Additionally, a teacher's choice of language plays a role in developing student comprehension. It seems to be common sense to state that simplifying the language used increases access to the content, yet we know that not every word in a text needs to be known by a reader for it to be understood. In fact, one content word in six can be replaced by a more difficult synonym without reducing its comprehensibility (Freebody and Anderson 1981: 3). Students are able to infer the meaning of new words, and allowing them to do so is a 'major avenue of vocabulary growth' (Nagy 1988: 3). This sits well with Brown and Armstrong's (1984: 132) notion that those who are good at explaining make higher cognitive demands on their pupils.

Three properties of effective vocabulary instruction are useful when planning teacher explanations. The first, *integration*, encourages students to form relationships between concepts and to their prior knowledge. This sets the context for the teaching of new vocabulary and the linking of detail to big ideas. The second, *repetition*, is perhaps the most pertinent in a section about redundancy and is seen as a way of prolonging processing time, thereby allowing the students to decode new words. It must be pointed out that being able to define a word does not mean that a student can recall it with the fluency and efficiency needed for comprehension. It is therefore important that conversations and activities dwell on new language so the students have an opportunity to practise using it. This segues neatly into the third property of effective vocabulary instruction, *meaningful use*. In short, students benefit more from thinking about the meaning of a word than from solely memorising its meaning (Nagy 1988).

This leads to further planning prompts:

- How complicated can I make the initial explanation? How will I prevent oversimplifying?

- What are the key words and phrases that students may need to practise with?

- How will these words be introduced? Is there an opportunity for inferring?

- When will these words be practised? In what context might these tasks/ conversations be meaningful?

- When will this language be reviewed?

Expert teachers are better at calling attention to the main ideas or revealing implicit ideas through gestures

Once we have identified the main the ideas in a topic, we must then draw the students' attention towards them. We do this by structuring explanations with framing and focusing statements. Framing statements are used at the beginning and end of each sub-topic and may define a problem, map the lesson ahead, make clear the purpose or emphasise what is important and what is not. Focusing statements may simply put stress on to an idea: 'It is important to remember ...' or, 'A vital aspect of this is ...' A focusing statement may actually come in the form of a question: 'What has been the most important idea today?' or, 'Why is it important that ...?' Focusing statements serve to emphasise key points in order to aid retention (Wragg 1993: 111).

Changes in speech patterns can also help to draw attention to important aspects of learning. We do this by varying tone and pace or even by shortening sentence length. It might simply be that we take a pause between ideas (though not within ideas); it might be a point when we note something on the board or choose to play a video clip or show a diagram or piece of text.

Gestures also play a prominent role in human communication and are deeply integrated with cognition. Gestures have been shown to 'have a huge impact on speech, perception and memory as they are used actively by listeners to interpret meaning' (Straube et al. 2011: 529). They provide information for students about the concept being taught (and vice versa – teachers can glean information about student understanding from reading their gestures). Hence, students are less likely to recall what a teacher has said when either no gesture at all or a mismatched gesture is used (Roth 2001: 373). Ergo, gestures are certainly something for teachers to consider while planning.

Gestures are either context dependent (e.g. pointing at a place on a map) or representative of an idea or concept, and both concrete and abstract ideas can be represented. For instance, raising your hand high can indicate both the concrete idea of Mount Everest's enormity and the abstract notion of aiming high in life's pursuits. Hand gestures, when timed with and tuned to speech patterns (e.g. pointing to the relevant part of a diagram or bit of text) can help students to perform better, particularly those who struggle to focus (Geng 2011: 26).

A modicum of caution must be used when considering which gestures may be useful. When teaching about different lenses, for example, I used a gesture that I hoped would reinforce the fact that light passing through a concave lens diverges (or spreads out), and I pointedly used the action to reinforce the pattern. In the following lesson, I asked the students what direction light travelled in after it had passed through a concave lens. One student immediately copied my hand gesture as he attempted to recall the answer. He had clearly forgotten what I had said but remembered the action (almost). (Incidentally, the improved longevity of the memory of gestures over speech seems to be a real thing (Cook et al. 2008).) However, as he put his gesture into words he overegged the action and, rather than move his two hands forward in a parallel fashion before separating them, he continued to separate his hands until his hands made a circle. He then answered 'In a circle.'

The clever use of gestures is about much more than politicians' empty hand movements to emphasise a disingenuous point. Research reveals that audiences favour those presenters with a greater variety of hand gestures, perceiving them as warm, agreeable and energetic (Goman 2010). Such gestures can be as simple as a palm down to invoke or suggest calm, or vertical palms to designate that something is exact, or of a regular rhythm or to add authority to what is said.

Related to the gestural is the teacher's movement around the classroom. I'm pretty sure we have all experienced the frustration of feeling the need to recap something and finding that, at that point, you are not at the front of the classroom. We try to get attention from our place away from the symbolic position of mastery (the front of the class), only to be ignored. It is easier to gain attention when we stand in our usual spot – the students become habituated to this and associate it with a signal to pay attention. Identifying a 'go to spot' for important dialogue seems like a remarkably simple bit of planning but inexperienced teachers often falter in this.

To plan better gestures to augment verbal descriptions:

- Look at your resources. What might you need to point at during an explanation?

- What ideas that are not in the classroom may need to be represented?

- How might the students interpret your gestures in a way that could lead to a misconception?[18]

- Where do you stand to deliver important information?

- How might you use gestures to draw attention to important points?

- How might you use gestures to refocus attention, move the students along, praise, admonish and so on?

---

[18] Body language expert Janine Driver provides some fascinating insights into the hand gestures and non-verbal cues of politicians in this clip from CNN: https://youtu.be/XqiRRIRhZoM. The example of the small hand signal while talking about the American Dream is a good illustration of how a gesture can lead to dissonance or confusion.

5. Expert teachers are better at improvising

Sawyer (2011: 19) describes great teaching as 'an artful balance of structure and improvisation'. This view prescribes that teaching involves more than a smidgeon of performance, where a teacher can 'draw upon an extensive repertoire of routines while playing out a scene' and echoes what we know about the two-way flow of feedback within classrooms (Borko and Livingston 1989: 475). It assumes that learning is emergent and is to be found within the course of instruction. It also assumes that learning is co-constructed, being built on students' pre-existing knowledge and in the dialogue of the classroom, where the teacher responds to student responses, learning as they go. In this way, 'teaching is an improvisational performance' (Borko and Livingston 1989: 483).

Education is a high structured entity that consists of overarching structures of curricula, syllabi, teaching and learning, assessment policies and so forth; it has many conventions, such as lesson planning and the teacher being at the front controlling the flow of ideas. Given that there are so many structures in place it might suggest that the need for improvisatory flair is somewhat limited. However, even the biggest of structures – the curriculum – has a deliberate, inbuilt vagueness that requires the teacher to interpret the intent.

There is always uncertainty in what happens in the classroom too: will Bob behave today? Will Bob complete this quickly or slowly? Will Bob understand the big idea? Although pedagogical content knowledge allows us to begin to predict what students' thoughts are likely to be, we cannot predict exactly how any classroom discussion will play out. We have to respond to what we hear to guide students in their learning. As such, lessons can be seen as structured conversations in which dialogue is largely improvised within an overall task and participation structure (Sawyer 2004: 16).

Teaching, as a performance orientated art form, can be argued to be a discipline (Sawyer 2011: 199). Our ability at it is not innate. It is a learnable craft. It is through awareness of the structures of teaching that we learn to identify when to improvise and how to do it. Yet talk of improvisation and on-the-spot decision making is all too rare in teacher training; we prefer to use our ability to plan the routines we use and the scripts we internalise for the teaching of content and the management of our classrooms as examples of, or proxies for, our expertise.

Pedagogical content knowledge is, of course, the bread and butter of our capacity to improvise, so identifying where this may be called on leads us to consider three areas of our planning:

1. How and where could we plan for contingencies?

2. How and where should we plan decision making in our lessons?

3. How can reflective practice help us to develop teaching expertise?

Expert teachers have more planned contingencies

It has been postulated that expert teachers share a belief that it is 'impossible to determine in great detail how a lesson should proceed'. Richard Feynman articulated this when he said, 'I have approximate answers and possible beliefs and different degrees of certainty about different things. But I'm not absolutely sure of anything.' He added, 'I don't have to know an answer. I don't feel frightened by not knowing things, by being lost in the mysterious universe without having any purpose, which is the way it really is, as far as I can tell – possibly' (*Horizon* 1988).

In short, we need to be reassured that we cannot plan for every eventuality. Our flexibility and ability to improvise are a big part of what we do, although it is well worth noting that more experienced teachers plan for twice as many contingencies as novice teachers do (Housner and Griffey 1985: 52). A teacher's flexibility while planning stems from their ability to identify and integrate the situational cues that the class, individuals and topic will require. Expert teachers are better at anticipating the difficulties students are likely to face and, therefore, are more likely to have a way of dealing with unthought-of situations; consequently, they are also more likely to deviate from their original plan than the novice is (Tsui 2003: 40).

Where might contingencies be needed in our planning? An overview of the structures used in planning may be a helpful start point and are outlined in the following table. Yinger and Clark (1979) identify two distinct areas: the use of instructional activities (the mainstay of planning) and the use of teaching routines.

Features of activities that can be planned	Suggested prompts to plan for contingency
Materials	What if I have misjudged the difficulty of the task? Does this matter?
	How might I support the students in completing it?
	How might I extend the students?
	Is the material as clear as I first thought?
Teacher instructional moves	How will I introduce and review the activity?
	Which parts of the activity may be misinterpreted by the students?
	What will they need to know before the activity?
	What could they then learn after the activity?
	How many times have the students interacted with this bit of content?
	Do we move on to a new idea, or do we need to look at the same content differently?
Context	Are the students novices or are they becoming expert in this concept or topic?
	Are the students practising with the idea?
	Am I going to assess or provide feedback as a result of the activity?
	Is the activity being run on a wet Thursday afternoon?
Location	Are the students being moved for the purposes of the activity? What problems might this bring?
	What problems might the room layout bring?
	How can the room be arranged to assist transition between these activities?

Features of activities that can be planned	Suggested prompts to plan for contingency
	What is the best way to group the students for this activity?
	If this does not work, what rearrangements can I make?
Structure	Is the activity too structured? Have the students been given enough space to think for themselves?
	Is the activity so open that the students will become confused or will not attend to the ideas properly?
	How could the structures be tightened or loosened, and why?
Sequence	Does the activity require the teaching of content before or can the activity be used to help the students work out some of the content themselves?
	What choice of activities should precede/follow this one?
	Do I have any if–then planning moments? (If this happens, we will then do this; but if this happens, we will do that.)
Duration	How long should this activity take for the quickest working students? For the slowest working students?
	How can I move them all on together?
	How could I extend the activity?
	What will I do if they get it too quickly?
	What will I do if they are slower than expected?
	What activities may be best left to start the next lesson?
Participants	What extra structure might (some) students need?
	What structure can I hold back to see if they can complete the activity without it?

Features of activities that can be planned	Suggested prompts to plan for contingency
	Is there any chance that I could have over-structured the activity so the students don't get to think about the content?
	How might I remove the structure during the lesson?
	What are my quick ways to get information from all about their understanding?
	How can I avoid using task completion as a form of assessing their understanding?

These two areas are then supplemented by four kinds of routines or processes. The following table shows the subdivisions of these areas.

Routines	Prompts for planning contingency
Executive planning	How can I improve my planning?
	How can I engage more with reflective practice?
	When in this lesson is it OK to improvise, and when is it not?
Coordination of activities	How can I improve turn taking?
	How can I improve the quality of student participation?
	Might ascribing each student a role in an activity help?
	How can I ensure that everyone is participating and encouraging each other to contribute?
Instructional (as in teaching) • Questioning • Instructions	What questions are key? Are there sub-questions that will lead up to the big idea?
	What content am I relying on them knowing already? What can I do if they don't?
	What am I expecting them not to know?

Routines	Prompts for planning contingency
	What can I do if they do?
	Which tasks and activities will need describing? What are the potential stumbling blocks in these processes?
	Is there any opportunity to let the students work out the instructions for themselves?
	What will I do if they don't get it?
	Are there any follow-on, extension, consolidation or practice tasks?
Management • Behaviour • Transitions	Where might potential behaviour problems occur in my seating plan? What are the alternatives?
	What aspects of poor behaviour (by individuals) can I ignore in the first instance?
	What aspects of good behaviour do I want to draw attention to?
	What behaviour scripts are useful for this class?
	• What is my clear opening? 'I've noticed [Bob] that you've had a problem starting this morning.'
	• How will I make clear my expectations? 'You know the rule on [completing all work to the best of your ability].'
	• How will I deliver the sanction clearly? 'You are going to have to see me for five minutes at break.'
	• How will I remind them about previous good behaviour. 'Can you remember how well you did last lesson?'[19]
	How long do I expect each activity to last?
	What activities are important enough to overrun these expectations?

---

[19] Adapted from a very useful podcast at Pivotal Education website: https://pivotaleducation.com/scripted-behaviour-interventions-pp1/.

Routines	Prompts for planning contingency
	How might I speed up slower than expected activities?
	How many transitions are there? Is this too many?
	How will I make the transitions flow?
	When will I be able to distribute material during the lesson? When might this lead to blind spots?

The big question for planning should be emphasised here. If you only add one question to your regular planning routine from this section of the book then let it be this one: 'When is it OK/valid/beneficial to improvise during a lesson, and when should the plan and the script be adhered to?' Unanticipated decisions are easier for experienced teachers as they have a variety of well-run routines they can draw on (Tsui 2003: 26).

A final source of improvisation may come from our rather large short-term memory. Expert teachers have been shown to remember a mental script of the key events that take place during lessons while simultaneously ignoring irrelevant details (Shavelson and Stern 1981: 484). This may be as simple as, 'Do you remember when Meera said that she thought electrons were negative? Well, she was right because ...' To do this more regularly requires us to consider potential student conversations and difficulties as well as finding moments where we can stop and weave them into our own inputs.

Expert teachers are better at generating on-the-spot examples (Zaslavsky 2014)

A consequence of deep pedagogical content knowledge is the ability to generate useful on-the-spot examples. Good examples for teaching are transparent, making it easy for us to direct students' attention to the key conceptual features, and they are readily generalised. In reality, we need to provide several examples for learning to take place. Along with the need for examples to be of the moment and responsive to student and task needs, this requires that we are able to regularly generate instant examples. Knowing when you and your subject tend to need on-the-spot illustrations is a good start point to planning. More often than not, my own example production takes place when a student either needs more proof that something is true or when they clearly do not understand the concept and I need to move them from an abstract idea back to something more concrete.

Choosing examples is not always easy; even as part of lesson preparation there is often a trade-off between the limitations of one example and those of another. By their very nature, examples tend to have a certain level of 'noise' about them that may distract students from the point you are trying to communicate. The implications of this vary between subjects and topics, but in some subjects, such as mathematics, the choice of examples is the difference between facilitating and hindering learning (Rowland et al. 2003).

Not being able to come up with ready-made on-the-spot examples is not really an option. So, to stave off anxiety, we must remember that examples are there for discussion. Giving an example and then asking a student to unpick the salient pieces will quickly tell you if they understand and whether the example has provided the intended learning. All examples, and not just those created during the lesson, require unpacking so the students get to see the properties, principles, concepts or ideas that the example should be encapsulating.

Expert teachers are better at directing learning

Treating the act of lesson planning as a single, standalone entity makes it more difficult for teachers to see the interlinked sequences, with different ways of arriving at the same goal. This pattern spotting ability can be planned for with the use of a simple concept mapping strategy (as discussed in Chapter 2). In moments when we need to improvise, seeing the whole picture means that teachers help students to 'concentrate on tasks relevant to goals', rather than filling a defined time limit or a lesson planning structure (Hattie and Yates 2013: 123).

Expert teachers use more routines and protocols to manage the classroom (Brophy 1986: 245)

Improvisation places a large cognitive demand on teachers' working memory, so it becomes more difficult for us to be aware of the detail of classroom interactions occurring around us. It is this that makes routines and protocols so important for busy classroom life. The act of teaching is often a juggling act between the managerial and pedagogical aspects of the classroom; as such, there is a need for us to orchestrate and organise activity. When we get this right, students behave well and spend more time thinking, studying and contributing to the learning of others. To do this, we must have a variety of procedures and flexible mental scripts that can be called on when problems arise. Routines are a way of simplifying the complex patterns of behaviour needed to teach effectively; they help to ensure a predictable, safe classroom environment by teaching the students specific behaviours for specific circumstances. Expert teachers establish these routines quickly, within the first four days of meeting a new class (Leinhardt et al. 1987: 136).

A key aspect of classroom dialogue is the establishment of speaking rights and listening responsibilities to determine who gets to speak when (Cazden and Beck 2003: 187). There is a certain amount of asymmetry to the traditional classroom, with the teacher selecting who speaks and this being heavily influenced by keen students waving their hands in the air. To ensure that all students have to engage and think about the content, or so that the conversation can dwell on an idea, teachers need strategies to manage these conversations. As with all routines and classroom protocols, once introduced it requires practice and maintenance throughout the year so the students see the benefit of it.

This is easily planned because, once we have determined when a strategy was used the last time, we can then decide if we need to re-explain it, remind the students of its value or just use it. The need for consistency in routines cannot be stressed enough. If teachers change the cues, the form of the procedure or allow the students to only partially follow the procedure, then several forms of the routine develop, taking teacher and class back to square one. Likewise, if only parts of a procedure or routine are taught, the students will inevitably be slow or inconsistent in their responses, losing time and the flow of the lesson. As a result, both teachers and students will need to put in the necessary effort to learn routines that are designed to save time within a classroom.

Leinhardt et al. (1987) categorise classroom routines into three varieties: management, support and exchange routines. *Management routines* include discipline and housekeeping, such as attendance registers and institutional activities (e.g. listening to school notices). To ensure that the classroom runs smoothly so that time and energy can be dedicated to the act of teaching and learning, it is important to remember that classroom management does not solely come from dealing with the negative, so a routine part of lessons should be providing positive consequences for students who are focused and following classroom protocols. *Support routines* that set up teaching and learning exchanges include gathering students around the board for a discussion and distributing materials or equipment. Finally, *exchange routines* permit the exchange of teaching and learning. These help to ensure that students engage successfully with the content and allow the teacher to monitor the learning taking place.

Oslin (1996) identified ten teaching and learning structures that involve routines. These are: presentations, shared presentation, review, drill, test, practice/homework check, transition, monitored practice, guided practice and homework assignment. Leinhardt et al. (1987: 144) suggest that routines are 'largely language contacts between teachers and students' and are often 'activity structure specific'.

For instance, collecting and checking homework requires a routine so that clear expectations can be set. My preferred method is to start the students on a task and ask them to have their homework on their desk ready to show me. I make my way around the classroom with my teacher record book and tick if each student has it. If the students have their homework with them, I say 'Thank you' and then quickly check the quality. If it is identifiable as a task done well and with care, I say 'Thank you' again, smile and move on. If it has obviously been completed on the bus on the way to school, or if a student has not completed it at all, I say 'I am disappointed' and then restate the purpose of the task (e.g. 'It was important to practise balancing chemical equations'), adding that we will discuss it further at break or lunchtime.

This routine allows me to quickly check that all the students have completed the homework and, importantly, conveys the expectation that 'we do homework around here'. Using a routine allows me to move on quickly and not get bogged down in the students' excuses about why they have not done the work. I find that most students tend to do their homework, so when a student lapses they more often than not apologise and say that they will stay in at breaktime to complete the task. For lessons that are not followed by a break or a lunchtime, this method is less effective. If I can, I try to set homework deadlines so this is possible. This routine is well practised so that everyone knows their role (Berliner 1986: 5).

Simply put, routines and procedures grant us time to make good decisions during the improvised parts of the lesson. Teachers make a phenomenal number of decisions during the act of teaching: around 0.7 per minute (Borko et al. 1990: 43) and between 1,200–1,500 unpredictable interactions with students per day (Jackson 1991: 149), so we need to be opportunistic in exploiting these moments for positive ends. We have the capacity to anticipate potential problems in upcoming lessons; Graham et al. (1993a) state that this can be improved by reflecting on previous experiences and through observing others. However, in the spur of the moment we rely on our ability to perceive and act on cues; we make in-lesson decisions about which instruction or what feedback is needed at that moment for the students in front of us. We are constantly predicting student learning.

Expert teachers listen intently to students seeking feedback about the activity and the associated learning taking place (Hattie and Yates 2013: 104)

We need to know what is going on before we can anticipate potential or arising problems and, consequently, make good decisions which ensure that the flow of the lesson can be maintained. Experienced teachers tend to take their cues and teaching decisions from:

- Student learning needs rather than behaviour and student interests.

- The goals of the lesson rather than being distracted by other ideas arising. They have a strong sense of direction.

- The important features within the class rather than taking singular individual responses as a source – a classic formative assessment tenet.

In addition, teachers require a rich repertoire of teaching tasks and knowledge of how these work from which they can make the astonishing number of decisions about what to do next. Many of our decisions are based on what we think students will accomplish from the task at hand, and when we get good at this we make fewer 'inappropriate' adjustments to our teaching (Berliner 1986: 7). The implications for teacher planning are that we must plan student activity not only for each lesson but also, to an extent, for what we will be doing in reaction to that student activity. To make good decisions, we need to seek out good or useful information and also create the time for considering that information and making appropriate decisions as a reaction to it. This is especially important in those moments when you have to decide what to do when you don't know what to do. Therefore, a vital part of our trade is planning for, or being able to identify, moments to slow down teacher activity to gain insight into the problem. This then presents us with a chance to figure out a potential solution and then orchestrate it.

Expert teachers possess finely tuned observational skills and perceptual abilities (Graham et al. 1993b)

Berliner (1986) suggests that novice teachers often overestimate the amount of learning that a student acquires in one lesson (although I might add that this issue is not entirely isolated to inexperienced teachers – learning is difficult to see). Teachers use a wide range of formative tools: exercise books, exams and question and answer responses, as well as keenly reading the facial expressions and other body language cues which signal that students are focused and attentive to the teaching. We use these tools to make decisions based on avoiding overloading students and, as a result of reading them, we make better decisions about where to head next. This takes years to hone but, thankfully, we can learn a lot from observing lessons. The following table highlights areas where a teacher can usefully observe their classroom, and those of others, in order to make useful decisions (adapted from Berliner 1986; Rink et al. 1994).

Management issues			
Student behaviour and learning	Support teachers	Time and space	Equipment and resources
Content development			
Selecting an appropriate task	Task individualisation	Purpose of task	Appropriateness of learning intentions
Teaching methods			
Student engagement	Checking understanding	What cues and signals to give	How to present new ideas
How to make ideas clear	Student independence	Ownership of knowledge	Clarity and constructive alignment of the activity
Student responses			
Quality of task completion	What feedback might help?	What feedback form is best?	On-taskness
Student effort	Student performance: quality of understanding	Student performance: retention of knowledge	
Teacher movement			
Scanning enough?	How to monitor class?	What to monitor?	Proximity to students
Social climate			
Student interactions	Teacher–student interactions	Characteristics of students	High expectations
Use of affective statements			

On the whole, teachers are poor at changing strategy when instruction is going poorly: we tend to do so only when interruptions occur (Tsui 2003: 28). It is therefore essential that we anticipate potential difficulties and, when we need to change tack, consider whether the new strategy does, in fact, return the students to the main concepts.

Teaching well is a complicated endeavour. We do not become expert teachers overnight; it takes many, many years. But a key part of it is becoming systematic, planning to master the complex skills and understanding the classroom through deliberate practice, feedback and reflection.

How can reflective practice help us to develop teaching expertise?

Rather than persisting with blindly planning and teaching in exactly the same way, day after day, regardless of whether it works or not, there must be moments in our working lives when we stop and take stock. Schön's (1983) idea of reflective practice is a professional responsibility and has a huge impact on our ability to 'improvise effectively within structure' (Sawyer 2004: 16). Expert teachers have more knowledge and more awareness of successful strategies and behaviours than novices, although the sheer volume and depth of an expert teacher's knowledge is too overwhelming to consider as part of your planning for each and every lesson. It therefore falls to our professional learning to embed these traits and behaviours into what is, in truth, an intuitive repertoire. Lesson planning must consequently include an element of professional learning. Selection of which area to focus on in which lesson is key, but it must be pertinent to you, your students and your school.

The Sutton Trust makes it clear that *sustained* professional learning is most likely to result when, firstly, teacher learning focuses on improving student outcomes and, secondly, when attention is paid to the learning rather than to the person or to comparison with others (Coe et al. 2014: 5). Teachers are continually encouraged to maintain their own commitment to being independent learners because professional learning and support is not always provided by a school's leadership. The United

States' National Board for Professional Teaching Standards (2016) rightly asserts that teachers should be part of learning communities that learn systematically from their experiences, but the provision of continued professional development has been described by one government sponsored commentator in the UK as suffering from 'low expectations … for too long' (Weston 2015).

There is one useful question that you can use in order to guide you: 'What do I want to get better at?' Crawford et al. (2005) extol the benefits of the 'effortful and time consuming' process of considered reflection as profoundly worthwhile. Experts reflect on their goals and on their limitations while reframing the problem in light of their observations and then considering alternative approaches. Through this process they continue to learn throughout the lifetime of their career, increasing their capacity to be flexible in how they work, adapting to difficulties and performing better. In addition, expert teachers become efficient: they are able to free up time and energy so they can focus on figuring out complex teaching problems while in the very flow of a lesson.

Seeing and hearing yourself teach has never been easier, with many useful web based video observation suites available. These all leave ownership of the film to you, and, as such, lie outside of the overbearing structures of formal, in-school lesson observations where the burden is on performance management, allocating numbers and evidencing school evaluations. Such structures have bollocks all to do with reflective practice, even if one of the outputs is for you, the observed teacher, to receive the thing they call feedback. The easiest way to improve is to film yourself, although a further very effective way is to become involved in a coaching relationship with colleagues to plan, observe and help each other to reflect and to see what learning is like in your lessons. Importantly, as the Teacher Development Trust (2015: 19) makes clear, 'A didactic model [of teacher training] in which facilitators simply tell teachers what to do does not lead to positive outcomes for participants or students.' This, in part, puts the ball very much in our court to teach, to learn and to enjoy our profession.

Summary

Teacher talk is far from simple. To do it well, we need deep pedagogical content knowledge to draw on in the sequencing, linking and construction phases of our explanations, which should be built around well-chosen representations, analogies and examples that inform and intrigue learners. Yet teachers must do more than simply engage an audience – we must help learners to construct an understanding of their own. As such, explanations are far from just the transmission of what we know. The ability to balance what students need to know with what the content demands is a critical consideration for planning. This is complex, so our explanations require a clarity that is derived from structuring both our interactions with the students and their interactions with the content.

But we also need highly honed communication skills to be able to deliver ideas. Planning what we say and how we say it is profoundly useful, of course, but to a large extent what we say is improvised. This is not to say that it is always made up on the spot, but we tend to improvise around structures and scripts that we have refined over the years. Critically, this professional learning is how we learn what to say and how to say it. It is for this reason that we must include it in our planning.

CHAPTER 5

The Act of Learning: Memory as a Process

Thus far in our exploration of pedagogical content knowledge, the 'complex and interwoven relationships' between a teacher's 'knowledge of content, teaching and learning' have become apparent (Loughran 2006: 2). The craft of lesson planning has many start points: it may be hidden structures in our subjects or aspects of our subjects that are difficult or easily misinterpreted that we ponder to figure out how to teach. As we seek to develop a deep, complex and contextual understanding in our students, we also consider how to structure and deliver explanations as well as the management of multiple exposures so that learning is likely to happen and is durable. We also spend a lot of time thinking about the students we teach, and so in the final two chapters we will turn our attention to perhaps the most important aspect of our pedagogical content knowledge – the learner.

At the heart of a teacher's pedagogical content knowledge is our (developing) understanding of how the memory works. On one hand, the relationship between learning and memory is straightforward; after all, 'If nothing has changed in long-term memory, nothing has been learned' (Kirschner et al. 2006: 77). We view memory as the destination for the learning process. However, to get information into our long-term memory we must think hard about the idea, and to do that we must hold the idea in our working memory. The working memory is 'probably ... where classroom experiences are stored as the student tries to make sense of them' (Nuthall 2007: 71). The following diagram summarises these two complementary memory systems: the short-term processing system (working memory) and the final destination of learning (long-term memory).

In this chapter we will look at memory as a process and in the final chapter at memory as a destination.

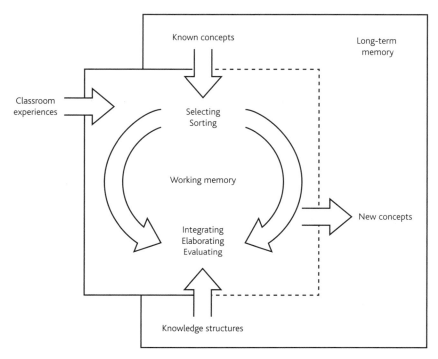

Source: Nuthall (2007: 71)

Working memory

What is working memory? The processing (or working) part of the memory holds and manipulates information in the mind for 'short periods of time' (Gathercole and Alloway 2007: 11). It helps us to:

- Learn new things.

- Remember instructions and what to do next.

- Read and understand.

- Select information.

- Organise and plan.

- Listen and respond.

- Restrain impulses.

Working memory plays an important role in our capacity to learn, but its capacity differs from person to person. Students with a poor working memory are at a high risk of educational underachievement (Alloway et al. 2009: 617). But no one has a perfect working memory. It is prone to distraction, it is ephemeral and it struggles to cope with large amounts of information. Without conscious efforts at retention, the information stored in the working memory disappears all too quickly.

The limitations of working memory are perhaps best demonstrated if we look at the Brown–Peterson test, an interesting psychological study in which the capacity to memorise a string of consonants was tested. (Bear in mind here that random or non-contextual information is difficult to remember.) Subjects were asked to memorise a sequence of consonants and then prevented from rehearsing them through a range of working memory heavy tasks, such as having to count down from 100 in threes. Astonishingly, recall accuracy decreased by 50% after only a paltry 6 seconds and by 18 seconds it had all but gone (Gathercole 2001: 335). Such fragility can be distressing for learners, particularly when the information has been removed for good.

The ability to store information also varies with age. Some research suggests that younger students can store two to four pieces of (random) information, while older students and adults can get nearer to seven pieces, and that these abilities are reduced during complex tasks or when retrieving information from long-term memory. We cannot underestimate the importance of the interaction between working and long-term memory for learning as it is in this that new knowledge is associated with prior knowledge. Having too many items stored overloads the working memory and, consequently, learning cannot occur. Typically, 10–15% of students in a mainstream classroom suffer from a poor working memory (Alloway 2008: 2); therefore, our planning should attempt to avoid overloading these students by asking for too many ideas to be processed at once. In fast paced, active classrooms potential over-loads are everywhere. Look out for:

- Multiple step instructions.

- Long lists of ideas that (from a student's view) may seem unconnected.

- Complex logical sequences.

- Tasks that require newly learned ideas to be applied.

- Asking a student to hold something in mind while doing something else that is mentally challenging.

Students with poor working memory will find these areas particularly difficult, so we must identify them. Such students may:

- Be slow in recalling information.

- Find remaining focused difficult – they are easily distracted.

- Appear not to have listened to instructions.

- Restart the work, resulting in numerous incomplete tasks.

- Regularly lose their place in a text.

- Tend to be quiet and not answer direct questions.

- Be frequently forgetful and lose items.

What can we do to support students' working memories during lessons?

Primarily, we should consider working memory as a focus for differentiating activities and materials for those with the weakest working memories. We can evaluate tasks for how many items or actions an activity entails and for where overload may occur. Inevitably, there are bits of content that are unavoidably complex, so for these, longer term planning across a topic might be most fruitful: reducing the number of items at the start and increasing these as the topic culminates.

Teachers naturally chunk information in order to reduce the number of items to be learned. This is best done by placing new knowledge in a meaningful context and making it clear how the key elements play a part. It may not have escaped your notice that the difficulties and limitations of working memory as described previously are linked to information that is presented in a random state. So, how the ideas in a lesson connect must become a distinct part of what is taught. We have already discussed how to do this – for instance, by using organisational structures to help students link concepts or by using worked examples to reduce the perceived randomness of the information. The SOLO taxonomy structure provides a useful model of how this might look when moving from single ideas, to multiple ideas, to joining them all up.

While learning, the ideas held in working memory require regular refreshing. Doing this using a variety of different methods seems a logical extension of Nuthall's (2007) multiple exposures guidance: we should aim to repeat the information three or four times over the course of a lesson. In the act of teaching, teachers should make full use of the whiteboard, flip charts and displays by recording important information or words as explanations and discussions develop. If tasks are likely to be extended and have complex ideas in them, then simple student resources such as memory aids that provide key words or definitions can help to reduce overload. It seems almost churlish to say this, but highlighting the resources that students have at their disposal to complete an activity is an important way of reducing the stress associated with poor working memory (Otto et al. 2013). This stress can be reduced by developing routines with the students. Regular use of a strategy allows the students to practise with it so that they become automatic, reducing future burdens on working memory.

Designing teaching strategies to support working memory

When designing tasks and activities, the incorporation of processing time is an important way of supporting the students' learning. This is especially important for content and activities that are cognitively intense. For this purpose, simple and short activities placed between difficult bouts of thinking suffice, as long as the students are given the opportunity for a 'cognitive break' (Willingham 2009: 15). This may be a simple review routine – for example, asking them to reread their notes and highlight key points or asking them to summarise the key idea learned. Even rote activities have their place at this stage of learning. Teachers normally tackle the cognitive workload by changing the pace of lessons – slowing down to give students the space to think – but we can also predict where a change of pace is necessary and plan a recapping activity that allows for a break.

There are many models we can use to structure exposure to knowledge and, at some point, all have their place, but when considering their impact on working memory some are clearly better than others. The following models, like all models, need to be taken with a pinch of salt. They do not represent a lesson planning structure but they are different ways in which the flow of ideas can be managed via our planning. They do not suppose a teacher or student centric view of pedagogy because new information can be given in a student centred way and student activity can be very teacher centred. Indeed, teaching models are much like a set of instructions for flat pack furniture: they will build you a wardrobe named after an obscure Scandinavian poet or type of Swedish omelette, but the end result will not be a hand crafted individual piece of furniture that future generations will lug along to the *Antiques Roadshow*.

Models that do not consider working memory

The Jack Kerouac Model – a telling model of instruction

Start	New information is explained	End

Crude description: Just like Kerouac's 'stream of consciousness' writing style, the teacher ruminates on the content, distilling it into pithy observations and contextualising it with tales of wonder. Explanation follows explanation.

Benefits for working memory: Easy to manage behaviour through dead-eyed stares and entertainment value. If narratives and analogies are used, they help the students to retain some of what is told.

Problems for working memory: The capacity of working memory is not considered in this model and it will result in overloading students with too many ideas. Students do not get an opportunity to fully interact with ideas before the next set comes along.

The Hit and Run Model – a top-loaded model of instruction

New information	Student activity

Crude description: All of the information is shared at the beginning of a lesson in a cathartic process[1] which allows the students to do some schoolwork during the remainder of the lesson.

Benefits for working memory: The students get a chance to interact with some of the ideas shared. These are likely to be the first ideas and last ideas offered. Teachers can sit behind their desks because their work is done.[2]

Problems for working memory: Once again, if a surfeit of ideas overload the working memory, it makes it impossible for students to assimilate much new knowledge.

---

[1] For the teacher.
[2] This is satire.

Models that consider working memory to varying extents

The Step-by-Step Approach – a chunked model of instruction

New information 1	Student activity	New information 2	Student activity

Crude description: The ideas being shared are split into smaller, more manageable chunks by the teacher on behalf of the students. Constructively aligned activities follow each new idea introduced.

Benefits to working memory: Students have less to hold in their working memory at any one time, making them more likely to think about the idea in a way that will lead to learning. Constructive alignment allows a greater time period for the students to contemplate the information.

Problems for working memory: This model does not consider the context of the knowledge, it does not review or activate prior knowledge and it does not consider the complexity or the sequence of the ideas being studied. It resembles the quantitative part of the SOLO taxonomy as the number of ideas being worked with is what matters.[3] Clearly, learners need to think about more things if they are to develop the deeper versions of understanding as represented by the higher levels of the SOLO taxonomy. It is well worth noting that one of the intentions of the SOLO taxonomy is to represent the demand on working memory.

The Mighty Oaks from Little Acorns Model – an incremental model of instruction

Basic idea explained	Student activity	More complex idea explained	Student activity

Crude description: It is rare that we will teach completely separate ideas in the same lesson, so this model is an adaptation of the previous one but now incorporates an

---

[3] From unistructural to multistructural.

increase in cognitive load. Again, the SOLO taxonomy gives us a useful way of thinking about this, with each level referring to the demand being placed on the working memory or attention span. Each level of response doesn't replace the previous set of ideas but adds to them. If the first task is unistructural or multistructural (e.g. listing, labelling, describing), this can be followed by studying a more complex version of the idea using a different set of tasks which ask the students to connect ideas together, moving though the SOLO levels of relational and extended abstract with explain, sequence and analysis tasks that have a concrete foundation.

Benefits for working memory: Although this model expects to place a large demand on working memory, it seeks to do so in an incremental way. Teachers are not only constructively aligning content and activities but have a plan for supporting developing working memory. There is also the inference that the idea will be repeated in subsequent teaching as ideas are built upon.

Problems for working memory: It is difficult to apply newly learned ideas to new situations, and this is what this model implies happens. Although we should be aware that it might appear that students haven't learned anything yet, we shouldn't panic because learning takes time. As with the previous model, this model does not take into account the usefulness of context and prior knowledge in helping the working memory.

Models that consider more than just working memory

The 9 O'Clock News Model – a deconstructed–reconstructed model of instruction

Big idea – context set	Basic idea	Student activity	More complex ideas explained	Student activity

Crude description: We are all familiar with the structure of a news broadcast: it starts with the big ideas, followed by a more detailed, nuanced and analytical look at the issues. The news moves from a basic idea ('Politicians are useless' or 'Gravy is nice') into complicated related ideas, such as a heartfelt apology from a politician ('I'm sorry we did not keep all our promises ...' or 'Before the election I know we said we would vote against any rise in tuition fees' or 'Why the North and South of Britain are growing apart is because of the North's insistence that gravy and chips do go together').

Benefits to working memory: The big idea provides a useful encoding category into which detail can be assimilated. Again, this model assumes that the starting ideas will be repeated when addressing the more complex ideas, helping to ensure multiple exposures, but now it has the 'headline' to help us chunk ideas together.

Problems for working memory: Although a context is provided for the learning to take place in, steps have not been taken to ensure that the concepts will be attended to too.

The Puzzling Model – an engagement chunked model of instruction

Problem on idea 1 set	Idea 1 explained	Idea 1 activity	Problem on idea 2 set	Idea 2 explained	Idea 2 activity
Puzzle	Enlighten	Learn	Puzzle	Enlighten	Learn

Crude description: The lesson is seen by the students as a series of problems to be solved. The term 'problem' does not necessarily imply a question (although it might do). The problem could be as simple as a true or false statement, a curious picture or an unexplained scenario. The purpose of the problem is to engage the students in the act of thinking about the content that is to be learned. Once the students have been enlightened as to the solution, they then have time to interact, assimilate and practise it. This supposes, of course, that time is available for children to learn things.

Benefits to working memory: 'Curiosity really is one of the very intense and very basic impulses in humans' (Singh 2014). It is in searching for meaning that memories are made, and curiosity can improve the efficacy of memory. A study of curiosity revealed that the more curious the learner, the more the knowledge is remembered. When students get to see a gap in their knowledge it is 'like an itch you just have to scratch' (Charan Ranganath, quoted in Sample 2014).

Problems for working memory: Thinking deeply to solve problems is hard and tiring work, so the students may start off a lesson replete with the mental agility of a Groucho Marx, but after long periods of thinking become fatigued and end up with the mental acuity of a Harpo.

There is an art in getting students to think about the right thing, and some ways of gaining students' attention might, in fact, distract them from the actual idea. Quick checks can save a lot of the effort of having to reteach:

- What are the students likely to think about?

- How might they interpret the activity differently?

- What needs to be in place to help them structure the correct interaction?

Another pedagogical difficulty is in finding the useful balance between developing curiosity and frustrating students. Simply setting a problem and then quickly following up with the answer does not develop curiosity. Indeed, there is an argument that deliberately making students confused can have beneficial effects. Physics researcher Jason Dowd from Duke University found that 'students who express more confusion tend to also perform better overall, as measured by final grade' (Dowd et al. 2015: 9), suggesting that there is some benefit in forcing students to experience confusion in the learning process. However, it must be acknowledged that a sure fire way of increasing student anxiety is to leave them in confusion for too long. Anxiety has a negative impact on the storage and processing capacity of working memory (Drake 1988). Our craft, as always, is to emulate an educational Wallenda: treading the tightrope between confusion and curiosity and the mental abyss of stress and anxiety.[4]

---

[4] The Wallendas, or Flying Wallendas, are a famous circus act of yore.

The Concise Crossword Model – an engagement model that includes cognitive breaks[5]

Problem on idea 1 set	Idea 1 explained	Idea 1 activity	Idea 1 review/ practice	Problem on idea 2 set	Idea 2 explained	Idea 2 activity	Idea 2 review/ practice
Puzzle	Enlighten	Learn	Break	Puzzle	Enlighten	Learn	Break

Crude description: This model is the same as the Puzzling Model but it takes a proactive look at providing a cognitive break for thinking students. Teachers normally tackle cognitive workload by relying on intuition to spot when to change the pace of lessons, slowing down to allow students the space to think.

Benefits to working memory: This model presupposes that students will be thinking deeply and that moments of respite will be beneficial in securing long-term learning. Although the idea of cognitive breaks can be applied anywhere, I have chosen to include them in this model to emphasise that they should follow the more taxing activities and thinking that we ask students to do.

Problems for working memory: Not many. This model is getting there, but it does not formally address the need to retrieve prior knowledge. Although the act of setting 'problems' will make students search their prior knowledge, it may not be the right prior knowledge as the problem is focused on future learning and is not purposefully about what they should already know.[6] When planning, we may need a cursory check to ensure that prior knowledge has been activated.

---

[5] Snappy title, eh?

[6] In reality it may well be, but since we are currently dealing with models this formally arbitrary stance is necessary.

The Ausubel Alchemical Model – a prior knowledge model

Activation of prior knowledge	Instruction on idea 1	Student activity on idea 1	Activation of prior knowledge	Instruction on idea 2	Student activity on idea 2

Crude description: The role of prior knowledge in learning gives it an almost alchemical quality – turning classroom activity into learning gold. Educational psychologist David Ausubel's assertion that teachers should find out what students know and then teach them accordingly also rings true for the learners themselves. They need to be aware of what they already know as they broach new learning.[7] Students need to interact with new information and reconcile it with their prior knowledge for learning to take place.

Benefits to working memory: Prior knowledge is the ultimate in retrieval cues and is naturally used as the hook on which to hang new learning.

Problems for working memory: Learning happens when a learner connects a new experience with an existing concept, which is thought to occur in the working memory. This is how we then interpret new experiences. This is not a straightforward event because old existing 'memories' or 'understandings' are extremely persistent (and are often referred to as beliefs). If the belief is incorrect, then learning will not take place as the incorrect belief is used to filter and interpret incoming information, so no sense can be made by the student. We must therefore tailor the activities to activate and correct students' prior knowledge before the new learning can occur.

As with all models, we have not dealt with the individual students we teach, and neither have we considered, in any direct way, how these models attempt to ensure that learning is lasting and durable – which is their long-term purpose. We can begin to do this by adding opportunities for repetition and/or practice into the model. This act provides our final model – modestly called Model Deluxe.

---

[7] Which is what working memory is!

Model Deluxe – or what the real world may be like …

Activation of prior knowledge	Big idea set in problem	Instruction on basic idea	Student activity on basic idea	Cognitive break	Reactivate prior knowledge	Instruction on more complex ideas	Student activity on more complex idea	Practise complex ideas

This is not a model as such but a combination of all the previous ones. The combination and sequence will change for different students and different lesson content. It imagines that the lesson starts with the students activating their useful relevant prior knowledge. A task incorporating the big idea into a problem (or other way of creating curiosity or confusion) follows, thereby causing thought. Basic principles are then explained or demonstrated and the students have a chance to work with this information. At this stage, the students should be engaged in deep thinking, both in terms of making sense of ideas and seeking connection to prior knowledge. A summary or practice task follows to allow the students to think less deeply and to dwell on the important ideas being learned. The more students practise with an idea, the less the demand placed on working memory, so before moving on, their prior knowledge and recently acquired knowledge are again brought to the fore so that the jump to the more complex version of the solution or concept becomes at least tangible.

Our planning requires us to be purposeful with every activity. Learning is not sequential, so nor should our planning be. As these models show, we must simultaneously consider prior knowledge, the number of items being worked with, the complexity of the ideas, how much cognitive work the students have done, whether they are in a 'new learning' or 'practice' phase and, of course, the capacity of the students themselves.

These models do not intend to be a lesson planning structure, but a tool to help you reflect on the sequencing and size of ideas, identifying when and how they will be revisited during a lesson and how they can be made more complex. They also introduce us to the idea of cognitive breaks that in a densely packed and fast paced curriculum will often be forgotten. As always, the content you are teaching and the students in front of you will tell you what is best. What follows are strategies and planning guidance in how the best practice of these models can be applied to your teaching.

What might the actual teaching be like? A useful start point is acknowledging the difference between recognition and recall. Recognition, with its many cues, is a much easier cognitive task than recall. Recognition tasks might (somewhat obviously) be a better way of activating prior knowledge. Note the difference in these two tasks.

1. Name three protagonists of the Fauvist movement.

2. Which three of the following were protagonists in the Fauvist movement?

    Derain

    Mead

    Picasso

    Matisse

    Vlaminck

With the first recall activity, even if you have studied this area, it would be hard to recall the artists without recourse to the internet or a book. In the recognition activity, you might find it fairly easy to recognise some or discount others, leaving you with potential answers. Even if you could only identify two potentially correct answers, you now have a start on the prior knowledge needed without too much exertion being placed on the working memory. At times, you might want to change the difficulty of the task depending on where you are in the teaching sequence or on the differing purposes of the activity: is it for thinking deeply? Is it a recap activity? Is it a test of student recall? Is it a test of student understanding?

Ultimately, students must be taught how to cope with the limitations of their working memory. A key part of developing this metacognitive knowledge can be achieved by showing how different teaching strategies help learners to learn, as well as encouraging self-monitoring. Self-monitoring is a critical skill to develop with all students but particularly those with poor working memories as it helps them to become better at the difficult task of remaining focused. Planning to aid those students with poor working memories through their ability to self-monitor is, perhaps, the ultimate application of our pedagogical content knowledge. Three questions can help here:

1. Does this task make the students think about the exact content I want?

2. How do I adapt it so that they do?

3. If it can't be adapted, what activity will focus the students on the exact content?

Traditional pedagogy can be readily adapted to achieve this. We all know how dictation works (or doesn't): the teacher reads out notes at such a pace that students are able to write down what is said. This places an enormous emphasis on working memory: the students must listen to what is said and store it so that it can be written down. This is how I was 'taught' eutectics at school. I have no bloody idea what eutectics are – that they have these weird looking graphs is my sum total of knowledge. Looking back, it was clear that I was afforded no time to think about them.

New dictation – an exemplar strategy to support working memory

New dictation is a strategy (i.e. it is *not* reading your notes at students), and it is rather good at supporting students with poor working memory with a well selected piece of text: an article is ideal for this purpose.[8] It initially encourages students to seek the big idea, before adding in the detail. It revisits content and allows students to support one another in the completion of the task, so that they talk about the material.

It works like this:

1. The teacher makes it clear to the students that the text will be read out twice: the first time it will be too fast to write anything down other than potential titles and/or subheadings. The second reading will be slower but still too fast to write down everything that is said and will only allow the students to bullet point their notes.

2. Read the text at too fast a pace to allow note taking. The students listen and are encouraged to pick out big ideas or come up with potential subheadings.

---

[8] This is based on the Project for Enhancing Effective Learning strategy of the same name; www. peelweb.org is still the best teaching strategy resource out there.

Pause purposefully between sections to allow the students to set out their own notes. With practice, they will stop writing all their headings in a list at the top of the page.

3. Read the text again, this time more slowly so the students can make brief notes, using the headings to structure these. There is an art to this, and students get better with practice, so encouraging them to put a bullet point with a single word is a great start point. The strategy accommodates for this in the next two steps.

4. When you've finished reading, allow the students to discuss their notes with one another, using this discussion to supplement them.

5. Give the students the text to review and allow a little time for them to further add to and amend their notes.

This strategy helps students to practise chunking and organising their ideas to support their long-term memory. Firstly, the teacher controls the rate at which new ideas are introduced, not only through the rate of reading but through the selection of appropriately challenging texts. The students are then allowed a risk-free chance to practise spotting the organising ideas through multiple exposures to the material. The students will eventually get this right. Using a full article gives them the information in a structure that chunks up ideas while also remaining connected. Listening and holding information in the working memory is hard cognitive work, so the discussion and review steps grant them an opportunity to take a 'cognitive rest'. When the students are checking their notes, the demand on working memory is greatly reduced because (in essence) the answers are in front of them.

How should teacher inputs be constructed to support working memory?

Nuthall's (2007: 126) research indicates that students need to be exposed to new material in a holistic, all-encompassing way so that they interact at least once with a full set of accessible information to ensure learning takes place. Teachers are in a prime position to emphasise the important information, and importance is easily stressed to the students through writing key ideas on the board as you discuss a topic or through having students underline ideas they consider important in a text.

However, underlining and highlighting have been shown to be fairly ineffective for student learning unless it is a high quality process (Dunlosky et al. 2013). Text coding strategies such as 'highlight the known and unknown information', 'circle key terms', 'double underline the important message' and 'annotate with question marks ideas that you require clarification on' help students to discriminate the information as well as isolating the important ideas, thereby making them more easily remembered. The art to this technique is for the students to actively interact with the text in the search for meaning, and by being selective they are not overwhelmed by a vast number of ideas to recall simultaneously. When using text coding with students, I make sure that the annotation codes are on prominent display so they do not have remember what the codes are, and I always select only one or two to work with at any point. I always start with circling unfamiliar words and question marking.

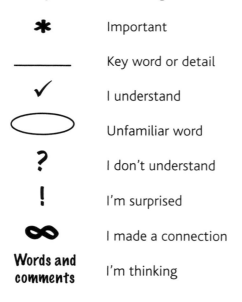

In Chapter 6, we will come across the split attention principle and its use in constructing resources for students that do not overwhelm the working memory. The basic idea is that we should place relevant information right where the students find it easiest to locate. They do not have to break their attention by going to 'look' for the information, and this minimises cognitive load. We can also help to maintain student attention on key concepts by not providing excessive quantities of information at any one time, even if it may be relevant at some point in the future. We can provide this information 'just in time'.[9] Just-in-time instruction involves withholding new information from learners until the moment it is required to complete a task. This may involve starting a task with only part of the necessary information; when skilfully done, it can be a very effective way of creating curiosity.

Good practice in sharing new information tends to make the links to prior knowledge clear and makes abstract ideas as concrete as they can be with examples and analogies that are seen as relevant to the learners. Explanations should move from simple to complex, though this doesn't necessarily mean we take a step-by-step approach. What may be more useful is a complete explanation that is a simpler version of a final desired one that we will then work towards. This simpler version provides a framework for all the further, more detailed elements of the fuller explanations to be pieced together. Planning for this involves identifying the parts of an explanation that can just about stand alone or, at least, that minimally interact with other parts. From here, we can sequence the ideas so that the amount of interaction increases as the explanation proceeds.

Although the research is a little unclear here, it seems best to present complex new information before the students actually start the learning tasks and for less complex information to be presented during the task (van Merriënboer et al. 2003). Each piece of content taught will be different, but thinking about when the students receive information based on how complex it is helps us to plan to keep the focus on the content being learned.

---

[9] I have used this strategy here, giving you a basic idea of the split attention principle but not too much information so as to distract you from the idea of just-in-time instruction.

The reduced goal specificity effect

Counter-intuitively, tasks that are considered goal free can help to reduce potentially excessive cognitive load on the working memory and engage students in learning. Goal orientated tasks have a specific measurable purpose in that they are generally assessment tasks, while goal free tasks are less specific and more open ended. A goal orientated problem may be as simple as 'find the value of angle X in the diagram.' Yet the demand such tasks place on working memory is high since novel problems mean that learners are unable to bring established schemas to bear. As a result, novice learners are most likely to revert to 'means end' strategies, spending time deducing how to solve the problem rather than learning the concept. In contrast, with a problem such as 'find all the angles in the diagram' (which is a less specific, more open ended task), learners are more successful at acquiring appropriate problem solving schemas (Sweller 1988: 259).

To be clear, goal free instruction does not seem fit for purpose as a whole model of instruction, but it is something that can be a useful part of it. Here are a couple of goal free problems from different subject areas.

Mathematics

The wonderful Bobby Bear game helps students to study probability by asking them to work out how many combinations of an outfit they can make.[10] The students get to choose the colour of his T-shirt and dungarees and can do this by dragging various items of clothing onto the bear, which then sports the colour combinations. The game informs the student when all of the combinations have been made and reveals the answer. At any point, the student can stop and work out the rule and apply it, answering in the box provided. If correct, the next problem is set up and the difficulty steps up. Questions sometimes feature fewer combinations, sometimes more. I played this in the interests of research (of course) and identified the rule within only a few games. My 8-year-old son worked it out rather quicker.

---

[10] The Bobby Bear game can be found at http://illuminations.nctm.org/Activity.aspx?id=3540.

Geography

This example uses the factors that cause human migration as listed below:

- Lack of services

- Lack of safety

- High crime

- Crop failure

- Drought

- Flooding

- Poverty

- War

- Higher employment

- More wealth

- Better services

- Good climate

- Good food supply

- Low crime rates

- Safer/less crime

- Political stability

- More fertile land

- Lower risk from natural hazards

The students are asked to classify these in as many ways as possible. Potential groupings include: natural and human causes; financial, climatic and safety conditions; or positive and negative. The comparisons help to drive the hidden (teacher) agenda – we are leading towards eventually classifying them as 'push' and 'pull' factors, which is the correct geographical nomenclature – but only after the students are familiar with all of the factors.

Fading guidance

Paas et al. (2004: 1) describe cognitive load theory as being primarily 'concerned with the learning of complex cognitive tasks, where learners are often overwhelmed by the number of information elements and their interactions that need to be processed simultaneously before meaningful learning can commence'. As teachers we need to be aware of placing any excessive or unnecessary demands on students' working memory. We can further support our students by using fading guidance strategies that seek to reduce the cognitive load on working memory. These focus on the key aspects of the learning and gradually increase the number of cognitive tasks. This is not unlike learning to ride a bike: I still have fond memories of my Raleigh tricycle on which I started off. This was followed by a Raleigh Budgie. I can still recall the day my dad took one stabiliser away – I have never leaned to one side so much in my life! Yet each of these steps helped me to ride a bike and become independently mobile. Two strategies work in tandem (pun intended) to help teachers to do this: worked examples and completion tasks.

Worked examples

Wholes are remembered better than parts. It is therefore important that students see the whole of a concept or text regularly. Worked examples and exemplars are an effective way of doing this, enabling students to see what the 'problem' is alongside the steps to the solution. This helps to reduce cognitive load and generates a solution or schema. Worked examples provide a form of scaffolding, working from a bigger picture to the constituent parts (in contrast to a 'framework' style scaffold which necessitates that students think about the individual parts before attempting to see the whole) – therefore, an exemplar paragraph is more useful than a writing frame. However, exemplars need to be used carefully: students should not be forced to study them methodically and, because they actually increase cognitive load, they should only be used while the students are struggling with the current problem. The teacher's job is to deconstruct the worked example so that the structure becomes clear to the students (van Merriënboer and Sweller 2009).

Completion tasks

An alternative to the worked example is the completion task. Completion tasks are an intermediary of worked examples and are independently completed. Students are provided with a partially filled in example and must finish it. In later examples, increasingly larger parts of the solution are left blank so the students must then complete more of the solution. For instance, a lesson may begin by students criticising a teacher-completed analysis of a historical source in order to gain an overview of what they have to do. The students could then go on to finish a partially completed analysis of a source before working up to a full independent analysis.

Linked to this is the fading guidance strategy, wherein tasks are initially scaffolded with step-by-step guidance and feedback, then with less feedback, then with none at all. Clearly, this principle is best applied to well-structured content – for example, physics or maths problems that have a specific process that is readily broken down into neat sections, or rules in English where a certain sentence construction is taught and then practised with increasingly less support.

Summary

Teachers have a variety of strategies to call on to support all students' working memories, which are key for those with poor working memories or when we are first teaching a difficult concept. Reducing the number of ideas being held in mind is the first port of call. However, with a full curriculum and limited teaching time, we may not always be able to use this approach as much as we would like, so it is helpful to look at this as a continuum: we gradually increase the number of items and provide some organisational scaffolding as we do so. This may occur as the students progress through the teaching of a topic or it may be a way of helping them to develop their working memories.

Teachers can also manage the sequence in which the concepts are taught, so that big ideas (such as threshold concepts and organisational ideas) come first. In this way, the students get an overview of the topic, and/or how a concept fits with others, before we proceed to break this down into its constituent parts. This may involve simplifying complicated processes before giving more elaborate explanations. For example, 'Red blood cells swell up and burst when placed in pure water as water moves in by osmosis across a partially permeable membrane' will progress to, 'Red blood cells swell up and burst when placed in pure water as water moves from a high water concentration to a lower water concentration across a partially permeable membrane by the process of osmosis' and eventually to, 'Red blood cells swell up and burst when placed in pure water as water moves from a low *solute* concentration to a high *solute* concentration across a *selectively* permeable membrane by osmosis.'

Even the non-science teachers among us will spot that as the number of ideas increases, the difficulty increases commensurately, especially as the last two explanations seem to contradict one another, which suggests that this change has something to do with the new idea of selectivity. Once a basic overview has been provided, the teacher can begin to add detail, opting either to teach the complexity and then break it down, or to teach a fragment (say, the idea of solute concentration) and then explain how this relates to the big idea. (In this instance, it would be harder for the students to learn about solute concentration first, without the overarching concept and direction.) This is not easy and it requires teachers to utilise several methodologies at once. These are summarised in the following table.

Early in teaching sequence/lesson	As the teaching sequence/lesson progresses
1. Have fewer items to work with and learn, but do this more deeply.	1. Provide organisational structures as the ideas become more complex.
2. Make sure new information is as integrated as possible.	2. Develop how concepts interact.
3. Activate prior knowledge.	3. Include extraneous information.
4. Use worked examples.	4. It becomes possible to elaborate on information.
5. Big picture first – provide an overview.	5. Use collaborative problem solving activities such as assertive questioning.
6. Concepts first.	6. Increase the number of open questions.
7. Remove extraneous information – simplify information.	7. Use completion tasks.
8. Avoid individual problem solving activities.	8. Use the fading guidance strategy.
9. Use a greater proportion of closed questions.	

CHAPTER 6

The Act of Learning: Memory as a Destination

We ask a lot of student memory. Over the course of a school career, a student is expected to learn between 2,000 and 3,000 words per year, such that they understand, remember and are able to apply them (Nagy 1988: 8). For argument's sake, let's say a student has to learn two new key words per lesson – in a 38 week academic year with five lessons per day they would learn 1,900 key words. However, this number speaks nothing of learning about the connections between these words. It is clear that a huge demand is being placed on students. Worryingly, schools tend not to manage learning on an institutional level; it is left to individual teachers who just so happen to have no idea of the simultaneous learning demands being placed on students in different subject areas. How many schools do you know of that seek to manage the quantity of ideas to which students are exposed? I don't know of any.

What is long-term memory?

Memory, in terms of school learning, has many possible meanings: memory skills and techniques, rote memory, short-term or working memory recall, finding patterns and connections between schemas within genres, storage and retrieval of information (triggers) or a way of making a response automatic.

Long-term memory is split into two functioning parts: one for declarative (factual) knowledge and the other for non-declarative knowledge (skills and procedures). We have one system for facts and another for skills and procedures; however, this takes no account of the fact that skills and knowledge interact or that skills are the application of knowledge, making up the sum of what we know and can do. Nevertheless, this distinction, though faulty, is useful background information. Declarative knowledge is subdivided into three categories which are neatly summarised by Bailey and Pransky (2014: 11):

1. *Episodic memory:* Rich, personal, multisensory memories of events.

2. *Autobiographical memory:* Stores our sense of self and has direct links to motivation.

3. *Semantic memory:* The storehouse of our knowledge of the world, including academic concepts. It is the part of the memory system most affected by culture.

Memory is probably best seen as a series of schemas. Schemas are theoretical maps that organise semantic content, specific concepts and the context in which the learning takes place (in other words, 'what I was doing when I learned that') and are a blend of episodic, autobiographical and semantic memory. The content and the students' experience of learning the content are inextricably linked.

What we learn is strongly influenced by the guiding schemas already in place, so we can expect students to recall the information that best fits their prior knowledge (Nuthall 2007: 80). In this regard, prior knowledge is the nightclub bouncer of memory.[1] Even if the knowledge turns up in the correct fashion statement, it can still be rejected if it fails to match the predetermined dress code in the eyes of the doorman. This makes it essential for teachers to make time to listen to what learners are saying. Student talk is full of clues about what they know and how they (believe they) know it. If we want to try to see beyond performance and find out if learning is taking place, then listening is essential. This is complex information, yet it is desirable because it affords us the opportunity to make better decisions about what happens in our classrooms. For the most part there is no such thing as a blank slate, so if a student has an incorrect schema then learning will not occur and, potentially, they may secure an existing misconception.

---

[1] Nightclubs are places where young people, and people who should know better, go to pretend to socialise, while being pummelled by both low quality, expensive beverages and a version of noise that some people term 'music'. Bouncers are employed to quell the overzealous mating rituals of males and to determine who is worth entering the social emporium – i.e. only those who meet certain standards.

With the potency of prior knowledge, thinking about teaching for understanding must come before we think about teaching for memory. Robustly addressing student misconceptions must come before any memory aid instruction, such as mnemonics. This actually mirrors how memories are made: when students are thinking about the concept at hand, learning creates the 'correct' (at least, that is the aim!) memory which can then be rehearsed, practised, drilled and memorised.

How is long-term memory different and how do we get there?

Memory does not have its own Dewey system organised for the benefit of others, such as a looming teacher or an inquisitive exam paper.[2] It sometimes serves us, sometimes fails us. As a gentleman of a certain age, I am forever putting down my spectacles, car keys and other assorted ephemera with the determined statement, 'I MUST REMEMBER THAT I PUT THESE HERE!' only to spend a considerable amount of time the next day searching frantically around the entire grounds of my palatial Gateshead villa for the lost item. Even with a conscious effort to activate it, our memory is fallible.

The same thing can happen in school – we aim to command an idea to be learned and remembered. We call this rote learning and its product rote knowledge. We surround learners with all of the scaffolds and prompts they need to be able to perform the knowledge, but when we take the scaffold away have they really learned anything? An example comes from my chemistry teaching. When I give students a template for writing chemical equations for an acid reaction with a metal, it is given in the hope that they can then substitute the name of the acid and metal and be able to write the chemical equation:

Scaffold: metal + acid → salt + hydrogen

Substitution: magnesium + hydrochloric acid → magnesium chloride + hydrogen

---

[2] The Dewey Decimal Classification is one of the numbering systems used in libraries so that books are easily found on the shelf. Bizarrely, I remember that books which start 580 are about plants from hours of strutting around university libraries in the days before the internet.

However, they always tend to forget that hydrogen gas is produced. My response, and I'm guessing many other science teachers' too, is to say, 'You've missed the gas made. We tested it ...' (inevitable silence). And now comes the drilled response, 'It goes pop ...' At which point, the students say 'Hydrogen', which is the correct answer. But is it? The students clearly recall that 'hydrogen goes pop', but do they know that hydrogen gas is produced when a metal and an acid react? I don't think they do. Of course, scaffolding such as a vocab sheet, point-evidence-explain paragraph structure or drilled responses can get students started. We just need to consider when to remove them.

At this point, it is worthwhile distinguishing between rote knowledge and what Willingham (2002) calls 'inflexible knowledge'. Rote knowledge is universally derided, and is defined as students recalling facts without understanding them. In contrast, inflexible knowledge has meaning, albeit on a superficial level, so students recognise where ideas are being applied. Without careful attention, some concepts will remain on a rote level and will not arrive at being flexibly used (which entails both recognising and restructuring an old problem into a new one).

Tempting as it seems, teaching in a way that promotes memorisation may not be the best method to gain fruitful long-term memory of the material. Teaching in a way that encourages the students to first understand the material must precede any practice or rote learning. Bahrick and Hall (1991) found that a major factor of memory is the extent to which students learn the material in the first place. We must therefore plan for understanding the material well and valuing performance, yet at the same time remaining acutely aware of its limitations.

Performance is distinct from learning. Learning is the long-term retention of information that can be applied to new contexts; therefore, learning exists beyond the act of teaching. On the other hand, performance is what can be observed and measured during instruction. They are not necessarily complementary – learning can be occurring even when no change in performance is evident (Soderstrom and Bjork 2015). However, the performance of the newly learned material gives us some indication that they are 'getting it' but not necessarily that they are learning it for the long term. Getting it can be done without the students attaining the knowledge at hand and is at the whim of the quality of our assessments. What if the assessment is a result of a skewed elicitation? Have I just asked, 'What gas goes pop?' or do the students know that when acids react with metals hydrogen is produced? Am I actually focusing on the content to be taught? Ensuring that students think about the material is consequently a big part of making learning durable. However, this alone does not aid long-term retention. Retention of newly learned material drops rapidly over the first few weeks, with the suggestion that what is left in our memory after 12 to 24 weeks will remain there pretty much for ever (Banikowski and Mehring 1999: 7).

The worst-case scenario would be that as these memories decay, our beliefs and misconceptions once more begin to come to the fore. Teachers can plan to avoid this by ensuring that students correct misconceptions and reconcile difficult and important ideas first, before we consider making the ideas stick. Most teachers know this and are snooty about rote learning and memorisation – except when it comes to covering an exam course which 'must be covered' and we just want them to know it. Teaching for understanding actually serves learning far better.

Planning must therefore couple teaching for understanding with planning to enhance the students' memories. The ingredients that appear to have an impact on remembering include the following interacting features of teaching and learning: organisation of knowledge and concepts, purpose, attention, contrasts, emotion and repetition.

Organising knowledge and concepts

Long before we can begin to plan the pedagogy for making the material memorable, we need to consider how we structure its presentation to our learners. Semantic knowledge of our subjects matters hugely in this respect. Expert teachers have a clearer and more connected view of their subjects, allowing them to avoid confusing interactions between ideas. Knowing what prior knowledge needs to be activated is part of this too.

The biological concepts of mitosis and meiosis provide a good example here. From the spelling of these words we can begin to see how these concepts might be muddled up by students: they share common processes and are readily confused. Firstly, in order to reduce potential confusion, it is important to ensure that they are not taught in consecutive lessons (I tend to place a different concept in-between them to split up these ideas). Secondly, using differing pedagogies helps to keep student experience of each concept distinct. Thirdly, and potentially most importantly, activating different prior knowledge and linking it to distinct big pictures is a way of teaching with the end in mind.

Teachers have a conceptual framework of how the knowledge of our subjects works together: we use it to plan sequences, identify where to dwell during lessons and what concepts to emphasise. Shulman (1987: 9) suggests that teachers have a 'special responsibility' as the 'primary source' of content knowledge for our subjects. Directly or indirectly, we communicate the 'truth' to students about how our subjects work: the facts, the concepts, the structures and how experts in this field think, act and find out information in the discipline. However, our concern with the procedures we use to convey the meaning of the content can sometimes override the subject knowledge itself. There is a subtle but useful distinction between understanding the content and understanding how the content is organised or learned.

Reflecting on what we really think about our subject and on how we perceive teacher knowledge, as distinct from that of experts in our field, can help. A quick look at Ball's (1988) research describing potential maths teachers' views on the nature of mathematical knowledge and how this knowledge is used is revealing:

View 1:   Mathematics is a mostly arbitrary collection of facts.

View 2:   Mathematics? I've never really thought about it.

View 3:   Doing mathematics means following set procedures.

View 4:   Doing mathematics means using remembered knowledge and working step by step.

View 5:   Mathematics is essential for everyday life.

View 6:   Mathematics helps one learn to think.

View 7:   Mathematics is just *there*, but it is necessary for progress in school.

These are very much the views of novices. As we teach and reflect, we develop more elaborate views about our subjects – although anything is more elaborate than not thinking about it or placing it in the silo of knowledge that is regarded as 'just for school'. It will not have escaped your notice that two of the views expressed here refer to the procedures of solving mathematics problems.[3] Indeed, teachers interviewed about 'dividing by zero' revealed the extent to which they think in terms of how to learn the process rather than how to think about the mathematics behind that process. Statements like, 'It is just something you have to remember' or something that 'Can't be done' reveal that the speakers of such drivel have received instruction on how to complete a problem or memorise a fact, but have not got very far in terms of interacting with the actual understanding of the content. Students often receive procedural teaching *about* mathematics but do not gain an understanding *of* mathematics. We can, as teachers, tend towards valuing procedural over declarative knowledge, yet both are needed.

When we come to present new information to students we must consider how the structure of the information is communicated. This meta-information is not normally communicated formally – it is rather abstract – but teachers should try to help students organise their new knowledge so that it is more readily and accurately retrieved. The world of social media has made the act more common: we do something similar when adding a #hashtag to a Twitter post – in doing so, we assign our tweet a link to a body of information.[4] Although hashtags are user generated, they tend to be shared and modified so that information can be compiled and seen holistically.

The school equivalent is when students title their work. But how do we ensure that this has meaning to the content and how do we make the details link too? Our knowledge of how topics are structured might be helpful in this regard: the 'big ideas' become organising concepts. Starting with big ideas and then looking at the constituent parts has been shown to be a better way of aiding later recall. For instance, do these big concepts help to provide useful titles or headings for student notes? Titles for work act as the simplest form of advance organiser and, like most simple things, the quality is difficult to get right. Consider the volume of sales of blended

---

[3] It may be useful to consider this as a limited version of the procedural knowledge domain of Bloom's taxonomy defined as discipline-specific skills. You may well be teaching procedures, but the conflict occurs when you are teaching a concept and all that is actually taught is the procedure.

[4] Being old, I am struggling to call it a 'body of knowledge'.

whiskey compared to single malts, or the availability of powdered coffee to single origin coffee beans: there is an art and craft in making simple products desirable and beautiful. It seems almost pretentious to say it, but the titling and structuring of the knowledge can help students to learn, so spending time thinking about how our titles and structures improve student learning is of benefit.

The following are potential titles for one topic in a science lesson:

Experiment to make hydrogen

Acids and metals

Salts

They are all accurate and include one important aspect of the lesson. However, on their own the lack of detail renders them unsuitable. By simply combining them, we can provide a succinct overview of the learning to come, so a title might be:

Reacting metals and acids to make hydrogen and salts

An alternative strategy might be to use subheadings. Books, newspapers and blog articles do this, but how often do we ask students to use subheadings?

This lesson therefore might be called:

Making salts

Followed by:

The reaction between acids and metals

Word equation for the reaction

Identifying the hydrogen gas produced

What is a salt?

Titling student work is not as easy as it seems. Look at these examples from one student's English book. They have been faithfully reproduced in order:

Descriptive writing

Chapter 14

Sentence types

'Island Man'

Villains

'Macbeth'

Apostrophes

'Macbeth' – who is the villain in this play and why?

They range from big ideas such as book titles and thematic concepts such as villains, and then on to grammatical structures. One is even called 'Chapter 14' – of what? Some of these are clearly pants, and some are more useful than others, but the list is far from random – if we look closely, the search for linguistic understanding becomes clear and this runs parallel to the study of literature. However, this list highlights the difficulty in making the sequence of student work either coherent or (at the very least) respectful to the content of the subject. A better approach may be to teach students to title their work well because this skill involves searching out big themes and connections.

An exemplar teaching procedure for organising student knowledge

To create an exemplar, start with a nicely written piece of text that has had its title and subheadings removed. Give the students time to read it. Ask them to title the piece and add helpful subheadings. Discuss and compare the quality of the titles using the following criteria:

- Does it contain a big idea?

- Does it serve as a useful summary of the text?

- Are all ideas encapsulated in a heading or subheading?

Do not underestimate the level of difficulty this causes students; it forces them to pay attention to the main ideas in a text. After practice with well-written texts, the same procedure can be used as a successful plenary with their own notes.

Key planning questions for organising student knowledge include:

- What are the big ideas that will help students to organise their knowledge?

- Are the big ideas presented before the smaller ideas?

- Do the titles, subheadings and learning intentions help students to organise their knowledge, or do they help to organise their 'work'?

- Have I considered how and when to present the connections in these ideas?

- Which is the right prior knowledge and what experiences should I remind students of? When is the best time to do this?

- What are the big ideas that must be revisited during the lesson/topic/year? Which ideas would be nice to revisit during the lesson/topic/year?

- Am I teaching knowledge about the subject or of the subject?

- Are similar ideas taught in different and distinct ways?

Making learning purposeful
– tending to the content

An infuriating truth about attention spans is that students will gladly remain engrossed in computer games for hours and hours without blinking or flagging. We might be inclined to discount these games as mindless violence but the problem solving behaviour the players exhibit is actually very mindful. It is clear that games designers have done their job well in creating experiences that motivate players to put huge amounts of time and effort into the interaction. It just happens to be the wrong type of mindfulness for learning a school curriculum because this type of learning is difficult and requires effort and motivation to organise complex concepts in ways that can be easily recalled. Our attention spans are short for this kind of hard cognitive work.

To state the obvious, our planning needs to encourage students to attend to the content being studied. However, in the light of understanding the limitations of working memory, we must keep in mind that the activities we set must allow students to grapple with the content. One of the things muddying the water for us is the fact that students learn the context of the classroom and therefore attend to the teacher and the processes as much as to the content. In addition, teachers do not always want their students to be just attending to the knowledge. Other legitimate educational intentions may include:

- Developing curiosity and motivation.

- Developing the skills and attributes of learners (e.g. learning how to construct concept maps).

- Developing a supportive classroom community.

- Developing student literacy and numeracy skills.

- Developing student passion for your subject.

Education has this richness. Sometimes we need to educate about the content and sometimes we need to educate the person; therefore planning must attend to the content and the operational conditions that allow both the content and person to flourish. Each and every task, activity or strategy has multiple pedagogical purposes. Our craft is how we plan to exploit them. Recall the heading and subheading activity in which students add these to a text. It is clearly rooted in the content, but it also develops students' abilities to organise their learning and work. Whether we choose to make this purpose explicit depends on many factors: the students, where they are in the topic, the time of day, which part of the lesson the task is being used in and so on.

Beware of volcanoes

Two aspects of cognitive load are being placed on working memory in the following exercise, one of which is entirely unnecessary. Can you spot the extraneous cognitive load?

Match the instrument to the definition. Use the numbers to do the matching.

Instrument	Write the matching number here	Definition
1. Banjo		Usually has 4 courses of doubled strings, making 8 strings. Can have 5 or 6 courses.
2. Guitar		Can have 18, 19 or 20 strings.
3. Sitar		Usually has 6 strings but varies between 4 and 18.
4. Mandolin		Usually has 4 strings but can have 5 or 6 strings.

Please note that this is a genuine task, which on the surface seems straightforward. Match the numbers to the definition. However, to do this the students have to remember the key word and its number and then figure out which is the correct definition. This may have to be done by deduction, adding a further demand. This is the extraneous load causing students to think about the task structure, not the content. We want the cognitive work to be done thinking about the content. The way the definitions have been written also adds to the demand, but in a more useful way with each definition being slightly ambiguous and therefore focusing the thinking on the differences between these stringed instruments.

Sometimes we fall foul of a task that appears to provide the required detail but misses. As an example, consider a group of students who have been asked to build and label a volcano to help them learn how it works. The students proceed to spend a large proportion of the time working out the best ratio of vinegar and baking soda to make the model erupt. The problem with this does not lie in the model building as such, but with the focus on making the models erupt with a chemical reaction and not on the pressure caused by tectonic action. The students spent their time thinking about vinegar and not about the nature of volcanoes.

Overall, if the aim of the task is to get the information into long-term memory, then removing any extraneous cognitive load that invokes additional thinking on top of the concepts being learned is beneficial.

Useful planning questions include:

- What is this task for?

- Does this task allow students to think about the content?

- What other purposes might this task have?

- Is there any conflict between the activity and the content?

- During this lesson, have the students had a chance to think about the ideas and the other benefits of this task?

- Is it opportune to exploit other purposes during this lesson? Where might this be better placed?

Using contrast to raise curiosity and interest, and other ways to gain attention

Before they have set foot in the room, students always notice that the desks have been rearranged. Their responses are always the same and always amusing: wide eyed stares, notes of incredulity, statements such as, 'Eh ... the desks have *moved*' and stunned accusations of betrayal. Even after nearly 23 years of teaching, the effect on students of changing the arrangement of my classroom still entertains me. Despite such fun, this is not the reason why I change the set-up of my desks. I do it for classroom management or to develop the class community, or as a way of signifying that something is going to be different in the lesson. We are sensitive to change and contrast.

Quick quiz: who do you associate with these 'catchphrases'?

- 'Ask not what your country can do for you – ask what you can do for your country.'

- 'It was the best of times, it was the worst of times.'

- 'Never was so much owed by so many to so few.'[5]

Easy, right? So, what makes these so memorable? Well, context certainly lends an air of importance, and this might explain why they are repeatedly quoted in the media. They all have an emotive quality too, but there is something else here that piques our interest: contrast. The use of contrast is widespread in our culture: 'Special offer – was £12.99, now £8'; nice contrasted with evil judges on reality TV talent contests;[6] Little and Large; Fat Boy Slim; Not only but also; I can't believe it's not butter; Apple's black silhouette characters with white iPods; the tortoise and the hare.

All these scenarios create conflict – and we pay attention to it. Closely related to this is the idea of cognitive dissonance where we hold two contradictory ideas in mind at once. This causes a lot of thinking and situational interest. Situational interest is short lived, is readily given to environmental stimuli and is seen as the mother of more

---

5 For the record: John F. Kennedy, Charles Dickens and Sir Winston Churchill.
6 For bellowing, yelping and screeching.

enduring personal interest. It is also interesting in that it is regarded by teachers as something that they can control and is their responsibility, while students see it as something that happens to them rather than something they can do anything about (Schraw et al. 2001: 212).

The degree of student interest has been correlated with elaboration and information seeking strategies. Elaboration involves students seeking connections with prior knowledge, looking for concrete examples, developing analogies and exploring the relationships between ideas, including the use of comparing and contrasting. Interestingly, rehearsal strategies, the mainstay of rote learning, have a negative impact on student interest (Schiefele 1991: 311).

This is readily achieved in the classroom through our behaviour and the structure of tasks as set out in the following table.

Examples of teacher behaviour for curiosity and interest	Examples of task structures for curiosity and interest
Tone of voice: volume, accent and rate.	A Venn diagram or other graphic organiser to make the types of thinking clear and distinct.
Changing the arrangement of the classroom.	Odd one out.
Questioning to raise awareness and curiosity: can nuclear power save the planet?	Spot the difference between two diagrams, sentences or graphs.
Make clear where counter-intuitive ideas are taking place.	Activities that explore prior knowledge.
Delay gratification by separating creating curiosity and providing an explanation and answer.	Good exemplars and bad exemplars.
Plan lessons using threshold concepts.	Write seven questions about …

Examples of teacher behaviour for curiosity and interest	Examples of task structures for curiosity and interest
When helping students to memorise content, make them recall rather than recognise content.	Provide a choice of activities.

Task designs to capture student interest are as diverse as the students themselves but more than likely involve:

- Something controversial.

- Something that jars or has contrast.

- Something that has a personal context or passion.

- Something novel or unexpected – for instance, a guest speaker or an unusual prop or fascinator.

- Something that they already know a little about but can see the gap in their knowledge.

- Something with a strong narrative.

It is clear that contrast really helps to structure teaching so that students find it difficult to avoid paying attention to the content. Complementary to contrast are the factors that have been shown to increase situational interest (Schraw et al. 2001). These include providing relevant information, utilising the split attention principle, and providing coherent information and the opportunity for students to make meaningful choices.

Providing relevant information

We provide information through the constructive alignment of learning intentions and tasks and through providing supportive and procedural information. When designing or selecting the supportive information it is well worth noting the 'modality principle'. This recommends that a spoken explanation is coupled with a visual source of information rather than a written explanation, so that students do not need to split their attention between two competing information sources.

The split attention principle

Moreno and Mayer (2000) suggest that when constructing presentations or handouts we should think about how visual information and on-screen text are integrated. The following example is from an A level biology lesson on potassium deficiency symptoms in plants. The slide on the right places the salient information in proximity to the action, making it easier for students to link the two pieces of information together. The split attention principle suggests that, although the same information is present in the slide on the left, it is split into two distinct parts and therefore the learners have to divide their attention between two mutually referring bits of information, thereby increasing cognitive load on the working memory.

This grape leaf shows classic potassium deficiency. It shows some of the typical signs of discolouring or scorched appearance of the leaves and chlorosis of the veins. Although not fully developed, the edges of the leaf tips are beginning to curl too.

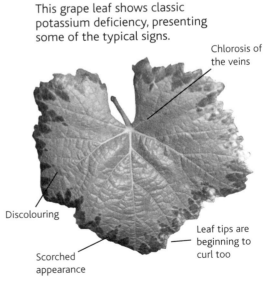

This grape leaf shows classic potassium deficiency, presenting some of the typical signs.

Chlorosis of the veins

Discolouring

Scorched appearance

Leaf tips are beginning to curl too

Source: https://commons.wikimedia.org/wiki/File:Grape_leaf_showing_nutrient_deficiency.jpg

In this next example, a chemistry teacher uses the split attention principle to reduce the cognitive load of his students as they tackle practical work by integrating the diagrams and instructions.

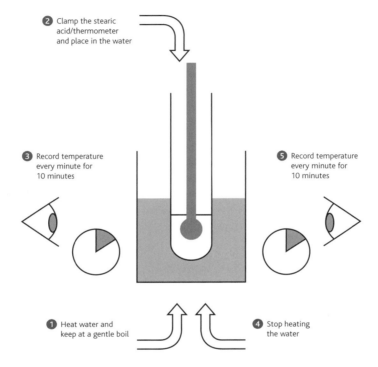

Source: David Paterson[7]

The positive effects of this kind of instruction cannot be overestimated, with students completing the tasks quicker, finding the tasks easier and developing a better understanding of the science involved, including the interpretation and comprehension of practical work (Haslam and Hamilton 2010). They also showed a more favourable attitude to laboratory work and showed greater manipulative and organisational skills (Dechsri 1997).

---

7   See David Paterson's excellent and well-thought-out blog post, 'Cognitive Load and Practical Work Research: An Update': https://dave2004b.wordpress.com/2018/01/03/cognitive-load-and-practical-work-research-an-update/.

Providing coherent information

As experts, it is easy to forget about the journey we had to take in order to develop that expertise. Concepts that seem obvious to you may not make much sense at all to your students. When designing materials for absolute novices, it seems that a single source of information is best, so a handout summarising a key idea would be the ideal place to start establishing what will be taught. As students begin to learn, they require differing pedagogy. At the drastic end of this is the 'expertise reversal effect' where the integration of the information, which was previously desirable, becomes undesirable and separate bits of information are more useful.[8] A sequence for teaching might look a little like this:

Arbitrary designation of knowledge level[9]	Form of information	Purpose
Novice	One source, preferably with visual and spoken explanation. High levels of integration. Use worked examples.	Gain basic understanding from a complete basic model.
Intermediate	A few sources. Integration still matters. Use completion tasks or partial clues.	Deepen understanding with examples. Use a more detailed complete model.
Expert	Multiple sources of information. Spoken explanation becomes less helpful. Use problem solving tasks or inferred information.	Transfer and apply concepts to new situations. Construct models piece by piece.

---

[8] As an aside, part of a student's experience must be to learn about how to use multiple sources of information. Otherwise, people will end up voting against their own interests as all they read is the *Daily Mail*.

[9] This may be thought of in traditional terms of age, but it may be more useful to think in terms of having just started a topic to the topic being almost completed.

The opportunity for students to make meaningful choices

Choice is an instrument that can be used to increase student ownership of learning. This ownership can take two forms: firstly, of the tasks and activities of the lesson and, secondly, over the ownership of learning. Choice brings with it intrinsic motivation, engagement and interest. It also conveys to students a clear message of trust. The potential for choice lies in two areas: what to study and how to study. What to study is, in reality, bound up in subjects, the curriculum and exam specifications, while how to study has rather more flexibility. However, even giving an illusion of choice can have the desired effect. Simply providing the right stimulus and asking students to ask questions about it can be used by us to direct activities, discussions and learning so the students feel that they have invested in the topic or lesson.[10] Even though the topic, stimulus and subsequent activities are devised by the teacher, the students' choice of what to study can help them to engage in the learning.

An important version of ownership involves students generating their own answers to questions created by the content. Answers that the students have worked out, deduced or generated for themselves are better remembered than the ideas that are merely read or told to them. This is readily applied to classrooms – for instance, if you are writing a review quiz to help students study a topic, making the quiz a 'fill in the blank' or short answer style test aids retention better than a multiple choice test does. The act of having forgotten and then struggling to recall is a great servant of memory (Bjork and Bjork 2011: 61).

Engaging the emotions

At the risk of sounding somewhat callous, I really do not mean in the 'we all remember where we were when Princess Diana died' (WARWWWWPDD) kind of way. Although the WARWWWWPDD method is highly durable, it tends to be beyond our control and can be a somewhat drastic technique for remembering the capital cities of South America. What we want for memorable learning to occur is an emotional investment from the students into the content or the task. Emotions are a sure fire way to add

---

[10] The hard part.

purpose to any learning activity, and students can be guided into making that commitment through a range of strategies. In terms of obtaining emotional investment, the following are of importance:

- *You and the culture of your classroom:* Students will work hard because you ask them nicely. They will invest in a task if they like you. The same *may* be true if they hate you and want to prove you wrong. However, this second option is less likely to work as it is liable to lead to apathy. Oddly enough, hatred is actually a better long-term strategy for learning. Two people, one a childhood bully and the other a chemistry teacher, both told me that I was incapable of getting into university. Although I still feel a bit angry about this pair of sad sacks, their actions and my response were very much like WARWWWWPDD – the effect on me was unintended but enduring. Building positive and honest working relationships with students, and between students, is a much more productive way of encouraging the commitment to learn.

- *Find the human element:* This is sometimes easy, sometimes difficult, but finding ways for students to see the relevance to humanity helps. People like people.

- *Be controversial:* As every tabloid editor knows, controversy is a useful attention grabber. Find a place for debate, argumentation and dialogue so that opinions can be aired, challenged and used to engage the students in wanting to know.

- *Make the concept tangible:* Rooting concepts in concrete objects, artefacts and experiences make them easier for students to believe and understand.

- *Make it personal:* Tell a personal story – or at least a made-up story about you. Can you weave in a story about the local community, local people, local history? I never teach electricity without reference to Joseph Swan, the inventor of the incandescent light bulb. Swan lived in Gateshead, and I use his story to engage students with the controversy of Thomas Edison's assumption of the title of inventor of the light bulb.

- *Act enthusiastically:* Telling children they have to learn stuff 'because it's in the exam' may well be the very reason for our existence and it may also work well enough for a selection of students, but any strategy is risky if it's the only one you've got. It is more likely that transmitting our enthusiasm, interest and curiosity about even the boring stuff is more likely to motivate students. We might manifest such enthusiasm for the usefulness of the concept, the process of learning or the final product. A serious part of the teacher's role is to act as an advocate for our subject content and be a model learner – and we should do this with the requisite passion, even on a Tuesday afternoon.

Hopefully, the contradiction between cognitive dissonance and cognitive load theory has leapt from the page: one says that holding two opposing ideas in your head will lead to confusion and that this is good for learning, and the other says that we should limit the amount of information held in the working memory at any one time. Both seem to have a positive impact on learning. It all comes down to teachers using dissonance to manage curiosity, attention and deep thinking about the material, while at the same time managing access and the amount of thinking done by students in order to maintain their motivation. In simple terms, we want moments when the students will feel emotionally and cognitively challenged (and which may not pay off for months or even years) but we also want moments when the students feel they are making progress in order to maintain their motivation and effort. Nuthall's (2007: 73) studies suggest that transfer to long-term memory will not occur until enough information has accumulated in the working memory; if insufficient information is present then learning is unlikely to occur. So, while repetition can be problematic it is an important part of lesson design.

Repetition as a strategy

The unit of a lesson is woefully inadequate as a device to scaffold the content that students need to learn. Ideas quickly decay from the memory if they are not used fairly soon after they have been learned, so it is imperative that we design lesson sequences that support students to:

- Clarify their understanding of the material.

- Revisit key ideas over time.

- Use activities to connect with prior knowledge.

- Develop from simple to complex explanations.

- Help them to remember the material.

- Perform tasks that allow them to demonstrate performance and learning.

Two guiding questions can help us to plan well:

1. When should the repeats take place, both in the session and across the curriculum?

2. How can changing the nature of the tasks help to avoid students being bored?

Using repetition as a strategy places several obstacles in the learners' way, not least the lack of motivation that comes from the boredom element of re-encountering previously studied material. However, familiarity is the more direct threat. When we face a previously experienced context, we automatically predict what knowledge will be needed in this situation. If the concept then fails to appear when we had strongly expected it to, we remember the context of the new idea less well (Kim et al. 2014).

As an example, one might make the assumption that a foolproof way to become a wine connoisseur is to quaff a whole bottle of Chianti and then, the next day, to guzzle down a bottle of Ribera del Duero and so on. It seems obvious that the deliberate and sustained bathing of our mouths in the delectable flavours of fruits, tannins and booze would educate our palates to the level of a sommelier. Apparently not – and we kind of know this, don't we? Most teachers will be well aware of the phenomenon of the 'second bottle of wine'. The second bottle of wine is a budgetary strategy whereby wine is purchased on the strength of it being either a first bottle or second bottle of wine for the evening. The first bottle is of premium quality and approaches £15 in price, while the second bottle is of inferior quality and noticeably cheaper, costing a more reasonable £4.79.[11]

---

[11] A heartfelt warning to colleagues: wine won in school fetes or given as gifts from leaving students is rarely of even second bottle quality. These wines must be returned to a different school fete to enter wine purgatory. These wines are clearly labelled with titles such as Pissy Hill, Le Poignet du Camp and Tendril du Fromage.

The underlying principle here is that even while perusing the aisle of a supermarket we are aware that, after the first bottle of wine has been drunk, we will have become in some ways *overfamiliar* with wine and we are aware that consuming a second bottle of wine of similar standing and price to the first may not be the best use of our money. The quality would be wasted on us as we will be half drunk. It is therefore recommended that tasters drink different wines of contrasting styles in each consecutive glass in order to become a master of wine. In this way, we learn how to discern the characteristics of the wine so that we can distinguish them. Anyone who has undertaken a wine tasting class will also remember to cleanse the palate with a glass of water in-between tastings.

Learning appears to share the benefits of this counter-intuitive approach (Birnbaum et al. 2013). The spacing effect – restudying something after a short delay – has been shown to lead to better long-term retention than restudying concepts in quick succession. When this is combined with the interleaving of the intentions (i.e. the learners study different concept categories) the effect is greater still, just as it is in alternating red, white and sparkling wine. This is possibly due to the fact that it prevents learners from assuming they know something merely because they have become familiar with it (or, in all likelihood, bored by it). Change is good for refocusing the mind. For clarity's sake, to optimise your ability to learn you cannot become too familiar with the content being learned: the risk here lies in assuming we know something.

Successfully planning the repetition of materials requires teachers to bring to bear all of their pedagogical content knowledge so that the learning narrative (or student experience of the material) is repeated at suitable intervals. This should be considered during and between lessons and especially over much longer time scales. Part of this narrative comes from the form of pedagogy used for each revisiting of a concept and how the idea is to be practised so that learning becomes durable.

Narratives of lessons: managing multiple exposures to concepts

Ideas (the things we teach) deserve narratives, and stories are a great memory tool for exploring the interconnections between ideas with purpose. Summarising, exploring and developing are what we really mean when we say we 'repeat ideas', and this is true both within a lesson and over longer periods of time. A review of the key points – the prior knowledge, as it were – seems prudent before moving on. But what do we mean by moving on? Do we mean moving on to a new idea? Do we mean moving on to a new task? Or do we mean moving on to a more complex version of the same idea? Although the answers to these questions have little common ground, they do, on occasion, help teachers to work out when it is best to repeat, or indeed manage, exposure to the ideas themselves.

There are times when we do not want to move the ideas on at all; rather, we want to dwell on a concept, exploring it from new angles to develop a deeper and more complete understanding. The following teaching sequence shows how this might look and how we can revisit ideas and build them into a narrative.

Number of exposures to ideas	Idea being studied: sources of finance
Idea 1 first exposure	Students listen to a brief teacher explanation of the three reasons why businesses require finance.
Idea 1 revisit	Students then read a business case study identifying the financial needs of the business.
Idea 1 built upon to establish idea 2	Students then read the same case study but this time identify the sources of finance.
Idea 2 is developed	Students watch a brief video on the sources of finance and compile a list of short-term and long-term sources.

Number of exposures to ideas	Idea being studied: sources of finance
Idea 2 is extended	Students define and identify the pros and cons of each source.
Ideas 1 and 2 are applied	Students answer a problem in which they have to identify the financial need of the business and suggest the best source of finance for this particular business.

Throughout this brief scheme, the main ideas are being revisited and reinforced. It is clear that each idea to be learned is studied, then is either studied again through a different method or is developed into a more detailed version. Just to be clear, this example aims to show how ideas can be both practised and extended when we revisit them with our students. It does not consider establishing a purpose, determining where the feedback might occur or linking it to a big idea.

Our pedagogical content knowledge allows us to see how the ideas in our subjects interact and develop, and we can apply this principle to design teaching sequences. These do not necessarily have to work from simple to more complex ideas, as we know that learning benefits from students seeing the big idea. However, it is worth considering how a basic idea taught in one activity may manifest itself in another activity later on.

We can illustrate this with an example which comes from my teaching about cell organelles – the functional parts that make up cells. Students first come across organelles when they study the structure of cells in Year 10. They learn the names of the parts, what they do and how to identify them in diagrams. For instance, mitochondria are small organelles that are the site of respiration – where we make the energy needed to do whatever living things do. In following lessons, they revisit the idea of organelles when they look at specialised cells, as different cells have different quantities of each organelle, which perform different functions. Inevitably, one of the cells they study are sperm cells, which have large numbers of mitochondria to provide the energy needed for motility. So, as part of the planning, the word 'organelle' becomes a teaching point and is then repeated, albeit in a new and more nuanced context.

Clearly, this sort of repetition is easier to achieve in a lesson than across the school year, although the students will encounter organelles again in Year 11 when studying the process of respiration (because mitochondria are the location for respiration). How can we plan to exploit these prior experiences? Might they have forgotten the previous learning by then? It is interesting to note that spacing out learning episodes can lead to long-term benefits for learners, and that even when material appears to have been forgotten, vestiges of the knowledge remain and appear to add speed to the new learning (Hattie and Yates 2013: 137). It is much easier for us to plan to do this in the short term because achieving multiple exposures of ideas within lessons is rather straightforward.

Deliberate practice

Experts achieve expertise not through their natural ability but through their capacity for intense practice and maintenance of performance, so the idea of deliberate practice comes from studying such experts (Ericsson 1993). This definition makes it clear that you do not necessarily become good simply by practising, but you can move from good to expert via this process. The principles of deliberate practice can also be applied to knowledge, provided that the design of the task allows for practice with the correct content. This sounds easy, but producing sufficient problems or scenarios for students to practise applying the same principle requires discipline on our part and resilience from the students.

Getting students to consistently practise a skill or the application of a bit of knowledge requires us to design tasks that subtly change the context for each practice, helping them to transfer their learning to new and novel situations. All the students need to bring to this practice is the willingness to practise. Repeatedly practising something requires motivation, which can be partially imbued by having an understanding of the benefits it will bring. Our assessments and feedback must take this into account.

Practice is not defined as simple repetition but as repetition with feedback. For feedback to be effective, the students must first understand the model or outcome they are working towards. Trial and error practising does not work well: the students need to be aware of how and what they are practising. This enables them to receive feedback and be reflective about how they can use this feedback to master the subject or skill. To this end, we must provide opportunities for students to be repeatedly exposed to the same information and then to repeatedly demonstrate their learning.

In Chapter 3 we saw that deliberate practice requires the following:

- A bigger problem that can be broken down into smaller ones.

- An understanding of the task at hand which allows investment into a conscious and focused effort.

- An element of choice or control over what is practised.

- A chance to deconstruct and restructure learning.

By way of an example, let's look at how deliberate practice can be applied to the essential skill of writing an essay. Martin and Rose's (2005) genre pedagogy cycle is incredibly useful for this:

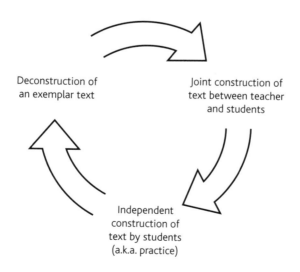

Deconstruction of
an exemplar text

Joint construction of
text between teacher
and students

Independent
construction of
text by students
(a.k.a. practice)

Source: Martin and Rose (2005: 253)

The skill of essay writing is complex and so naturally fits into something that can be broken down into smaller parts. The first step of the genre pedagogy cycle is to deconstruct an exemplar piece of text that is ideally closely related to the topic the students will practise with independently. This prevents them from merely copying the teacher and is an opportunity to revisit prior knowledge. This is followed by a joint construction stage in which the teacher, through questioning, involves the students in the co-construction of a text. This will inevitably be a collection of student ideas which the teacher improves and talks through in the process of recording those ideas. It is vital that the teacher shares their internal monologue while doing this, saying what they think and why certain sentence structures work and so on. Next, the students are sent away to practise writing independently. The students will require large amounts of feedback during and after the writing process, along with multiple opportunities to write academically to fully develop this essential skill.

In preparation for writing an essay on 'Where does new human life come from?' in which they are asked to use connectives to sequence the action (e.g. next, firstly, following that, this leads to, then), the students, with guidance and teaching, break down a couple of paragraphs on external fertilisation in amphibians:

> External fertilisation is a form of reproduction when the female's ovum is fertilised by the male's sperm outside of the female body. Since sperm need to swim and the developing egg must be moist, external fertilisation always occurs in water. Elaborate courtship rituals are sometimes used to ensure that the sperm and the eggs are released close enough together to ensure fertilisation. It is therefore unsurprising that fish and amphibians are the organisms that use this method to create new life.
>
> External fertilisation has many advantages, especially for the parents. After fertilisation, many species of fish and amphibians do not expend effort in looking after the young. This allows them to feed and breed again so that they produce large numbers of offspring to increase the chance of some surviving to adulthood.

The purpose of this is to identify the strategies, styles and rules that must be focused on while writing. As a rule, I always start by recording student observations and comments before moving on to any aspect of teaching, which allows me to start where the students are at. I then begin to model that this is a collaborative process, which, in turn, sets up one of the main requirements necessary for deliberate practice to take place – namely, that the students need to understand the task so they have some element of control. I find that this helps to invest the students in the conscious and focused effort needed for success. If the students do miss something, then the example (if it is well planned) should show them how to write scientifically. A list of the characteristics evident in the example might include:

- Written in the third person.

- Each paragraph starts with a topic sentence that says what something is and what it does.

- Each topic sentence includes a topic noun early in the sentence.

- Written in the past or present tense.

- Is specific in describing where and when something occurs.

- Sequences the processes using time connectives.

Only after the students have this understanding will I present the task they are to complete. This will highlight the content to be included and the writing skills I expect to see – in this case:

Extended writing task: Where does new human life come from?

Your task is to write a report about how the male and female reproductive systems develop and how they work in the conception and development of new life.

Content criteria

The report must include the following:

- Name the organs involved, correctly spelled, and describe their role.

- Describe the process of puberty for your gender and the opposite one.

- Explain how fertilisation and implantation is more likely on certain days of the menstrual cycle.

- Name the sex cells and explain how they come together.

- Describe each stage of how a fertilised egg grows into a baby during pregnancy.

- Explain how the placenta and the mother's blood supply provide the oxygen and the nutrients needed for the baby to grow.

Report criteria

Writing to inform

To inform means to give facts to another person.

When writing to inform / report, make sure:

- Language is clear, factual and impersonal.

- You use short and clear sentences.

- You break up the writing with diagrams, illustrations, pictures and subheadings.

- Topic nouns organise the text.

Writing to explain

To explain means to make clear, to show the meaning or to account for – you are trying to say how or why something happens.

- Writing to explain is generally in the third person and in the past or present tense.

- Use clear and factual language.

- Use sentences that link a cause and an effect.

- Use connectives to compare (e.g. whereas, though, while, unless, equally, however).

The next phase of the genre pedagogy cycle is to jointly construct some writing with the students. Once more, the control of this activity is seemingly with the students, but it remains an opportunity for me to model, when necessary, how I would go about completing the task. I start by giving the students a minute or two to come up with a potential topic sentence.[12] I then either take multiple examples and write them up on the whiteboard (or type them up) or take one and seek to improve it.

The process may take student writing through the following developments:

Skill being practised	Co-constructed sentences
Start	The organs are the ovaries, uterus and testes.
Addition of detail	The main organs are the ovaries, uterus and testes.
Locating when this is occurring	The main organs involved in reproduction are the ovaries, uterus and testes.
Adding detail – linking back to the topic sentence	The main organs involved in reproduction are the ovaries, uterus and testes. The ovary releases the egg.
Locating the action	The main organs involved in reproduction are the ovaries, uterus and testes. The ovaries are where releases the egg.

---

[12] I tend to provide planning support for the content in the form of key words for each concept to be written about in order to focus the students as much as possible on the complexities of writing.

Skill being practised	Co-constructed sentences
Checking and correcting grammar	The main organs involved in reproduction are the ovaries, uterus and testes. The ovaries are where the egg is released.
Adding detail	The main organs involved in reproduction are the ovaries, uterus and testes. The ovaries are the place where the egg is developed and released.
Applying sentence structure and going back over to add further (locating) detail	The main organs involved in reproduction are the ovaries, uterus and testes. The female's ovaries are the place where the egg is developed and released. The male's testes is the place where the sperm are developed and released.
Final – interestingly worked backwards to add more detail and connectives to emphasise detail	The main organs involved in reproduction are the ovaries, uterus and testes. The major female organs are the ovaries and uterus. The ovaries develop and release the egg, whereas the uterus grows and develops the embryo. The male testes develop and release sperm cells.

The process continues, building up each sentence and paragraph until it is complete or it is clear that the students are ready to practise independently. This is clearly a slow and time consuming task. This particular task (which is for Year 7s) takes about 45–60 minutes before they get to practise independently. However, the conditions for deliberate practice have now been established and the students are therefore more likely to set about practising and writing to a high(er) standard.

The process of practice is hard work. During this phase, it is important to focus on whether the students are aware of what it is they are being asked to do rather than on the quality of what is being written. Having the success criteria and examples available makes this a much more tangible thing for the students to understand and therefore deliberately practise.

Opportunities to demonstrate learning

There are two purposes in planning this kind of learning activity. Firstly, it acts as another exposure to the information but it also serves to transfer the knowledge to subtly new situations, taking the student from novice to expert. Secondly, the type of feedback required for this type of activity will be more academic or content based, as opposed to the procedural or 'how to' feedback that practice requires.

Even simple strategies such as completing an exam question can achieve this, providing the students have the chance to rehearse the ideas, elaborate on them, recall them and then reflect on them with constructive feedback. The feedback a teacher provides should be a combination of content based comments and guidance on how to do something. This includes considering how the knowledge is organised.

Planning exposures to knowledge

It is during lesson planning that we can plan multiple exposures to individual ideas, but even at this level of planning it is a difficult task. We must prioritise ideas and content that require revisiting, deconstructing and reconstructing. These may include common student misconceptions, difficult content, threshold concepts or other important content in the subject. The scale of ideas becomes the instant problem, so much so that teachers mainly delegate this responsibility to those who design the national curriculum, exam specifications and course textbooks.

Narratives in subjects: revisiting concepts over longer periods of time

Overcoming the problems of massed practice

Way back in Chapter 3, we looked at the spacing effect, which states that if 'practice is spaced out over time, it generally leads to superior learning', and stands in contrast to massed practice or accumulating the practice straight after the initial learning experience (Kang 2016: 13). Although massed practice is helpful in learning, it poses a difficulty for teachers: it can give the illusion of mastery.

During massed practice of, for instance, ratio problems in mathematics, it is easy for the students to simply follow the prescribed procedure to produce an answer. Yet when they are faced with a mixed set of problems to solve in an examination or need to transfer their knowledge to a new course, they may struggle. Massed practice misses the important first step of problem solving: being able to identify the type of problem that is to be solved so that we can apply the correct strategy or knowledge. Massed or blocked practice is common in many lesson plans and in the structure of many school textbooks: ideas are followed by practice problems about the same ideas, and this has the effect of reducing the difficulty of the problems (Rohrer and Taylor 2007).

Imagine, if you will, a set of maths subtraction problems and question 6 says this:

> Bob has baked 12 cupcakes. His science teacher eats 8. How many cupcakes remain?

Since this question does not include the usual command words ('subtract' or 'difference'), even students who are able to subtract may not be able to infer that they should. However, if this problem follows other problems requiring subtraction, the students know the strategy in advance. In fact, they could solve this problem without reading anything other than the numbers (Rohrer et al. 2015). Put another way, blocked practice sometimes allows students to not do any of the hard thinking required for learning to occur.

One simple solution is to interleave the types of problems used during student practice. This does not mean an increase in the number of practice questions, more a consideration of when the students practise. In reality, we would want to combine the benefits of both massed and interleaved practice.

Our schemes of work and practice activities would ideally be built to do both. This can be done simply as the following study undertaken by Rohrer et al. (2015) shows. Over a three month period, the students involved in the study received their normal lessons. Cleverly, the experimenters had the students change the type of practice for the two different problem types being studied (slope and graph problems). Half the classes involved were given weekly homework that used blocked practice for slope questions while interleaving the graph questions with questions from a previous topic. This enabled the researchers to compare the effects of interleaving, which showed a 25% improvement in the interleaved problems after one day and a 76% improvement after one month. The conclusion, according to Pan (2015), was that the effect of interleaving was found to be 'strong, stable, and long-lasting', as it helps improve our ability to distinguish between similar concepts.

This methodology is readily applied across the curriculum, as the science homework example that follows shows. The topics selected are ones which students readily confuse, so being able to discern which topic area they are thinking about becomes an important part of their learning.

Respiration and photosynthesis mixed questions

- What are the products of aerobic respiration?

- What are the reactants of photosynthesis?

- What do plants store glucose as?

- What are the products of anaerobic respiration?

- What are the reactants of aerobic respiration?

- What are the products of photosynthesis?

The Act of Learning: Memory as a Destination

- What are the reactants of anaerobic respiration?

- What do animals store glucose as?

- What subcellular structure does photosynthesis take place in?

- What subcellular structure does anaerobic respiration take place in?

- What subcellular structure does aerobic respiration take place in?

- Which process of life is endothermic?

- Which process of life is exothermic?

- What is the word equation for anaerobic respiration?

- What is an oxygen debt?

- What is the word equation for aerobic respiration?

- What is the word equation for photosynthesis?

- What is the word equation for the breakdown of lactic acid?

- What problems does lactic acid cause in muscles?

- Name three uses of the energy released by respiration.

- In what direction does active transport move substances?

- How are palisade cells adapted for photosynthesis?

- What three conditions could limit the rate of photosynthesis?

- Why do plants need nitrate ions?

Interleaving within a topic or term

The skill for teachers is to use their pedagogical content knowledge to identify where interleaving will have the biggest impact, but designing a series of homework tasks to follow your usual scheme of learning seems like a prudent and manageable first step. This can be as simple as the term's worth of homework shown in the following table. The key ideas are a combination of what will be taught during this time and some necessary exam skills practice that is pertinent to the content. Some ideas need to be understood before others, and some are more important or more difficult. The basic principle is that the students will get a chance to revisit the content straight after the lessons, so that the practice is massed at some point, and at least once more throughout the remainder of the term so there is some interleaving. Key ideas and difficult ones have been prioritised and are revisited on three separate occasions.

GCSE science: biology (Year 11, term 2)	Weeks										
Key ideas	1	2	3	4	5	6	7	8	9	10	11
Hormones – examples and compare to nervous coordination		X			X				X		X
The role of the pituitary gland		X				X					X
Pancreas – insulin and glucagon			X						X		X
Negative feedback systems			X	X					X		X
Treating type 1 and type 2 diabetes				X				X			X
Hormones and puberty					X		X				X
Hormones regulating the menstrual cycle					X		X				X
Artificial control of fertility						X				X	X

GCSE science: biology (Year 11, term 2)	Weeks										
Key ideas	1	2	3	4	5	6	7	8	9	10	11
Mock exam review	X	X									
Data handling questions			X		X				X	X	
Evaluation questions				X		X	X				
Plant hormones – auxins and tropisms								X		X	X

Interleaving across a syllabus or year

Interleaving can also be performed on a much grander scale. Pan (2015) identifies that interleaving of content 'strengthens memory associations' as our brains are 'continuously engaged at retrieving different responses and bringing them into short-term memory'. This is enhanced when 'repeating that process' over longer time periods as 'neural connections between different tasks and correct responses' are strengthened, which results in 'enhanced learning'. Unlike blocked practice, the correct solution to an interleaved problem cannot be found in the structure and prompts of the other problems, as each problem is focused upon a different concept or problem type. Indeed, exam board syllabi are now much more orientated towards this, building curricula around big ideas that can be interleaved over the duration of the course, as the following example, worked up to form a 5 year science curriculum, shows.

Year 7	Year 8	Year 9	Year 10	Year 11
Particle model M	Elements M	Atomic structure M	Structure and bonding M	Electrolysis E3
Interdependence E4	Digestion O	Energy resources E2	Cell transport and specialisation Respiration Organisation in animals O	Organic chemistry R
Energy E2	Speed and work E2	Cells O	Forces Motion F	Digestion O
Separating mixtures M	Periodic table M	Periodic table M	Chemical changes R	Photosynthesis E4
Cells O	Breathing O	Forces Hooke's law F	Energy transfer by heat E2	Forces F
Forces F	Pressure F	Communicable diseases Preventing disease O	Nervous system O	Molecules and matter M
Metals and non-metals R	Types of reaction R	EM waves W	Electricity E1	Rates of reaction and equilibrium R
Movement – organisation O	Respiration E4	Earth's atmosphere E3	Energy changes E2	Respiration E4
Current and potential difference E1	Heating and cooling E2	Conservation of energy E2	Organising plants O	Hormonal coordination Reproduction G
Acids and alkalis R	Chemical energy R	Adaptation, interdependence E4	Radioactivity M	Electricity E1
Reproduction G	Photosynthesis E4	Earth's resources E3	Cell division and stem cells G	Light triples W
Earth structure E3	Electromagnetism E1		Alkanes and alkenes M	Chemical analysis M
Variation G	Earth and climate change E3		Waves W	Variation and evolution G
Waves (light and sound) W	Inheritance G		Polymer triples M	Genetics and evolution G
Universe	Waves W		Non-communicable diseases O	Space triples E3

Key to science themes				
Forces F	Electromagnetism E1	Energy E2	Waves W	Matter M
Reactions R	Earth E3	Organism O	Ecosystem E4	Genetics G

The big ideas are the organising principles of our subjects. Organising principles are simply a generalising concept that holds smaller linked ideas together. Consider the Key Stage 3 national curriculum for mathematics. It is organised around the following organising principles which we instantly recognise as topics.

- Working mathematically

- Number

- Algebra

- Ratio, proportion and rates of change

- Geometry and measures

- Probability

- Statistics

This grouping allows teachers to crudely plan spacing and interleaving:

Half term 1			Half term 2			Half term 3		
Number	Algebra	Working mathematically	Algebra	Statistics	Number	Working mathematically	Algebra	Statistics

But do they make for useful organising principles for learning? Well, for experts such as teachers, yes, but not necessarily for students. As adults who have experienced a whole mathematics course, we will at least be able to name some ideas that would be taught within each topic. For instance, statistics would include tally charts, percentages, scatter graphs and correlations. As a young teacher, I was always befuddled when students asked if what they were studying was biology or physics. It took me a while to realise that they asked this because they did not know – they just knew that they were studying a 'science' course. Rather than see this question as a distraction, I realised that it was an attempt to begin to organise their knowledge. This organisation is vital for recall. However, the topics of 'biology', 'statistics' or '19th century literature' do not have the deep contexts for our students that they have for us, and, ultimately, inculcating such contexts is one of the aims of our teaching.

In fact, even these topics contain a rich variety of content. Here is the Department for Education (2013: 9) curriculum statement for one section of Key Stage 3 statistics: 'Construct and interpret appropriate tables, charts, and diagrams, including frequency tables, bar charts, pie charts, and pictograms for categorical data, and vertical line (or bar) charts for ungrouped and grouped numerical data.' Although some of the entries here share common ideas, some are unique in their construction. Knowing that something is part of the thing called 'statistics' will not necessarily help you to recall the rules for a specific example. What holds these ideas together is their intended use: constructing and interpreting with categorical data. For the students, the organising principle is therefore more about using categorical data that is common to all the different methodologies. For teachers, this shows us the level of planning we would need to undertake to help students organise their knowledge and to plan our repeats and revisits of concepts.

Ultimately, structuring your curriculum plans around organising principles that will need to be revisited, explored and developed is a useful start, especially in helping you to identify where detail and nuance is needed in planning individual lessons. Again, the concept maps we constructed in Chapter 2 to understand how concepts are built upon and where they have come from are useful here. The English exam board OCR (2015: 4) sagely adds this advice:

> The beauty of interleaving is that you can embed it as little or as much as you like and tailor the interleaving to your students. You can also mix blocking most of your lesson content with interleaved homework tasks that complement current learning and develop deeper understanding of prior topics.

The biggest benefit will come from identifying the concepts that are big enough to be generic but specific enough to be useful. For instance, the statistics topic we discussed may be better served by using the smaller organising principle of 'using categorised data' to plan the spacing and interleaving of concepts.

Half term 1			Half term 2			Half term 3		
Number organising principle 1	Algebra organising principle 1	Working mathematically principle 1	Algebra organising principle 1	Statistics organising principle 1 – using categorised data	Number organising principle 1	Working mathematically principle 2	Algebra organising principle 1	Statistics organising principle 1 – using categorised data

It is clear even from this simple example that interleaving is a messy affair with a vast number of principles which need to be plotted throughout a course. Sometimes you will want to return to the smaller principle within the bigger topic, and sometimes you will want to look at a different aspect. We rely a lot on our pedagogical content knowledge here, but in our busy schedules this is easily lost. The process of interleaving works much better when completed during departmental planning time on a 'conceptual level', supporting all teachers to exploit what we know about how learning happens. Even broad brush strokes at this level help to prompt more detailed thinking for lesson planning. This need not be an excessively onerous task during planning – it is key knowledge that allows you to revisit the ideas at a time when the students may have forgotten a substantial part of these ideas (i.e. most of them).

Summary

In this chapter, we have discussed how we can help our students to retain their knowledge in the long run. Although, it may not be an actual place in the brain, the long-term memory provides a useful proxy for the destination of learning. It is based on the notion of schemas – organised and interconnected chunks of knowledge. As we have seen, building a knowledge schema is effortful for students and teachers alike. Expert teachers draw students' attention to, and help them to engage with, the big chunky organising ideas of the schema so that the chance of retention is enhanced. We do this when we ensure that the content being taught is coherent and tangible. We also do not forget the powerful effect of emotion on memory. We do this when we exploit the apparent controversy of an idea or when we place one idea in stark contrast to another idea.

Simultaneously, we are mindful of and act to counter the limitations of working memory – the processing part of the brain which can only pay attention to around four ideas at any one time. Expert teachers identify and remove any excessive, untimely or unnecessary ideas so the students can focus on the big idea at the right time. This can be achieved by utilising the split attention principle – for example, integrating written information with supportive visuals when designing student materials.

Expert teachers also think about the long-term delivery of content so that it is revisited often. We know that some ideas have an exalted status over others – we discussed threshold concepts in Chapter 3. We can use these ideas to build a coherent narrative not only during a lesson but throughout a students' experience of the subject too. There is evidence that students benefit from a slightly fractured course narrative; the interleaving of concepts means they are forced to remember an idea before it fades completely. However, even with interleaving, it seems sensible to ensure that students get to see a complete and coherent set of information (Richland et al. 2005). That is to say, it is better to teach a number of short topics within a lesson rather than change topic each lesson. It is also prudent to understand that topics which are more closely related are more likely to benefit from being interleaved (Hausman and Kornell 2014: 159). This suggests that the true benefit comes from the spacing effect that interleaving brings about (Kornell et al. 2010), so short time frame interleaving strategies (like the mixed respiration and photosynthesis questions beginning on page 280) represent the best way to structure course content.

This leaves us with the following planning questions:

- What are the organising principles of the content? How are they communicated?

- How will the content be attended to? Where are the moments for the students to be confused and search for meaning? Where are the moments for clarity?

- Do the activities engage the students in the content? How does the teaching overcome the problem of familiarity?

- Has the extraneous cognitive load been removed?

- Who owns the learning? How can the lessons become more student centred?

- How will the pedagogy change as the students become more expert?

- What is the narrative of the lesson?

- What is the narrative of the content?

- How will the exposures be managed within an individual lesson or a lesson sequence?

- How will the exposures be managed over a course or topic? Is it interleaved and spaced?

- How will the content be presented? Is it clear, coherent and engaging? Is it tangible, emotional, contrasting, controversial or unexpected?

- Is there an opportunity for the students to practise with the material? Is there an opportunity for the students to demonstrate new learning?

Conclusion

What started as an attempt to explore the lesson planning process has, I hope, turned into a celebration of teachers' professional wisdom – the knowledge that makes us experts. This unique, beautiful, complex and nuanced intelligence is still too undervalued for me. We do not speak of these things enough. Back in 1986, Lee Shulman (1986: 6) reflected that teaching is 'trivialised, its complexities ignored and its demands diminished'. I think he was right to assert that part of the difficulty the profession faces is that we, as teachers, find it hard to articulate our professional knowledge and how we know it. He attributed this to the quality of the research base.[1] 'Portrayals of expertise in teaching are rare' and when they do exist they 'dwell on the teachers' management of the classroom ... [while] few give full attention to ... the management of students ... [or] the management of ideas within classroom discourse' (Shulman 1987: 1). For this reason, Shulman gave us pedagogical content knowledge.

Pedagogical content knowledge encapsulates the rich conceptual understanding of our subjects and how they are learned. This involves us having a wide repertoire of teaching procedures and protocols and knowing how to develop them to suit the students in front of us. To do this we need to comprehend why a procedure works and match this to the support needed by our students in order for them to learn. We need to know how to represent ideas through analogies, images, examples and well-structured explanations. Yet one analogy or one way to explain is not enough; we need alternative ways for each and every lesson we teach. Teaching is a dialogue, so we must be able to adapt in response to the students' changing needs and how a lesson or topic progresses. We learn to do this through our professional development, our reading, our own experience of planning and designing lessons – and, indeed, from the act of teaching itself. It must be emphasised that this is not a soft *and*: it means in combination with, alongside, as well as, including – and from this we can identify what makes topics difficult and for which students.

---

[1] And, in part, the political motivations behind it. I will leave a dignified 'no comment' here.

There are many truths about what works in teaching, some of which are apparently contradictory. Take, for example, the suggestion that rehearsal strategies are bad for interest and motivation and are therefore detrimental to learning. Yet we also know that rehearsal strategies are good for the memory. What matters here, pedagogically, is when and how we use them. We learn to do this through our experience. Ascertaining students' prior knowledge is also a big part of a teacher's expertise because with this knowledge we can plan and prepare for the misconceptions that students arrive with in our classrooms. We can then be 'fruitful in reorganising the understanding of learners, because those learners are unlikely to appear before [us] as blank slates' (Shulman 1986: 9–10).

In short, we need to understand both learners *and* the process of learning. This is difficult because it is an invisible process. Nuthall (2005: 925) describes a 'mythical belief that engaging learning activities transfers the content of the activity to the mind of the students' so that 'learning is not encapsulated in the visible here and now of classroom activities'. He adds that since learning takes place in the minds of students, teachers have 'little direct evidence or little possibility of obtaining direct evidence, of what individual students are learning as they make the moment by moment decisions by which they run their classrooms'. This is indeed a challenge. Yet we must take comfort from knowing that it is the fruit of our pedagogical content knowledge that enables students to learn.

Shulman (1987: 8), rather tongue-in-cheek, suggested that 'if teacher knowledge was organised into a handbook, an encyclopaedia or some other format for arraying knowledge' that the category headings would at minimum include: content knowledge; general pedagogical knowledge; pedagogical content knowledge; knowledge of learners and their characteristics; knowledge of educational ends, purposes and values; knowledge of educational context and, I would humbly add, knowledge of assessment and feedback. Clearly, this book has not dealt with all of these categories: it is obvious that there is much more to say on the role pedagogical content knowledge plays in teacher expertise. Even from the inception of pedagogical content knowledge, Shulman knew it to be, let us say ... extensive. But we have explored some of its richness in terms of how it helps to conceptualise the teaching of our subjects, our expert teaching skills and how learning takes place. Pedagogical content knowledge provides the professional language for teachers to discuss and share best practice, and ultimately learn from each other.

Looking back on the chapter headings of this book, it does seem rather ambitious, but it is what we do daily as teachers – we think about a lot of things simultaneously. I hope that within the pages of this book I have captured the interdependence of each aspect of teacher expertise to some extent. Reviewing each chapter in reverse order will hopefully make this clear: by starting with where we want to be, we can consider how our knowledge helps our students.

The long-term memory is the destination of student learning, so our awareness of how to ensure that new knowledge will eventually arrive there – and remain there – is essential. Our expertise comes from knowing how to sequence and arrange learning over time. But it can only take place if our students understand the content and have an opportunity to process it. How students deal with this information, and the limitations of working memory, is a key aspect of teacher knowledge, but the real skill comes from balancing this proficiency with the complexity of the subject matter being taught.

Structuring the new information that students' encounter is a crucial element in granting them access to the beauty of our subjects. Without this, learning will not occur. Our teacher knowledge involves creating representations of our subject so that it can be understood. Our expertise lies in knowing how to make wise choices about how to explain, demonstrate, illustrate and exemplify the ideas we want our students to learn. Yet our representations do not live and die by how well they are structured, but also by how well we communicate them. We must be expert orators and listeners, creating clear narratives and frequently checking how well the students are following us. The skill of communication is part of our teaching practice and involves managing the flow of ideas, being responsive to changing student needs and selecting the most effective way of explaining a particular concept at this exact moment in time. The ability to plan is where teachers develop and utilise this know-how.

Our curricula are full of things we want to teach our students – so full that we need to make choices about where to spend our lesson time. This is a start point for planning, not a call to hijack the intended curriculum. By accepting that time is limited and that some concepts within a subject are more important than others, we have a huge responsibility. Expertise is needed in order to understand which concepts help students to organise other pieces of information and which are essential to learn before other concepts can be tackled (e.g. threshold concepts). In turn, we need to know what students find difficult and why, and how we can make things easier for them. This is pedagogical content knowledge. This is what non-teaching subject specialists do not have, and even what teachers of different subjects do not completely share.

Often, to make concepts easier for our students to digest, we break them down into meal-size pieces. Yet in doing so we may deny them a view of the complexity we are trying to convey. As expert teachers, we do a lot of chunking down and joining back up again. Placing knowledge into context increases student engagement and, speaking as a science teacher, it allows me to teach the interesting parts of my subject, which are the interactions between concepts. Enabling students to see how our subjects are joined up can help to set a direction and purpose for our teaching and their learning. Again, this is another aspect of pedagogical content knowledge that permits us to make good decisions about what and how to teach and when to teach it.

Deciding what, when and how to teach is not as straightforward as it seems: at the heart of our expertise is our understanding of our students and their prior knowledge, and how this may be incorrect and how we can help them to correct it. Our experience with assessment tools and a variety of pedagogical approaches is needed here in order to supplant long held student ideas about phenomena. And thus we complete the loop. We are back to long-term memory – but this time to consider how we can change what students think they know.

In the introduction, I quoted chef Claudia Roden who told us that there are no true recipes because ingredients vary greatly and lack exactness. She told us to weigh with the eye and to taste as we go. This is exactly what our pedagogical content knowledge allows to do: it gives us the language to discuss, share, prepare and deliver great lessons, regardless of our students' start points, our preferred pedagogical style or the content of the lesson. It is *our* expertise.

Now go cook ...

References and Further Reading

Akyeampong, K., Ampiah, J., Fletcher, J., Kutor, N. and Sokpe, B. (2000) Learning to Teach in Ghana: An Evaluation of Curriculum Delivery. MUSTER Discussion Paper No. 17. Centre for International Education, University of Sussex.

Alloway, T. P. (2008) Effective Screening Tools for Children with Working Memory Impairments. Paper presented at the British Educational Research Association Annual Conference, Heriot-Watt University, Edinburgh, 3–6 September.

Alloway, T. P., Gathercole, S. E., Kirkwood, H. and Elliott, J. (2009) The Cognitive and Behavioural Characteristics of Children with Low Working Memory. *Child Development* 80(2): 606–621.

Anderson, V. and Hidi, S. (1988) Teaching Students to Summarise. *Educational Leadership* 46(4): 26–28.

American Association for the Advancement of Science (2013) *Atlas of Science Literacy: Mapping K–12 Science Learning*, Vols 1–2. Available at: http://www.project2061.org/publications/atlas/.

Bahrick, H. P. and Hall, L. K. (1991) Lifetime Maintenance of High School Mathematics. *Journal of Experimental Psychology* 120: 20–23.

Bailey, F. and Pransky, F. (2014) *Memory at Work in the Classroom: Strategies to Help Underachieving Students*. Alexandria, VA: Association for Supervision and Curriculum Development.

Ball, D. L. (1988) Knowledge and Reasoning in Mathematical Pedagogy: Examining What Prospective Teachers Bring to Teacher Education. PhD dissertation, Michigan State University.

Banikowski, A. K. and Mehring, T. (1999) Strategies to Enhance Memory Based on Brain-Research. *Focus on Exceptional Children* 32(2): 1–16.

Barmby, P., Bolden, D., Raine, S. and Thompson, L. (2013) *Developing the Use of Visual Representations in the Primary Classroom*. London: Nuffield Foundation.

Barnes, D. and Todd, F. (1977) *Communication and Learning in Small Groups*. Abingdon: Routledge and Kegan Paul.

Beadle, P. (2013) *The Book of Plenary: Here Endeth the Lesson* (How to Teach). Carmarthen: Independent Thinking Press.

Beadle, P. (2015) *Literacy: Commas, Colons, Connectives and Conjunctions* (How to Teach). Carmarthen: Independent Thinking Press.

Berliner, D. (1986) In Pursuit of the Expert Pedagogue. *Educational Researcher* 15(7): 5–13.

Berliner, D. (2004) Expert Teachers: Their Characteristics, Development and Accomplishments. *Bulletin of Science, Technology and Society* 24(3): 1–23.

Biggs, J. (2003) *Aligning Teaching for Constructing Learning*. York: Higher Education Academy.

Biggs, J. and Collis, K. (1982) *Evaluating the Quality of Learning: The SOLO Taxonomy*. New York: Academic Press.

Birnbaum, M. S., Kornell, N., Bjork, E. L. and Bjork, R. A. (2013) Why Interleaving Enhances Inductive Learning: The Roles of Discrimination and Retrieval. *Memory & Cognition* 41(3): 392–402.

Bjork, E. L. and Bjork, R. A. (2011) Making Things Hard On Yourself, But In a Good Way: Creating Desirable Difficulties to Enhance Learning. In M. A. Gernsbacher, R. W. Pew, L. M. Hough and J. R. Pomerantz (eds), Psychology and the Real World: Essays Illustrating Fundamental Contributions to Society. New York: Worth Publishers, pp. 56–64.

Black, P. and Wiliam, D. (1998) *Inside the Black Box: Raising Standards Through Classroom Assessment*. London: King's College School of Education.

Borko, H. and Livingston, C. (1989) Cognition and Improvisation: Differences in Mathematics Instruction by Expert and Novice Teachers. *American Educational Research Journal* 26(4): 473–498. Available at: https://journals.sagepub.com/doi/10.3102/00028312026004473.

Borko, H., Livingston, C. and Shavelson, R. J. (1990) Teachers' Thinking About Instruction. *Remedial and Special Education* 11(6): 40–49.

Brophy, J. (1986) Research Linking Teacher Behavior to Student Achievement: Potential Implications for Instruction of Chapter 1 Students. *Educational Psychologist* 23(3): 235–286.

Brophy, J. (2008) Developing Students' Appreciation for What is Taught in School. *Educational Psychologist* 43(3): 132–141.

Brophy, J. and Alleman, J. (1991) Activities as Instructional Tools: A Framework for Analysis and Evaluation. *Educational Researcher* 20(4): 9–23.

References and Further Reading

Brophy, J. and Good, T. (1984) Teacher Behavior and Student Achievement. Occasional Paper No. 73. Ann Arbor, MI: Institute for Research on Teaching, Michigan State University.

Brophy, J. and Good, T. (1986) Teacher Behavior and Student Achievement. In M. C. Wittrock (ed.), *Handbook of Research on Teaching*. New York: Macmillan, pp. 336–391.

Brown, G. A. (2006) Explaining. In O. Hargie (ed.) *The Handbook of Communication Skills*, 3rd edn. Abingdon: Routledge, pp. 195–228.

Brown, G. A. and Armstrong, S. (1984) Explaining and Explanations. In E. C. Wragg (ed.), *Classroom Teaching Skills*. Abingdon: Routledge, pp. 121–148.

Brown, G. A. and Atkins, M. (1997) Explaining. In O. Hargie (ed.) *The Handbook of Communication Skills*, 2nd edn. Abingdon: Routledge, pp. 199–229.

Brown, G. A. and Manogue, M. (2001) AMEE Medical Education Guide 22. Refreshing Lecturing: A Guide for Lecturers. *Medical Teacher* 23(1): 231–245.

Brown, S. and Salter, S. (2010) Analogies in Science and Science Teaching. *Advances in Physiology Education* 24(4): 167–169.

Calderhead, J. (1984) *Teachers' Classroom Decision Making*. London: Holt, Rinehart & Winston.

Calderhead, J. (1993) The Contribution of Teachers' Thinking to Professional Development. In J. Calderhead, P. Denicollo and C. Day (eds), *Research on Teacher Thinking: Understanding Professional Development*. Abingdon and New York: Routledge, pp. 11–18.

Calfee, R. C. (1986) *Handbook of Research on Teaching*. New York: Macmillan.

Camp, E. (2006) Metaphor in the Mind: The Cognition of Metaphor. *Philosophy Compass* 1(1): 154–170.

Carney, R. N. and Levin, J. R. (2002) Pictorial Illustrations Still Improve Students' Learning from Text. *Educational Psychology Review* 14(1): 5–26.

Cazden, C. and Beck, S. (2003) Classroom Discourse. In A. C. Graesser, M. A. Gernsbacher and S. R. Goldman (eds), *Handbook of Discourse Processes*. Mahwah, NJ: Erlbaum/Taylor Francis, pp. 165–198.

Chi, M. T. H., Bassok, M., Lewis, M. W., Reimann, P. and Glaser, R. (1989) Self-Explanations: How Students Study and Use Examples in Learning to Solve Problems. *Cognitive Science* 13(2): 145–182.

Chi, M. T. H., De Leeuw, N., Chui, M. and LaVancher, C. (1994) Eliciting Self-Explanations Improves Understanding. *Cognitive Science* 18: 439–477.

Chilcoat, G. W. (1989) Instructional Behaviours for Clearer Presentations in the Classroom. *Instructional Science* 18(4): 289–314.

Chinn, C. A. and Brewer, W. F. (1993) The Role of Anomalous Data in Knowledge Acquisition. *Review of Educational Research* 63(1): 1–49.

Chui, M. (2008) Statistical Discourse Analysis of Group Problem Solving: Evaluations, Wrong Ideas, Rudeness, Justifications, and Micro-Creativity. *Contemporary Educational Psychology* 33: 382–402.

Clement, J. (1993) Using Bridging Analogies and Anchoring Intuitions to Deal with Students' Preconceptions. Special Issue: The Role of Analogy in Science and Science Teaching. *Journal of Research in Science Teaching* 30(10): 1241–1257.

Coe, R. (2013) Improving Education: A Triumph of Hope Over Experience. Inaugural lecture, Durham University, 18 June. Available at: http://www.cem.org/attachments/publications/ImprovingEducation2013.pdf.

Coe, R., Aloisi, C., Higgins, S. and Major, L. E. (2014) *What Makes Great Teaching? Review of the Underpinning Research*. London: Sutton Trust.

Coker, H., Medley, D. and Saor, R. (1980) How Valid Are Expert Opinions About Effective Teaching? Special Issue: Teacher Education – Time for Reform? *Phi Delta Kappan* 62(2): 131–134.

Cook, M. (2011) Teachers' Use of Visual Representations in the Science Classroom. *Science Education International* 22(3): 175–184.

Cook, S. W., Mitchell, Z. and Goldin-Meadow, S. (2008) Gesturing Makes Learning Last. *Cognition* 106(2): 1047–1058.

Corno, L. (1981) Cognitive Organizing in Classrooms. *Curriculum Inquiry* 11: 359–377.

Cotton, K. (2001) Close Up #5: Classroom Questioning. School Improvement Research Series 3. Available at: https://educationnorthwest.org/resources/school-improvement-research-series.

Crawford, V. M., Schlager, M., Toyama, Y., Riel, M. and Vahey, P. (2005) Characterising Adaptive Expertise in Science Teaching. Paper presented at the American Educational Research Association Annual Conference, Montreal, 11–15 April.

Dalby, D. (2014) The Connections and Contradictions in Student Responses to Contextualised Tasks. *Research in Mathematics Education* 16(1): 75–76.

de Winstanley, P. A. and Bjork, E. L. (1997) Processing Instructions and the Generation Effect: A Test of the Multifactor Transfer-Appropriate Processing Theory. *Memory* 5(3): 401–421.

de Winstanley, P. A. and Bjork, E. L. (2004) Processing Strategies and the Generation Effect: Implications for Making a Better Reader. *Memory & Cognition* 32(6): 945–955.

Dechsri, P. (1997) Effect of a Laboratory Manual Design Incorporating Visual Information-Processing Aids on Student Learning and Attitudes. *Journal of Research in Science Teaching* 34(9): 891–904.

Department for Education (DfE) (2013) *Mathematics Programmes of Study: Key Stage 3. National Curriculum in England*. London: DfE.

Department for Education and Skills (DfES) (2004) *Pedagogy and Practice: Teaching and Learning in Secondary Schools. Unit 8: Explaining*. London: DfES.

Dowd, J. E., Araujo, I. and Mazur, E. (2015) Making Sense of Confusion: Relating Performance, Confidence, and Self-Efficacy to Expressions of Confusion in an Introductory Physics Class. Physical Review Special Topics. *Physics Education Research* 11(1): 010107-1–010107-10.

Drake, S. (1988) Cognition and Emotion. *Anxiety and Working Memory* 2(2): 145–154.

Driver, R., Guesne, E. and Tiberghien, A. (eds) (2000) *Children's Ideas in Science*. Buckingham: Open University Press.

Duffy, G. C. (2002) The Case for Direct Explanation Strategies. In C. C. Block and M. Pressley (eds), *Comprehension Instruction*. New York: Guilford Press, pp. 28–41.

Duffy, G. C. (2009) *Explaining Reading: A Resource for Teaching Concepts, Skills and Strategies*, 2nd edn. New York: Guilford Press.

Dunlosky, J., Rawson, K. A., Marsh, E. J., Nathan, M. J. and Willingham, D. T. (2013) Improving Students' Learning with Effective Techniques: Promising Directions from Cognitive and Educational Psychology. *Psychological Science in the Public Interest* 14(1): 4–58.

Dwyer, F. (1970) Exploratory Studies in the Effectiveness of Visual Illustrations. *AV Communication Review* 18(3): 235–249.

Edwards, J. A. (2005) Exploratory Talk in Peer Groups: Exploring the Zone of Proximal Development. School of Education, University of Southampton. Available at: https://eprints. soton.ac.uk/18139/1/Edwards_J_CERME4_paper.pdf.

Ennis, R. (2011) Critical Thinking: Reflection and Perspective. *Inquiry* 26(1): 4–18.

Ericsson, K. A. (1993) The Role of Deliberate Practice in the Acquisition of Expert Performance. *Psychology Review* 100(3): 363–406.

Fadel, C. (2008) *Multimodal Learning Through Media: What the Research Says*. San Jose, CA: CISCO.

Fliessbach, K., Weis, S., Klaver, P., Elger, C. E. and Weber, B. (2006) The Effect of Concreteness on Recognition Memory. *Neuro Image* 32: 1413–1421.

Foos, P. W. (1992) Test Performance as a Function of Expected Form and Difficulty. *Journal of Experimental Education* 60(3): 205–211.

Freebody, P. and Anderson, R. C. (1981) Effects of Vocabulary Difficulty, Text Cohesion, and Schema Availability on Reading Comprehension. Technical Report 225. Urbana, IL: University of Illinois at Urbana-Champaign, Center for the Study of Reading.

Frymier, A. B. and Shulman, G. (1995) What's In It For Me? Increasing Content Relevance to Enhance Students' Motivation. *Communication Education* 44: 40–50.

Gathercole, S. (2001) *Short Term and Working Memory*. Hove: Psychology Press.

Gathercole, S. and Alloway, T. (2007) *Understanding Working Memory: A Classroom Guide*. London: Harcourt Assessment.

Geng, G. (2011) Investigation of Teachers' Verbal and Non-Verbal Strategies for Managing Attention Deficit Hyperactivity Disorder (ADHD) Students' Behaviours within a Classroom Environment. *Australian Journal of Teacher Education* 36(7): 17–30.

Glaser, R. and Chi, M. T. H. (1988) Overview. In M. T. H. Chi, R. Glaser and M. J. Farr (eds), *The Nature of Expertise*. Hove: Psychology Press, pp. xv–xxviii.

Goman, C. K. (2010) Great Leaders Talk With Their Hands. *Forbes* (21 September). Available at: https://www.forbes.com/2010/09/21/body-language-hands-gestures-forbes-woman-leadership-communication.html#13ade48028bc.

Graham, G., Hopple, C., Manross, M. and Sitzman, T. (1993a) Novice and Experienced Children's Physical Education Teachers: Insights Into Their Situational Decision Making. *Journal of Teaching in Physical Education* 12(2): 197–214.

Graham, K. C., French, K. E. and Woods, A. M. (1993b) Observing and Interpreting Teaching–Learning Processes. *Journal of Teaching in Physical Education* 13(1): 46–61.

Hamaker, C. (1986) The Effects of Adjunct Questions on Prose Learning. *Review of Educational Research* 56(2): 212–242.

Hamm, P. (2005) *Teaching and Persuasive Communication: Class Presentation Skills. A Handbook for Faculty, Teaching Assistants and Teaching Fellows*. Providence, RI: Harriet W. Sheridan Center for Teaching and Learning, Brown University.

Harden, H. and Crosby, R. (2000) AMEE Guide No 20: The Good Teacher Is More Than a Lecturer – 12 Roles of the Teacher. *Medical Teacher* 22(4): 334–348.

Hargie, O. (2006) Communication as a Skilled Performance. In O. Hargie (ed.) *The Handbook of Communication Skills*, 3rd edn. Abingdon: Routledge, pp. 7–29.

Hargie, O. and Dickson, D. (2003) *Skilled Interpersonal Communication: Research, Theory and Practice*. Hove and New York: Routledge.

Harries, T., Bolden, D. and Barmby, P. (1992) The Importance of Using Representations to Help Primary Pupils Give Meaning to Numerical Concepts. Available at www.directory-mathsed.net/download/Harris.pdf.

Haslam, C. Y. and Hamilton, R. J. (2010) Investigating the Use of Integrated Instructions to Reduce the Cognitive Load Associated with Doing Practical Work in Secondary School Science. *International Journal of Science Education* 32(13): 1715–1737.

Hausman, H. and Kornell, N. (2014) Mixing Topics While Studying Does Not Enhance Learning. *Journal of Applied Research in Memory and Cognition* 3(3): 153–160.

Hattie, J. (2009) *Visible Learning: A Synthesis of Over 800 Meta-Analyses Relating to Achievement*. Abingdon and New York: Routledge.

Hattie, J. and Yates. G. (2013) *Visible Learning and the Science of How We Learn*. Abingdon and New York: Routledge.

Hiller, J. H. (1971) Verbal Response Indicators of Conceptual Vagueness. *American Education Research Journal* 8: 151–161.

Hiller, J. H. (n.d.) Communication Vagueness Dictionary. Available at: https://prov-alisresearch.com/products/content-analysis-software/wordstat-dictionary/communication-vagueness-dictionary/.

Hirschman, E. and Bjork, R. A. (1988) Generation Effect: Two-Factor Theory. *Journal of Experimental Psychology: Learning, Memory and Cognition* 14(3): 484–494.

Hofstadter, D. (2001) Analogy as the Core of Cognition. In D. Gentner, K. J. Holyoak and B. N. Kokinov (eds), *The Analogical Mind: Perspectives from Cognitive Science*. Cambridge, MA: MIT Press, pp. 499–538.

Hogan, T., Rabinowitz, M. and Craven, J. A. (2003) Representation in Teaching: Inferences from Research of Expert and Novice Teachers. *Educational Psychologist* 38(4): 235–247.

Horizon (1988) The Pleasure of Finding Things Out [video]. BBC Two (27 March). Available at: http://www.bbc.co.uk/programmes/p018dvyg.

Housner, L. and Griffey, D. (1985) Teacher Cognition: Differences in Planning and Interactive Decision Making between Experienced and Inexperienced Teachers. *Research Quarterly for Exercise and Sport* 56(1): 45–53.

Huckstep, P., Rowland, T. and Thwaites, A. (2003) Primary Teachers' Mathematics Content Knowledge: What Does It Look Like in the Classroom? Paper presented at the British Educational Research Association Annual Conference, University of Exeter, 12–14 September.

Jackson, P. (1991) *Life in Classrooms*. New York: Teachers College Press.

Kang, S. H. K. (2016) Spaced Repetition Promotes Efficient and Effective Learning: Policy Implications for Instruction. *Policy Insights from the Behavioral and Brain Sciences* 3(1): 12–19.

Keller, M., Newmann, K. and Fischer, H. E. (2013) Teacher Enthusiasm and Student Learning. In J. Hattie and E. M. Anderman (eds), *International Guide to Student Achievement*. Abingdon and New York: Routledge, pp. 247–249.

Kim, G., Lewis-Peacock, J. A., Norman, K. A. and Turk-Browne, N. B. (2014) Pruning of Memories by Context-Based Prediction Error. *Proceedings of the National Academy of Sciences of the United States of America* 111(24): 8997–9002.

Kirschner, P. A., Sweller, J. and Clark, R. E. (2006) Why Minimal Guidance During Instruction Does Not Work: An Analysis of the Failure of Constructivist, Discovery, Problem-Based, Experiential, and Inquiry-Based Teaching. *Educational Psychologist* 41(2): 75–86.

Kornell, N., Castel, A. D., Eich, T. S. and Bjork, R. A. (2010) Spacing as the Friend of Both Memory and Induction in Young and Older Adults. *Psychology and Aging* 25(2): 498–503.

Krathwohl, D. R. (2002) A Revision of Bloom's Taxonomy: An Overview. *Theory Into Practice* 41(4): 212–218.

Kulkofsky, S. (2008) Do Better Stories Make Better Memories? Narrative Quality and Memory Accuracy In Preschool Children. *Applied Cognitive Psychology* 22: 121–138.

Kunter, M., Tsai, Y-M. Klusmann, U., Brunner, M., Krauss, S. and Baumert, J. (2010) Students' and Mathematics Teachers' Perceptions of Teacher Enthusiasm and Instruction. *Learning and Instruction* 18: 468–482.

Kyriacou, C. (1997) *Effective Teaching in Schools: Theory and Practice*. Cheltenham: Nelson Thornes.

Learning Scientists (2017) Spaced Practice [podcast] (4 October). Available at: http://www.learningscientists.org/learning-scientists-podcast/2017/10/4/episode-4-spaced-practice.

Lee, H. W., Lim, K. Y. and Grabowski, B. (2007) Generative Learning: Principles and Implications for Making Meaning. In M. Spector, D. Merrill, J. V. Merriënboer and M. Driscoll (eds), *Handbook of Research on Educational Communications and Technology*. New York and Abingdon: Routledge, pp. 111–124.

Leinhardt, G., Weidman, C. and Hammond, K. M. (1987) Introduction and Integration of Classroom Routines by Expert Teachers. *Curriculum Inquiry* 17(2): 135–176.

Lemke, J. (1998) Multiplying Meaning: Visual and Verbal Semiotics in Scientific Text. In J. R. Martin and R. Veel (eds), *Reading Science: Critical and Functional Perspectives on Discourses of Science*. Abingdon and New York: Routledge, pp. 87–113.

Limb, C. J. and Braun, A. R. (2008) Neural Substrates of Spontaneous Musical Performance: An fMRI Study of Jazz Improvisation. *PLoS ONE* 3(2): e1679. Available at: https://journals.plos.org/plosone/article?id=10.1371/journal.pone.0001679.

Loughran, J. (2006) *Developing a Pedagogy of Teacher Education: Understanding Teaching and Learning about Teaching*. Abingdon: Routledge.

Loughran, J., Berry, A. and Mulhall, P. (2012) *Understanding and Developing Science Teachers' Pedagogical Content Knowledge*. Rotterdam: Sense Publishers.

McBer, H. (2000) *Research into Teacher Effectiveness: A Model of Teacher Effectiveness.* Research Report 216. London: Department for Education and Employment.

McComas, W. F. and Abraham, L. (2004) Asking More Effective Questions. Rossier School of Education, pp. 1–16.

Martin, A. and Dowson. M. (2009) Interpersonal Relationships, Motivation, Engagement, and Achievement: Yields for Theory, Current Issues, and Educational Practice. *Review of Educational Research* 79(1): 327–365.

Martin, J. and Rose, D. (2005) Designing Literacy Pedagogy: Scaffolding Democracy in the Classroom. In R. Hasan, C. Matthiessen and J. Webster (eds), *Continuing Discourse on Language: A Functional Perspective*. London: Equinox, pp. 251–280.

Marzano, R. (2004) *Building Background Knowledge for Academic Achievement: Research on What Works in Schools.* Alexandria, VA: Association for Supervision and Curriculum Development.

Marzano, R. (2010) The Art and Science of Teaching/Representing Knowledge Non-Linguistically. *Educational Leadership: The Key to Changing the Teaching Profession* 67(8): 84–86.

Mayer, R. and Gallini, J. K. (1990) When Is an Illustration Worth Ten Thousand Words? *Journal of Educational Psychology* 82(4): 715–726.

Mercer, N. (2008) Three Kinds of Talk. Available at: https://thinkingtogether.educ.cam.ac.uk/resources/5_examples_of_talk_in_groups.pdf.

Merrill, M. D. (2008) Reflections on a Four-Decade Search for Effective, Efficient and Engaging Instruction. In M. W. Allen (ed.), *e-Learning Annual*. San Francisco, CA: Wiley/Pfieffer, pp. 141–167.

Meyer, D. (2010) Math Class Needs a Makeover, *TED.com* [video]. Available at: https://www.ted.com/talks/dan_meyer_math_curriculum_makeover.

Meyer, J. and Land, R. (2003) Threshold Concepts and Troublesome Knowledge: Linkages to Ways of Thinking and Practising within the Disciplines. ETL Project Occasional Report 4. Available at: http://www.etl.tla.ed.ac.uk/publications.html.

Mishra, H. (2011) In Praise of Vagueness: Malleability of Vague Information as a Performance Booster. *Psychology Science* 22(6): 733–738.

Moreno, R. and Mayer, R. E. (2000) A Learner-Centered Approach to Multimedia Explanations: Deriving Instructional Design Principles from Cognitive Theory. *Interactive Multimedia Electronic Journal of Computer-Enhanced Learning* 2(2): 12–20.

Muijs, D. and Reynolds, D. (2011) *Effective Teaching: Evidence and Practice*. London: SAGE.

Nagy, W. (1988) Vocabulary Instruction and Reading Comprehension. Technical Report No. 431. Children's Research Center, University of Illinois at Urbana-Champaign.

National Board for Professional Teaching Standards (2016) *What Teachers Should Know and Be Able to Do*. Arlington, VA: National Board for Professional Teaching Standards.

Noghabi, R. K. and Slawinski, E. B. (2006) Instructional Clarity: The Effect of Bilingualism and Instructor's Preparation. *Europe's Journal of Psychology* 2(2). Available at: http://ejop.psychopen.eu/article/view/328/html.

Novak, J. D. and Gowin, D. R. (1984) *Learning How to Learn*. Cambridge and New York: Cambridge University Press.

Nubold, P. and Turner, M. (1987) *Death is the Mother of Beauty: Mind, Metaphor, Criticism*. Chicago, IL: University of Chicago Press.

Nussbaum, E. M. (2008) Collaborative Discourse, Argumentation, and Learning: Preface and Literature Review. *Contemporary Educational Psychology* 33: 345–359.

Nuthall, G. (1997) Learning How to Learn: The Social Construction of Knowledge Acquisition in the Classroom. Paper presented at the Seventh Biennial Conference of the European Association for Research in Learning and Instruction, Athens, Greece, August.

Nuthall, G. (2005) The Cultural Myths and Realities of Classroom Teaching and Learning: A Personal Journey. *Teachers College Record* 107(5): 895–934.

Nuthall, G. (2007) *The Hidden Lives of Learners*. Wellington: NZCER Press.

OCR (2015) *AS and A Level Teacher Guide: Psychology. Spaced Review and Interleaving: An Introduction*. Cambridge: OCR.

Ofsted (2018) *School Inspection Handbook* (September). Ref: 150066. Available at: https://www.gov.uk/government/publications/school-inspection-handbook-from-september-2015.

Odora, R. J. (2014) Using Explanation as a Teaching Method: How Prepared Are High School Technology Teachers in Free State Province, South Africa? *Journal of Social Sciences* 38(1): 71–81.

Ord, W. (2012) Great Learners: Learning, Not Just Knowing [video]. Available at: https://www.youtube.com/watch?v=vCWd3nrEwT8.

Orgill, M. and Bodner, G. (2004) What Research Tells Us About Using Analogies to Teach Chemistry. *Chemistry Education: Research and Practice* 5(1): 15–32.

Osler, J. and Flack, J. (2008) *Whose Learning Is It? Developing Children As Active and Responsible Learners*. Rotterdam: Sense Publishers.

Oslin, J. (1996) Routines as Organizing Features in Middle School Physical Education. *Journal of Teaching in Physical Education* 15(3): 319–337.

Otto, A. R., Raio, C. M., Chiang, A., Phelps, E. A. and Daw, N. D. (2013) Working Memory Capacity Protects Model Based Learning from Stress. *Proceedings of the National Academy of Sciences of the United States of America* 110(52): 20941–20946.

Paas, F., Renkel, A. and Sweller, J. (2004) Cognitive Load Theory: Instructional Implications of the Interaction between Information Structures and Cognitive Architecture. *Instructional Science* 32: 1–8.

Pan, S. C. (2015) The Interleaving Effect: Mixing It Up Boosts Learning. *Scientific American* (4 August). Available at: https://www.scientificamerican.com/article/the-interleaving-effect-mixing-it-up-boosts-learning/.

Paterson, D. (2018) Cognitive Load and Practical Work Research: An Update. *Thoughts on Chemistry and Education* (3 January). Available at: https://dave2004b.wordpress.com/2018/01/03/cognitive-load-and-practical-work-research-an-update/.

Perkins, D. (2009) *Making Learning Whole: How Seven Principles of Teaching Can Transform Education*. San Francisco, CA: Jossey-Bass.

Petty, O. S. and Jansson, L. C. (1987) Sequencing Examples and Non-Examples to Facilitate Concept Attainment. *Journal for Research in Mathematics Education* 18(2): 112–125.

Petty, R. and Cacioppo, J. (1986) The Elaboration Likelihood Model of Persuasion. *Advances in Experimental Psychology* 19: 124–192.

Pitkäniemi, H. (2010) How the Teacher's Practical Theory Moves to Teaching Practice in Education. *Enquiry* 1(3): 157–175.

Posner, K. A. and Strike, G. J. (1992) A Revisionist Theory of Conceptual Change. In R. A. Duschl and R. J. Hamilton (eds), *Philosophy of Science, Cognitive Psychology and Educational Theory and Practice*. Albany, NY: State University of New York Press, pp. 147–176.

Putnam, A. (2015) Mnemonics in Education: Current Research and Applications. *Translational Issues in Psychological Science* 1(2): 130–139.

Rhem, J. (2013) Before and After Students 'Get It': Threshold Concepts. *Stanford University Teaching Commons* (6 November). Available at: https://teachingcommons.stanford.edu/teaching-talk/and-after-students-get-it-threshold-concepts.

Richland, L. E., Bjork, R. A., Finley, J. R. and Linn, M. C. (2005) Linking Cognitive Science to Education: Generation and Interleaving Effects. In B. G. Bara, L. Barsalou and M. Bucciarelli (eds), *Proceedings of the Twenty-Seventh Annual Conference of the Cognitive Science Society*. Mahwah, NJ: Lawrence Erlbaum, pp. 1850–1855.

Richland, L. E., Kornell, N. and Kao, L. S. (2009) The Pretesting Effect: Do Unsuccessful Retrieval Attempts Enhance Learning? *Journal of Experimental Psychology: Applied* 15(3): 243–257.

Rink, J. E., French, K., Lee, A. M. and Solmon, M. A. (1994) A Comparison of Pedagogical Knowledge Structures of Preservice Students and Teacher Educators in Two Institutions. *Journal of Teaching in Physical Education* 13(2): 140–162.

Roberson, R. (2013) Helping Students Find Relevance. *Psychology Teacher Network* (September). Available at: http://www.apa.org/ed/precollege/ptn/2013/09/students-relevance.aspx.

Roden, C. (2005) *Arabesque: A Taste of Morocco, Turkey and Lebanon*. London: Ted Smart.

Rohrer, D. and Taylor, K. (2007) The Shuffling of Mathematics Problems Improves Learning. *Instructional Science* 35: 481–498.

Rohrer, D., Dedrick, R. F. and Stershic, S. (2015) Interleaved Practice Improves Mathematics Learning. *Journal of Educational Psychology* 107(3): 900–908.

Roth, W. M. (2001) Gestures: Their Role in Teaching and Learning. *Review of Educational Research* 71(3): 365–392.

Rothwell, W. and Kazanas, H. (1998) *Mastering the Instructional Design Process: A Systematic Approach*. San Francisco, CA: Wiley/Pfieffer.

Rowland, T., Thwaites, A. and Huckstep, P. (2003) The Choice of Examples in the Teaching of Mathematics: What Do We Tell the Trainees? *Proceedings of the British Society for Research Into Learning Mathematics* 23(2): 85–90.

Sample, I. (2014) Curiosity Improves Memory By Tapping Into the Brain's Reward System, *The Guardian* (2 October). Available at: https://www.theguardian.com/science/2014/oct/02/curiosity-memory-brain-reward-system-dopamine.

Sawyer, R. K. (2004) Creative Teaching: Collaborative Discussions as Disciplined Improvisation. *Educational Researcher* 33(2): 12–20.

Sawyer, R. K. (2011) *What Makes Good Teachers Great?* Cambridge: Cambridge University Press.

Schiefele, U. (1991) Interest, Learning, and Motivation. *Educational Psychologist* 26(3–4): 299–323.

Schön, D. (1983) *The Reflective Practitioner: How Professionals Think in Action*. New York: Basic Books.

Schraw, G., Flowerday, T. and Lehman, S. (2001) Increasing Situational Interest in the Classroom. *Educational Psychology Review* 13(3): 211–225.

Scott, C. (2009) Talking to Learn: Dialogue in the Classroom. *The Digest* 2: 1–17.

Seguin, R. (1989) *The Elaboration of School Textbooks: Methodological Guide*. Paris: Division of Educational Sciences, Contents and Methods of Education, UNESCO.

Shanteau, J. (1992) Competence in Experts: The Role of Task Characteristics. *Organizational Behaviour and Human Decision Processes* 52(2): 252–266.

Shavelson, R. and Stern, J. (1981) Research on Teachers' Pedagogical Thoughts, Judgments, Decisions, and Behavior. *Review of Educational Research* 54(4): 455–498.

Sheehan, C. (2008) Developing Elementary Teachers' Ability to Design and Implement Multiple Representations of Science Content. Dissertation, State University of New York at Albany.

Shulman, L. (1986) Those Who Understand: Knowledge Growth in Teaching, *Educational Researcher* 15(2): 4–14.

Shulman, L. (1987) Knowledge and Teaching: Foundations of the New Reform. *Harvard Educational Review* 57(1): 1–23.

Singh, M. (2014) Curiosity: It Helps Us Learn, But Why? *NPR* (24 October). Available at: https://www.npr.org/sections/ed/2014/10/24/357811146/curiosity-it-may-have-killed-the-cat-but-it-helps-us-learn.

Smith, L. and Land, M. (1981) Low-Inference Verbal Behaviors Related to Teacher Clarity. *Journal of Classroom Interaction* 17: 37–42.

Smith, L. and Sanders, K. (1981) The Effects on Student Achievement and Student Perception of Varying Structure in Social Studies Content. *Journal of Educational Research* 74(5): 333–336.

Smith, L. R. (1982) Training Teachers to Teach Clearly: Theory into Practice. Paper presented at the Annual Meeting of the American Educational Research Association, New York, 19–23 March.

Smith, M. (2016) The Benefits of Spaced Practice in the Classroom: Four Tips for Teachers. *TES* (30 September).

Snyder, S. (1991) The Effect of Instructional Clarity and Concept Structure on Student Achievement and Perception. Paper presented at the Annual Meeting of the American Educational Research Association, Chicago, 2–6 April.

Soderstrom, N. C. and Bjork, R. A. (2015) Learning Versus Performance: An Integrative Review. *Perspectives on Psychological Science* 10(2): 176–199.

Stahl, R. J. (1994) Using 'Think-Time' and 'Wait-Time' Skillfully in the Classroom. *ERIC Digest* ED370885: 1–6.

Straube, B., Green, A., Bromberger, B. and Kircher, T. (2011) The Differentiation of Iconic and Metaphoric Gestures: Common and Unique Integration Processes. *Human Brain Mapping* 32(4): 520–533.

Suffian, H. and Rahman, S. (2010) Teacher's Choice and Use of Examples in the Teaching and Learning of Mathematics in Primary School and Their Relations to Teacher's Pedagogical Content Knowledge. *Procedia-Social and Behavioural Sciences* 8: 312–316.

Sweller, J. (1988) Cognitive Load During Problem Solving: Effects on Learning. *Cognitive Science* 12: 257–285.

Teacher Development Trust (2015) *Developing Great Teaching: Lessons from the International Reviews Into Effective Professional Development*. London: Teacher Development Trust.

Thinking Allowed (2016) Weather Forecasting, Young People and Politics [audio]. BBC Radio 4 (15 February). Available at: http://www.bbc.co.uk/programmes/b06zttbs.

Thorndyke, P. W. (1977) Cognitive Structures in Comprehension and Memory of Narrative Discourse. *Cognitive Psychology* 9: 77–110.

Titsworth, S. (2010) Translating Research Into Instructional Practice: Instructor Clarity. Available at: https://www.tamdistrict.org/cms/lib/CA01000875/Centricity/Domain/55/PDF-TRIP-Instructor_Clarity.pdf.

Tsui, A. (2003) *Understanding Expertise in Teaching: Case Studies of Second Language Teachers*. Cambridge: Cambridge University Press.

Turner, F. (2008) Beginning Elementary Teachers' Use of Representation in Mathematics Teaching. *Research in Mathematics Education* 10(2): 209–210.

Turner, F. (2009) Kate's Conceptions of Mathematics Teaching: Influences in the First Three Years. Proceedings of CERME 6, Lyon, 28 January–1 February.

Ugur, G., Dilber, R., Senpolat, Y. and Duzgun, B. (2012) The Effects of Analogy in Students' Understanding of Direct Current Circuits and Attitudes Towards Physics Lessons. *European Journal of Education Research* 1(3): 211–223.

van Merriënboer, J. and Sweller, J. (2009) Cognitive Load Theory in Health Professional Education: Design Principles and Strategies. *Medical Education* 44(1): 85–93.

van Merriënboer, J., Kirschner, P. A. and Kester, P. (2003) Taking the Load Off a Learner's Mind: Instructional Design for Complex Learning. *Educational Psychologist* 38(1): 5–13.

Watson, P. (2002) The Role and Integration of Learning Outcomes into the Educational Process. *Active Learning in Higher Education* 3(3): 205–219.

Weston, D. (2015) 'For Too Long, Schools Have Accepted a Culture of Low Expectations for CPD'. *TES* (9 June). Available at: https://www.tes.com/news/too-long-schools-have-accepted-culture-low-expectations-cpd.

Wiggins, G. (2010) What's My Job? Defining the Role of the Classroom Teacher. In R. J. Marzano (ed.), *On Excellence in Teaching* (Bloomington, IN: Solution Tree Press), pp. 7–30.

Wiliam, D. (2009a) Content Then Process: Teacher Learning Communities in the Service of Formative Assessment [video]. Available at: https://www.youtube.com/watch?v=029fSeOaGio.

Wiliam, D. (2009b) *Embedding Formative Assessment: A Professional Development Pack for Schools* [DVD]. London: SSAT.

Willingham, D. T. (2002) How We Learn: Inflexible Knowledge: The First Steps to Expertise. *American Educator* 26(4): 31–33.

Willingham, D. T. (2009) *Why Don't Students Like School? A Cognitive Scientist Answers Questions About How the Mind Works and What It Means for the Classroom*. San Francisco, CA: Jossey-Bass.

Wilson, T. C., Pfister, F. C. and Flery, B. E. (1981) *The Design of Printed Instructional Materials: Research on Illustrations and Typography*. Syracuse, NY: ERIC Clearinghouse on Information Resources.

Wit, E-J. and Gillette, M. (1999) What is Linguistic Redundancy? Gillette Technical Report, University of Chicago, pp. 1–17.

Wittrock, M. C. (1991) Generative Teaching of Comprehension. *Elementary School Journal* 92(2): 169–184.

Wragg, E. C. (1993) *Primary Teaching Skills*. London and New York: Routledge.

Wragg, E. C. and Brown, G. A. (2001) *Explaining in the Secondary School*. Abingdon and New York: RoutledgeFalmer.

Yinger, R. and Clark, C. (1979) Three Studies in Teacher Planning. Research Series No. 55. East Lansing, MI: Institute of Teaching Research, Michigan State University.

Zaslavsky, O. (2014) Thinking With and Through Examples. In P. Liljedahl, C. Nichol, S. Oesterle and D. Allan (eds), *Proceedings of the Joint Meeting of PME 38 and PME-NA 36*, Vol. 1. Vancouver: PME, pp. 21–34.

Index